HAPPINESS IS LIKE A CUR DOG

THE THIRTY-YEAR JOURNEY OF A
MAJOR LEAGUE BASEBALL PITCHER AND
BROADCASTER

Nelson J. King

authorHOUSE®

AuthorHouse™
1663 Liberty Drive
Bloomington, IN 47403
www.authorhouse.com
Phone: 1-800-839-8640

First published by AuthorHouse 9/21/2009

ISBN: 978-1-4490-2547-2 (sc)
ISBN: 978-1-4490-2548-9 (hc)

Library of Congress Control Number: 2009909207

Printed in the United States of America
Bloomington, Indiana

This book is printed on acid-free paper.

I dedicate this book to:

My wife Bernadette, who, despite the solitary life of being married to a professional baseball player and broadcaster, was dedicated to raising three loving, intelligent, and responsible children.

My three daughters, Laurie, Leslie, and Amy, whose encouragement, love and support made this book a reality.

Walter Earl, my brother-in-law, whose friendship and assistance when times were difficult is treasured beyond measure.

Jack Berger, former Public Relations Director of the Pittsburgh Pirates, who, in 1959 at a most distressing time in my career, changed the direction of my life by recommending me for what became a lengthy and rewarding career in radio broadcasting.

TABLE OF CONTENTS

FOREWORD

Nellie King can't help himself. He is still Pittsburgh's King of baseball lore. He just *has* to tell his stories about his days in baseball, and few can spin a tale better than this former Pirates' pitcher and broadcaster. He was 80 years old in the winter of 2009 when I last spoke with him, and had battled several health challenges the previous two years, but he's bounced back in big-time style to the amazement of his family, many friends, and followers.

"The so-called 'golden years' can kiss my behind," joked King during one of my visits.

King can swap stories about Roberto Clemente, Ralph Kiner, Paul Warner, Bob Prince, Dick Groat, and just about any name you can find in the *Baseball Encyclopedia*. Honus Wagner of the Pirates, a charter member in Baseball's Hall of Fame in Cooperstown, once said, "There ain't much to being a ballplayer…if you're a ballplayer."

The same can be said of storytellers. King has the knack for sharing insightful and humorous stories about the people he met while playing for the Pirates and later as a sidekick to Bob Prince in the broadcasting booth. There are people who make their living as baseball broadcasters who have yet to tell a story on the airwaves, but King was a natural at it.

He knew a story when he saw one—the first requirement—and he knew how best to craft that story.

King frequently receives friends such as Steve Blass, Dave Giusti, and Kent Tekulve, all former Pirates' pitchers who live in Upper St. Clair. They brought Bob Friend from Fox Chapel and Bobby Del Greco from Brookline with them on one of their visits to participate in a Pirates' Alumni program at Friendship Village. "If there were a Hall of Fame for nice guys," offers Steve Blass, "Nellie King would be a charter member."

Nelson Joseph King, who was born in Shenandoah, Pennsylvania on March 15, 1928, pitched for the Pirates for four seasons (1954 to 1957) and shared the Pirates' broadcast booth with Bob Prince for nine years (1967-1975). King is often the butt of his own baseball stories. He's quick to make fun of himself, and readily admits that he never had a hit in the major leagues in 23 plate appearances. "I came close once; I should've had a hit," he'll say with a big smile. He had a 7-5 record as a pitcher, and came up one year short of earning a baseball pension.

He likes to tell a story about how he threw one pitch to become the winning pitcher in a game against the Chicago Cubs, while Jim Brosnan of the Cubs, best known for authoring a wonderful book called *The Long Season*, was the losing pitcher while throwing one pitch. He has another story about how he was the losing pitcher for the Pirates while touring the Grand Canyon, which he retells with humor in these memoirs.

King worked as a sports reporter for WTRA in Latrobe in the early 1960s. He interviewed many of the Pirates just before the World Series in 1960, and asked them who they thought would be the hero of the World Series. "Only one of them named Bill Mazeroski," recalled King. "That was Harvey Haddix. When I asked Haddix why he thought it would be Maz, who'd be batting eighth in the lineup, he said, 'Because

they'll pitch to him. They wouldn't get cute or too careful with him'."
That turned out to be a mistake on the Yankees' part.

I know King's classic stories, and which buttons to push to get him
to tell the details of what he did or witnessed many summers ago. He
remembers whether he threw an inside curve or a fastball high and
outside. It's sparkling stuff. Most pitchers are pretty good at giving you
those kinds of details, but King does so with élan.

Nellie lived in a modest red brick home on James Place in Mt. Lebanon
for 35 years. He and his wife Bernadette raised three daughters—Laurie,
50; Leslie, 48; and Amy, 45. King is proud to tell you that Laurie has
a Ph.D. in Anthropology and teaches at Georgetown University, Leslie
has a Masters in nursing, and Amy is in television production work,
and has been an angel in looking after his needs the last few years. All
three daughters and his wife earned degrees at Duquesne during the
30 years King worked there as the sports information director and the
men's golf coach.

King said he learned who his friends were during his long battle
with health problems. "Pete Dimperio, the great football coach at
Westinghouse High in Pittsburgh, used to say that there were three
stages of life," said King. "You're young, you're middle-aged, and you're
lookin' good. Right now, I'm looking good!"

I am so happy that Nellie King has written his stories and now
has his own book chock-full of fun and games and insights into some
memorable ballplayers and characters. King's book will be competition
for my books about Pittsburgh, but anyone who cares about this
wonderful gentleman has to cheer this achievement. After all, I've gone
to him countless times when I needed anecdotes about somebody in
baseball. Nellie has never let me down.

—Jim O'Brien

ACKNOWLEDGEMENTS

An act of kindness, no matter how small,
is never wasted.

I humbly and gratefully thank everyone who showed me kindness, encouragement, and generosity during my baseball journey: Lefty Hallman, director of the YMCA in Lebanon, PA, and Jimmy Kercher, the manager of the first organized team on which I played in 1945. Charles "Pop" Kelchner, the St. Louis Cardinal Scout who signed me to my first pro contract in 1946. Roy Dissinger, the baseball scout who signed me to my second contract in 1946, and a third one in 1947 at Geneva, AL, where I began my 12-year pro career.

In Geneva, AL, second baseman "Cotton" Bosarge gave me invaluable advice on how to throw a sinking fastball, thereby opening the door to the Major Leagues. Clyde MacAllister, catcher, and our manager, Francis Hecker. Pete McGarry, a veteran catcher who made me a major league prospect when I won 20 games in 1948 at New Iberia, LA. My Louisiana teammates George Kinnamon, Mike Turturro, and Joe Kaczowka.

At York, PA in 1949, manager Frank Osceak's confidence increased my skills when I led the Inter-state League with in ERA of 2.25. My York teammates, Jim Dean, Chuck Fedoris, Bill Plate, and Fred Uhlman.

Andy Cohen, manager at Denver, CO in 1953, used me as a short reliever, as a result of which I won 15, lost 3 and saved 17 games with an ERA of 2.00, enabling my promotion to the major leagues in 1954.

My Denver teammates: Jake Thies, Harry Pritts, Curt Roberts, Gus Gregory, Jack Sheppard, Barney Schultz, Pat Haggerty, and Whitey Reis.

Manager Bobby Bragan at Hollywood in 1955 and teammates Joe Trimble and Ben Wade. Danny Murtaugh, manager at New Orleans in 1954. His confidence in my role as a starter led to a 16-5 record and a league leading ERA of 2.25. Teammates Pete Peterson, Danny Kravitz, George and Gene Freese, Dale Coogan, Roy Face, Lenny Yochim, Bobby DeGreco, and trainer Tiny Tunis all enriched my experience.

With the Pittsburgh Pirates' organization in 1956, Dale Long hit a record setting 8 home runs in 8 games. His leadership moved us into first place in mid-June. I thank all of my teammates: Dick Groat, Bill Mazeroski, Roberto Clemente, Bob Skinner, Elroy Face, Bill Virdon, Vern Law, and clubhouse man John Holihan.

Jack Berger, public relations director for the Pirates, changed my life after baseball in December 1959 when he recommended me to Joel Rosenblum, owner of three small stations outside of Pittsburgh who was looking for a former player to do sports reporting. I earned the job, working for stations in Kittanning, Latrobe, and Greensburg. Thanks are also due to Tom Johnson, Hugh J. Brenna, Warren Koerbel, and others for helping me learn the job from the ground up.

To Iron City Beer, KDKA, and the Pirates for selecting me to replace Don Hoak on Pirates' broadcasts from 1967 to 1975. Thanks to KDKA producer Ed Young for his professional work and to George

Kleeb and Mel Check, who handled the engineering for the broadcasts. Thanks to the friendship of Rege Cordic, Bob Trow, Bob McCully, Ed and Wendy King, Tom Bender, Paul Long, Mike Levine, Vince Lashied, and Dean Steliotes

Years shared with sportswriters: Charlie Feeney, Les Biederman, Jack Hernon, Al Abrams, Bob Smizik, Gene Collier, Chuck Finder and Chilly Doyle. The friendship of TV sportscasters: Sam Nover, Stan Savran, Myron Cope, Bill Hillgrove, and Bob Pompiani.

Friendships with players and their families, Dave and Ginny Giusti, Steve and Karen Blass, Bill and Milene Mazeroski, Willie Stargell, Roberto and Vera Clemente, Dave and Barbara Ricketts, Sally O'Leary, Jean Donatelli, PA announcer Art McKennan, and Pirates' alumni, Joe Billadeaux, Monica Robinson and the players who have created a special bond among former teammates.

Thanks to John "Red" Manning, former athletic director at Duquesne University, and alumnus Jim McDonough, for offering me the position of Sports Information Director in December 1975. Special thanks to Ray Goss, a true friend with whom I worked on Duquesne Dukes basketball broadcast from 1974 to 1998. Coaches John Cinicola, Jim Satalin and trainer Bob Milie for friendships that remain strong to this day. Assistant Sports Information Director Jim Lachimia, current Duquesne athletic department members, Greg Amadio, Paul Hightower, Dave Saba, George Nieman, Cindy Morton and previous secretaries, Pixie Sohn and Betsy Bjalabok.

To Ellen Smith and my daughter Laurie for their editing assistance.

To Joe Garagiola, Ralph Kiner, Arnie Palmer, and Mark Bowden for their testimonials, and Jim O'Brien for the foreword and his encouragement over the years, I extend my deepest gratitude.

INTRODUCTION

The Biblical saying, "for where your treasure is, there will your heart be also," sums up my varied career. It is rewarding to look back over the 80 years of my life and realize that following my heart has always led me to happiness and satisfaction. From the time I graduated from high school until today, there were only four years when I was not doing what I truly wanted to do: two were spent in the army during the Korean War, and two were devoted to trying to make a living selling mutual funds after the end of my baseball career. All the other years I found joy, satisfaction, and success by listening to my heart and doing things I truly loved.

True to the paradox many discover as they grow older, my overall memory has become less acute, while my recollections of long-ago games, events, and relationships are increasingly vivid and cherished. One memory in particular stands out: on a brilliant summer day in 1941 when I was 13 years old, I saw my first major league game. My older brother Bill and my uncle Nelson (for whom I am named) took me to Philadelphia to see the Phillies and Reds play at Shibe Park. The Cincinnati Reds had won consecutive National League titles in 1939 and 1940, so they grabbed my attention much more than the Phillies that day. I recognized pitchers Paul Derringer and Bucky Walters, as well as their manager, Bill McKechnie. The most recognizable of all, though, was Ernie Lombardi, the Reds' huge catcher.

I barely noticed the Phillies' double play combination that day. Danny Murtaugh was playing second and Bobby Bragan was at shortstop. As a child sitting in Shibe Park, I could never have imagined our paths would cross in the major leagues just 13 years later. Danny Murtaugh was my manager at New Orleans in 1954, and later with the Pirates in 1957. My wife, Bernadette, and I were honored when Danny later became the godfather of our first daughter, Laurie.

Years later, as a radio and television broadcaster for the Pirates, I was fortunate to renew my association with Danny when he managed the 1971 Pirates to a World Championship. I pitched for Bobby Bragan in 1955 at Hollywood, and in 1956 with the Pirates. Bragan's confidence in my ability to throw strikes enabled me to enjoy my brief success at the major league level before an arm injury forced my retirement in 1957.

Seeing my first major league game with my uncle and brother was certainly memorable, but what happened after the game that day in Shibe Park remains particularly vivid. In those days, you could exit the old ballparks from the field. As a kid, I was completely enchanted to be that close to the diamond on which the players had moved, seemingly larger than life. As I walked, starry-eyed, past the visiting team's dugout on the first base side, my brother said, "Hey, Nels—Babe Ruth and Lou Gehrig sat in this dugout!"

Fourteen years later, on April 24, 1955, I was sitting in that very same dugout, wearing a Pirate's uniform, about to make my first appearance as a starting pitcher in a major league game. From the perspective of the boy who first saw Shibe Park in 1941, the chance of this ever happening would have seemed as remote as making it into baseball's Hall of Fame!

Recalling my brother's words on that summer day gave me a deep feeling of satisfaction that words can never describe.

This is the story of the wonderful journey that took me from the Milton S. Hershey School for Boys to the minor leagues, and then to a major league career as a relief pitcher for the Pirates. As such, it is a story about finding happiness, or rather, letting happiness find me.

Among the great teachers I had during my years in baseball, one stands heads and shoulders above the rest: Pirates' General Manager "Branch" Rickey, a baseball genius as well as a master rhetorician.

I first became aware of Mr. Rickey's unparalleled ability to communicate and inspire when he gave a talk to the entire Pirates' team during spring training in 1954 at Fort Pierce, Florida. The topic was happiness, and with his inimitable wisdom and simplicity he said: "Some people believe you can think or will yourself into happiness, but that's not true. You can't get up in the morning and say to yourself, 'I'm going to be happy today!'" Mr. Rickey explained this assertion by comparing happiness to a "cur dog:"

A commercial painter began painting a garage door when he noticed a cur dog nearby. Fascinated with the dog, he reached down and tried to pet the animal. But as soon as he did, the dog ran away. The painter went back to his job, and soon the dog returned. Again the painter reached down and tried to pet the dog, and the dog ran away. The painter returned to his task and soon became so immersed in his work that he began whistling. So involved in painting, he was oblivious to anything but his work. The 'cur dog' had returned, but the painter was unaware the dog was nudging his leg; the man kept painting and whistling. Suddenly, he felt the dog reaching up and pawing at his thigh. That's what happiness is. You can't

go out looking and searching for it. If you do, it will escape
you and run away, just like that cur dog. But if you go about
enjoying and focusing on your work, happiness, like that dog,
will remain there beside you.

The dog Mr. Rickey chose to symbolize happiness was not a purebred show dog, but rather, your everyday mutt or cur—what Pittsburghers might call a "Heinz-57-variety" dog. This allegory immediately made sense to me, because happiness always seemed to sneak up unexpectedly through a mongrel mix of frustrations and successes.

Psychologist Abraham Maslow has a term for those moments in life when your senses are completely open to everything that is going on around you. He calls them "peak experiences." Your mind is completely at ease and immersed in the "now," while your senses are soaking up everything in vivid detail. How wonderful it is—and how rare—in a life in which our enthusiasm and energy is all too often sapped by our day-to-day obligations, worries about the future, and fears rooted in past experiences. When love and satisfaction with one's work come together, peak experiences can happen.

I enjoyed my first peak experience in the summer of 1948. I was pitching for the New Iberia, Louisiana Pelicans in the Class "D" Evangeline League, and enjoying a truly successful season, winning 20 games and pitching 284 innings. I woke up early one morning after another winning game with a feeling of peace and serenity that was new to me. The mugginess of the bayou had not yet engulfed the day. A cooling breeze was lightly stirring the white lace curtains of the window near my bed, wafting in the sweet smells of the flowers opening outside. I was all-alone. The pleasing songs of birds only accentuated the quiet.

I lay there for several minutes, completely enthralled with the sensation of profound contentment. "This is how life should be lived,"

I thought. But the more I tried to hold on to the experience, the faster it ebbed away, until it finally evaporated. Yet, it was such a wonderful moment that I can relive it in my mind to this day. I've enjoyed other peak experiences in baseball, when moments are simply allowed to just happen and unfold. As a pitcher, I was deeply involved in "the now," with no anxiety.

Later, as a broadcaster alongside Bob Prince, whose charisma was a force-field in and of itself, I was to know peak experiences in which language became charged with the excitement on the playing field, and then that spark was passed along to thousands of unseen fans listening in their homes, on porches, in their cars, or at a local bar.

In my years of association with Pittsburgh Pirates' baseball from 1948 to 1975, I've seen the organization go through the whole gamut of human emotions. Pittsburgh is no stranger to hardship, and the Pirates have known their years "in the cellar." Like the city itself, the team emerged from the darkness and soot of the 1950s to enjoy two shining decades that Bob Prince called "the halcyon days" of Pirates baseball.

Surely, it was a peak experience for the entire western Pennsylvania region to be a part of Bill Mazeroski's dramatic home run at Forbes Field, clinching the 1960 World Series. Pittsburghers also enjoyed the honor of witnessing the excellence of legendary players like Roberto Clemente and Willie Stargell. How lucky I was to have played and broadcast during these halcyon days of Pirates' baseball!

In the following pages I attempt to capture an era in baseball that is rapidly fading. During my brief major league career I played against such Hall of Fame greats as Stan Musial, Ernie Banks, Hank Aaron, Eddie Matthews, Jackie Robinson, Frank Robinson, Ken Boyer, Roy Campanella, Duke Snider, Pee Wee Reese, Don Newcombe, Sandy Koufax, Don Drysdale, Warren Spahn, Robin Roberts, and many others. As a broadcaster I was privileged to view and describe the excellence of

Roberto Clemente, Bill Mazeroski, Willie Stargell, Bob Gibson, Johnny Bench, Joe Morgan, Tony Perez, Lou Brock, and many more.

Committing these memories to paper has been personally satisfying. I hope you will enjoy reading them as much as I did living them. My wish is that you, too, will always find the "cur dog of happiness" by listening to your heart.

CHAPTER ONE

A Survivor

I was born on March 15, 1928, in Weston Place, PA, the youngest of five children. Our family lived in a two-storey duplex house owned by the Locust Mountain Mining Company, where my father was employed. My earliest memory is that of lying in a crib positioned between the dining and living room over a big grate opening in the floor that provided the central heat for the house. A nurse in an unusually bright uniform was looking down at me. Later in life, when I described this memory to my mother, she told me that I had contracted pneumonia as a toddler and that they had feared I would not recover. Evidently, the moment I remember is the moment I came out of my delirium. I've been a survivor ever since.

My mother, Amelia "Millie" Miles, was born on March 16, 1887. My father, Charles Vincent King, lost his father in a train accident when he was young and was raised by an uncle. At the age of 12, he began working as a slate picker in the coalmines. My mother was sixteen when she fell in love with "Charlie" King, who was ten years her senior. His background as a Lithuanian Catholic with few family ties, coupled with the disparity in age and the difference in religions, did not charm my grandmother, Emma Rebecca Miles. A fervent Protestant of Welsh-German ancestry, she decided that a sure-fire way to end the romance was to send her daughter across the seas to visit relatives in Wales. Absence just made the heart grow fonder, and upon her return, Millie married Charlie on January 31, 1906. My grandmother would eventually be won over by the caring and loving relationship my parents shared.

Monday was always washday at our house. When I was just learning to speak, my mother delightedly told her friends how I recited the days of the week: "Sunday, *WASHDAY*, Tuesday..." it was a long, hard day for my mother. Doing the wash for a family of seven was difficult enough, but added to that work order were my father's work clothes, filthy from his shifts in the mines. We were fortunate enough to have one of the very early washing machines, but it still required my mother to feed the sopping clothes into the ringer, and then hang them outside to dry. Clothes would freeze almost as soon as they were hung out to dry in the cold winters on top of the mountain. But there was a deliciously clean fragrance when the clothes were brought inside to thaw out—a smell that can't be duplicated, even with the technology we have today.

My mother relished telling the story about the arrival of electricity to our family house. She invited my grandmother to visit and see this wondrous invention. Emma, my grandmother, was awestruck as she witnessed electric lighting for the first time. She turned to my mother and said, "My God, Millie, isn't it amazing? No candles, no gas lights, I can't believe it! The next thing you know, we'll be shittin' in our own houses!"

I have few memories of my father; I was only five years old when he died. What I learned about him came through stories told by my family, especially my Uncle Nelson. By the time I was born, my father had worked his way up from a 12-year-old slate picker to mine supervisor. Self-educated, with a curious and active mind, he applied for and was granted a patent by the U.S. Patent Office for a coal-sifting device. Despite his limited education, my dad was an active citizen who left a mark on his community, serving on the board that established the Locust Mountain Hospital—the first hospital in the Shenandoah area—and acting as Grand Exalted Ruler of the B.P.O.E. Elks Club. On rare occasions, he took me to the club, where I would bask in his importance.

My father's true passion was baseball. I learned later in life that he pitched on a semi-pro team in the hard coal region. Working in the mines for 12 hours Monday through Friday and then a half-day on Saturday left little time for leisure. Maybe that's why people truly appreciated and made the most of their idle hours. Every summer, my father eagerly planned one or two trips into Philadelphia in his 1928 Willys Knight to see the A's or the Phillies play Sunday doubleheaders at Shibe Park. The distance from Weston Place was 100 miles each way, which took well over three hours driving on two-lane highways devoid of bypasses, hamlets, or towns. Because he had to drive that distance, he made sure he was going to see as much major-league baseball as possible. Money was tight, and fans of that era enjoyed the value of getting two games for the price of one. I never heard my father complain about how long a game lasted; it meant that there was more to see, remember, and talk about for the rest of the summer and through the winter.

From the 1920s to the late 1940s, baseball earned the title of "America's National Pastime." Semi-pro baseball teams commanded the attention of every small town in America and the percentage of people playing and watching the game of baseball was larger then than ever before—or since. You could see a semi-pro game (played in twilight weekdays and afternoons on weekends) in every city, town, or hamlet in America. Players on these semi-pro teams were locals, so they didn't require numbers on their uniforms to identify them. Their shirts served as advertising space for enterprising local businesses.

My brother Paul, an excellent shortstop, played for Minersville and then Tremont, two of the top semi-pro teams in the anthracite coal region. On Sunday after church and lunch (which always included my mom's nourishing eggnog), our family would pile into the Willys Knight to see Paul play. My dad always arrived a bit early to see fielding practice so he could assess the visiting team's talent. He diligently kept a scorecard, which he later used as a reference to discuss the games with Paul.

One of the best visiting players was a left fielder for Pine Grove named Pete Gray. Although Pete had lost his right arm in a childhood accident, he had developed an amazing ability to hit, catch, and throw a baseball. He would catch a fly ball, flip it up in the air, tuck his glove under the stub of his right arm, and catch the ball with his left hand and throw, all in one motion. He hit from the left side of the plate and always put the ball into play. Blessed with great running speed, Pete was a constant threat on the bases, where he also took advantage of his handicap—or so his opponents believed.

My brother Paul recalled that he was a "dirty" base runner who always came into second base with his spikes up high like Ty Cobb, trying to cut the infielder making the tag. "He knew he could get away with it," Paul said. "Who the hell was going to start a fight with a guy who had only one arm!?" Pete later attracted nationwide attention by playing in the major leagues for the St. Louis Browns during World War II. In 245 times at bat against major-league pitching, he struck out only eleven times!

Signed to a minor-league contract in the early 1930s, my brother Paul played briefly at Charleroi (PA), Harrisburg (PA), and later at

Ogdensburg (NY). His decision to get married, coupled with the Depression economy, extinguished his pro ball career. He went on to work as a draftsman while continuing to play at the semi-pro level, a compromise that he found financially and personally satisfying.

Paul followed with pride the career of Harry Gumbert, who was his roommate at Charleroi. Gumbert went on to have a successful and lengthy career, pitching 15 years in the National League for New York, St. Louis, Cincinnati, and Pittsburgh. Paul would later follow my success in baseball, but I often sensed he wondered what might have happened had he been able to continue pursuing his own baseball dreams.

It was Paul's example—and equipment—that fostered my earliest interest in the game. One of my solitary pastimes as a kid was using an old piece of wood to hit stones into the woods below our home. Playing a make-believe game in which I inserted my brothers into the line-up, I would judge each successfully hit stone by the distance it traveled as a single, double, triple, home run, or out. It was the first time I became aware of my competitive nature, since I always got hits, but my brothers didn't. Later, I started using one of Paul's baseball bats, which made me much more skillful at hitting stones, until he angrily informed me, "You don't use my game bats to hit stones!"

In the first five years of my life, I enjoyed a happy childhood. Everyone knew one another in a small village like Weston Place, and it was never a problem finding other kids with whom to play. Summers were meant for walking barefoot through the woods and streams in search of tadpoles, bird's nests, and small animals; or taking a foray into the woods with my friends, Pete Stockett and Sam Walacavage. One day we stumbled upon a secluded spot littered with discarded white balloons. We would learn much later that these were condoms.

Winter on top of the mountain always brought big snowfalls. With few cars and no snowploughs, conditions were ideal for sledding. I had a Flexible Flyer, the Cadillac of sleds. The superb location for sled riding started at the top row of homes in the village. If the snow was packed tight and you got a good run—and were able to negotiate one particularly sharp left turn—you could sail two miles, all the way into downtown Shenandoah. The downside was that you had to walk all the way back. I remember those happy days in Weston Place all the more clearly because, like that long, fast run down the hill on my sled, they were about to end in the coming winter.

My journey from Weston Place has been filled with many defining moments, most of them rewarding, except for one—the death of my father, who passed away at the height of the Depression when I was just five years old.

The early end of my childhood

December 4, 1933 was a leaden day. I was sitting on the floor of my parent's bedroom, my knees pulled up near my chin. The shades were pulled down and the only glow in the room came from a dimly lit lamp on a dresser at the foot of the bed on which my father lay. My mother and others were gathered around the bed. I didn't know what was happening, but there was a kind of quiet you feel just before a bad storm.

The loud crying and weeping came suddenly. My father, suffering from pneumonia, had just died. I can still see my mother running from the room and up the attic steps, for what I still don't know. Perhaps she wanted to be by herself. My next-older brother Charles, who came home from school, approached the bed and quickly ran into his room. I went to follow him and couldn't find him until I heard his sobbing. He was hiding under his bed. I could not make sense of what had happened. I felt as if I were outside of a picture looking in, no one was aware of me. Maybe for this reason, I still remember the event as if it were captured on film.

During the days before my father's burial our home was full of people. In those days, the viewing was held in the living room of the family home. Weston Place included just two rows of company houses. Automobiles were rare in that Depression period, but the two streets were crowded with cars. People came to pay their respects to my father and share in my mother's grief. With a gray sorrow shrouding everything, the adults told me to "go out and play." It seemed inappropriate to be playing and having fun when everyone was so sad. I thought there must be something terribly wrong with me.

As the funeral service at our home was ending, something happened that became indelibly seared into my memory. The minister asked the family to say their final good-byes to my father. Everyone did so individually. My mother turned to me and said, "Nelson, walk up and give your dad a kiss goodbye." I pulled away, too frightened to kiss my dead father's body. My mother continued to plead with me to do as she commanded.

As the silence grew heavier, I sensed that all the mourners were watching and waiting impatiently for me to carry out my mother's command. My fear paralyzed me, and I could not move until led to the casket. I didn't kiss my dad, but touched his hand to end the humiliation I was feeling. It was my first experience with performance anxiety. Despite years of therapy, and successful careers in baseball, broadcasting, and public speaking, that moment is so strongly imprinted on me it remains a constant and unwanted companion until this day.

With the death of my father, our life and family fell apart. People who did not experience the Depression have no idea of how difficult it was. There were no safety nets, no unemployment compensation, no medical or retirement benefits, and no social security. All you had was your job. My dad had always had steady work (when "steady" meant only two or three days a week). He was able to do something that so many others could not: put food on the table for his family. I remember men coming to our back door, asking if they could sweep the porches, rake leaves, or anything. They weren't looking for money to pay off credit cards. Struggling to survive from meal to meal, they only wanted a sandwich!

Those who berate government assistance programs never experienced those terribly difficult years of want, fear, and humiliation. The benefits we now enjoy are taken for granted, as if they were always part of our lives. To use a baseball metaphor, too many people in this country have been born on third base, yet think they've hit triples! As a nation and people, we have become increasingly more arrogant and less tolerant of the less fortunate.

The Iron Gates

My father's death left our family barely in the on-deck circle. With the dire economic situation facing my mother, it became obvious she could not keep the home and the family together. The age difference between my siblings and me was wide. Bill was 25, Paul, 23, Emma, 21 and Charles was 17. Except for Charles, the others were beginning lives and households of their own. Devastated by the loss of her true love, and burdened with caring for her senile father, my mother had agonizing decisions to make, chief among which was what to do with me. Difficult family decisions were made without my involvement. I reasoned that they thought it would be too painful for me. But as years have gone by, I understood it really was the other way around.

I remember driving to Philadelphia with my mother and brother on an overcast winter day in 1935, unaware of where we were going or why we were making the trip. It turned out to be a visit to Girard College, a home for orphans. To get into the grounds, we had to drive the car through a large iron gate, similar to the ones you see in old prison movies. Or at least that's what it looked like to me. I spent the day taking physical and intelligence tests, anxiously hoping I had failed both. The most memorable part of the day was leaving the grounds. I vividly recall looking out the back window of the car as the large iron gates were closing. It felt so good to know that I was going home.

My mother learned a few weeks later that I would not be accepted because they had they discovered I had a heart murmur. I didn't care what the reason was. I was just glad I wouldn't be going through the ominous iron gates of Girard College again.

During a pleasant summer day when I was eight, a very charming lady came to visit our home in Weston Place. Her name was Bertha Harm, and she worked at the Hershey Industrial School, an orphanage for "poor Caucasian boys" in Hershey, PA. She spent the afternoon talking to my mom and giving me written tests. I never heard anything more about it, until late in November when my mother informed me that I had been accepted at Hershey Industrial School. After my reprieve, the difficult decision had finally been made.

A Traumatic Day

Ironically, exactly three years from the date of my father's death, on December 4, 1936, I was admitted to the Hershey Industrial School. Like the day of my Dad's passing, the weather was dreary, wet, and chilly. My brother Charles and my mother drove me to Hershey, PA, the central Pennsylvania town named for the chocolate magnate, Milton S. Hershey. At the school, I was introduced—or rather, re-introduced—to Miss Harm. Recognizing her, I now put all the pieces of this nightmarish reality together. I had a physical exam at the hospital, and as we were getting into the car to go back to the main building, I slammed the door on my mother' hand. I don't think it was intentional, but deep in my unconscious it may have been my way of continuing my family's non-verbal response to difficult situations. I felt guilty for the harm I caused her, and all the words I might have offered to change the way things were unfolding stayed trapped inside me.

By the afternoon, I was separated from my mother and brother. They told me I was going to be measured for clothing and that my mom would meet me at Kinderhaus, where I would be living. By the time I was fitted for clothes, it was near dinnertime. The meals, like most of the services for the school, were all prepared at the "Main," as it was called. I was informed that I would be transported on a bus to Kinderhaus with the evening meal. All alone on this bus, the prepared food my only fellow "passengers," I was looking forward to seeing my mom and brother when I arrived. What a disappointment it was when I got off the bus, all the kids and the house parents were waiting on the porch to see the new kid.

I very much wanted to say goodbye to my mother and brother. I searched through all the faces, looking for them, but they were not there. I was frightened, then angry and crushed, when told that they had returned home. One of the housemothers informed me that they had wanted to stay, but had been encouraged to go, so that I wouldn't have to experience the sadness of saying goodbye. I've felt anger, disappointment, and loneliness in my life, but never have I felt them with the searing intensity I did on that December day in 1936.

Being admitted to Hershey Industrial School was similar to the experience I had when drafted into the Army during the Korean War. You join a group of complete strangers, and immediately, you are expected to get into the routine. But this adjustment is less traumatic at age 21 than it is at age 8. I spent two years at Kinderhaus with Miss Barker and Miss Cramer, two very loving and caring, but exacting, housemothers. I was enjoying the friendships that I had developed with boys my age at Kinderhaus. However, I couldn't say the same about the next move I experienced.

Following the end of the fifth grade in 1937, I was transferred from Kinderhaus to farm home #48, called Valley View. The home was one of many dairy farms where students ranging from 11 to 18 years of age lived. There were two sets of "house parents" who, while trying to control 18 boys, had children of their own to care for. They were able to deal with our basic needs for food, clothing, and shelter, but had little time for close personal relationships. While the housemothers tried to be nurturing and caring, their husbands were not so inclined. Their main concern was getting the farm work done.

Living among boys of various ages created a miserable atmosphere ripe for physical and emotional abuse by the older boys. Orphanages serve a worthy social purpose, but believe me, there is, as Dorothy declares in *The Wizard of Oz,* no place like home. There was no lap to climb up on for comfort or to discuss problems and concerns. You learned early on not to make waves and to follow the rules. I didn't *live* those early years at Valley View; I simply *survived* them.

Milton S. Hershey, the founder of the school, thought it was important for youngsters like us to learn the "work ethic." At Valley View we had a herd of 30 Holstein cows, one huge bull, four mules, two large workhorses, and a multitude of chickens. The one thing you must know about a dairy farm is that cows don't take holidays or weekends off. They must be milked morning and evening, and that added up to 60 milkings a day for our herd. Cows do little but eat, sleep, and produce milk. They also drop an awful lot of manure. I found out nothing could wake you up faster than being hit in the face by a tail full of cow manure early in the morning.

The Milton Hershey School subscribed to the old maxim, "idleness is the devil's workshop." Dairy farms in those days were labor-intensive, so we boys had no chance of ever getting into the devil's workshop. We did most tasks by hand. Using pitchforks to move hay from the field to horse-drawn wagons and then to storage in the hay lofts; cutting down corn stalks by hand, tying them into stacks, and untying them later to husk the corn for transport to the barn; following the machine that cut the wheat and bound them into sheaves that we stacked (and if it rained, we had to un-stack them) before bringing them to the barn, where a machine separated the wheat from the chaff.

The most tiresome and useless chore was hoeing corn. If you have driven on country roads or on Interstate 70 through Ohio and Indiana, you've noticed those long, endless rows of corn. You can't appreciate how endless they are until you and a dozen other boys start out on a hot summer morning and spend the entire day hoeing the weeds from the corn. Down one row, then back, then down another row and back again until IT WAS TIME TO MILK THOSE DAMN COWS AGAIN!

A usual day started at 5:30 AM, actually a half-hour earlier if you were one of the two boys who had to go out to the pasture and bring the cows into the barn for milking. We had time after the morning milking to wash up for breakfast. That began with boys taking turns each morning to read morning devotions and saying a prayer before eating. We had little time to eat as we then had additional chores at the barn and house before getting dressed to wait for the school bus. I had the chore of cleaning the ashes from the huge furnace that heated the home. It took me too long to handle this chore. I was always anxiously hurrying to get cleaned up and dressed, afraid I was going to miss the school bus — which I and two other kids did and had walk some six miles to school. I have never forgiven that damn bus driver.

Like the army, life at Hershey was organized and disciplined. You followed orders and did not make waves. Get out of line at school and you served detention, usually at noon, so you missed the movies shown in the auditorium. School ended at around 3:30 and we caught the bus back to the farm home and began MILKING THOSE DAMN COWS AGAIN.

The Solace of Summer Baseball

You may not believe it, but during the long summer evenings we found time to play baseball. I enjoyed it, even though the field we played on was full of stones and ruts and weeds. Baseballs were treasured items and despite the field of wheat adjacent to the ball field, we never lost one, but trampled down a helluva lot of wheat searching for them. We also learned how to lengthen the life of the ball by re-sewing the cover when it came loose. After the leather cover wore out, we used black friction tape to keep them usable.

We played in a loosely organized farm-home baseball league against other farm homes located nearby. "Nearby" in farm language means that it was a mile or two away: no bus rides. We walked, carrying our equipment with us. No fancy uniforms, just those same bib overalls we wore when working on the farm. The only change in our attire was for those of us lucky to get a pair of baseball cleats for Christmas. The other kids wore their work shoes full of cow manure. This was the extent of my high school baseball career. Given the restrictions on gas and travel during World War II, there were no high school baseball teams at Hershey Industrial School.

Having started school in Weston Place at age five, I was a year younger than my classmates and seemed always to be swimming upstream physically when competing with them. This caused me to change my course of study. My mother's dream was that I would learn a trade at Hershey. I had planned to take the sheet metal and heating course when I went into the tenth grade. However, because of my lack of physical strength, I was put into the commercial course. I was informed that I would have to spend one extra year at school if I wanted to take the sheet metal course. I did not want to spend one more year there—I wanted out—so choosing the commercial course was a "no-brainer." Later, during my time in the Army during the Korean War, I would realize that this was a life-saving choice.

I was to graduate in June of 1945 from Hershey Industrial School. But because of World War II and the need for workers in factories supplying the "Arsenal of Democracy," I was allowed to leave school before graduation. In March of that year, I moved into the home of my sister Emma, her husband Al Sincavage, and my mother in Lebanon, PA. Emma and her husband were both teachers at Lebanon High School. My sister, who had aspired to be a dancer, was a graduate of East Stroudsburg College, the only one in our family to have attended college. Al, who had played college football and graduated from Lebanon Valley College in Annville, PA, served as the assistant football coach at Lebanon High School. He was one of the early professional football players, a linebacker in the 1930s for the Shenandoah Presidents. In those days, helmets did not include face guards, and Al had the face to prove it. His nose was broken so many times that surgeons never could get it straightened.

That spring, I began my first job, earning seventy-five cents an hour as a clerk in the large warehouse of Bethlehem Steel in Lebanon, PA. They made every size of nuts and bolts imaginable—all in great demand during World War II. But the job failed to fill the empty space in my heart. My affection for the game of baseball was growing stronger each day.

CHAPTER TWO

The Siren Call of Baseball

Investing your life in any profession involves great love, and love is blind! I'm sure those closest to me in the summer of 1945 questioned my decision to invest my life in the game of baseball. Standing six feet, six inches tall and weighing only 165 pounds, I was not what anyone would call "physically developed." The likelihood of my making the major leagues were less than my chances of winning a national lottery, but at age 17, what did I have to lose? Throughout my life, I have found that listening to my heart has always led me to my treasures. That didn't mean financial wealth, but it led me to something you will never find listed on your paycheck: Satisfaction!

In the summer of 1945, I tried out for my first organized baseball program, formed by "Lefty" Hallman, director of the Lebanon, PA YMCA. I pitched well and was selected to play for Kercher's Machine Shop, one of six teams in the league. Thanks to the YMCA League and the support of local businessmen, my pitching caught the attention of Charles "Pop" Kelchner, a long-time St. Louis Cardinal scout who resided in Lebanon. That fall, he signed me to a Cardinal minor-league contract to play at Lynchburg, TN. The contract was for $100 a month. I didn't care about the money; I was now a professional baseball player—or so I thought.

In March 1946, I asked for and got a leave of absence from my job at Bethlehem Steel to report to the Cardinals' minor-league camp in Albany, Georgia. I was in for some early surprises and disappointments. Raised in the regimented all-boys school at Milton Hershey, I was unbelievably naive about the world. For the first time in my life, I was on my own—without house parents or family, traveling by bus from Lebanon, PA to Albany, GA.

Raised in an all-white, northeastern school for boys, that bus ride to Georgia opened my eyes to a world I had never seen before. The scenes of ramshackle houses and the poverty of Black people seemed never-ending as the bus sped through the rural South. The squalor I viewed from the bus became more palpable when I arrived in Albany. Each day on my way to the ballpark, I had to walk on the dusty red clay streets through the "colored" section of "Al-benny" (as it was pronounced). For the first time in my life, I witnessed the profound injustices of the world in which I was living.

During the next nine summers of baseball and two years in the U.S. Army, I would meet people from every social, economic, educational, ethnic, and racial stratum of society. Travel and baseball provided me with the finest liberal education I could ever receive. I became more socially aware and active, while developing a greater understanding, tolerance, and compassion for people. I would recommend travel to all young people. It does broaden one's appreciation and acceptance of other people and their cultures.

My stay as a professional baseball player in Albany was brief. Young and naive, I didn't know that the number given me indicated my ranking as a prospect. I should have realized that when I was given a three-digit number to attach to the back of my uniform.

Despite my brief stay, there were moments of great joy and satisfaction. As a youngster at Hershey Industrial School, I was an avid Cardinal fan, amassing two huge scrapbooks filled with clippings and photos from 1940 through 1945. I can still feel the delight I felt on the first day of camp, putting on the shirt with the historic "Cardinals" in script writing. They were the original St. Louis Cardinal uniforms worn by the major-league players. As I was about to tuck in the shirt, I noticed some embroidered writing on the bottom of the right shirttail. It looked like an autograph. I quickly pulled up the shirttail and I couldn't believe what I read: *"SLAUGHTER."* God, I was wearing Enos Slaughter's shirt! *Can it get any better than this?* I thought.

My first manager was "Specs" Garbee. Baseball nicknames are derived from physical characteristics, and to nobody's surprise, Specs wore glasses. He spent his entire baseball career pitching in the minors, but he knew a lot about pitching. Dealing with very young pitchers, his instructions were similar to those of an Army platoon sergeant. He began with the basics, and I'm talking *real* basics. For instance, how to stand on the mound: "Look and act like a professional, dammit! The mound is your office. This is where you work. You stay on the mound, ready to make the next pitch!"

He then would describe what you *did* not do: "After each pitch, you don't walk fifteen feet toward the catcher—get the ball—walk around to the back of the mound—pick up the rosin bag, toss it ten feet behind the mound—then walk back up the mound to the pitching rubber to get a sign from the catcher." With sound reasoning, he continued. "Hell, you have just walked about 50 feet and thrown the rosin back where you can't reach it. Do you know how many pitches you will make during a game? Multiply that by 50 feet on every pitch and you'll walk miles during a game. Do you think you're not going to use up a lot of energy on a hot day? You bet your ass you will!"

Specs also reminded us that such posturing movements would "annoy the hell" out of our fielders and fans. He then put it in economic terms: "You don't get paid by the hour. If you can get the game over in an hour and a half, you still get the same amount of money." Major-league pitchers and managers today could benefit from this minor-league wisdom.

In my first spring training camp, we practiced six hours a day. I didn't know there was so much to conditioning and learning your trade, but, damn, I loved it—until I was plunked hard in the right shoulder while batting. My arm was so sore I couldn't throw for days. Since they didn't have time to wait for a "three-digit number" like me to get over an injury, I received my first pink slip after only two weeks in camp. I still have the brief telegram I sent to my mother that day: "I was released and will be home next week." They asked for my shirt back—my Enos Slaughter shirt. Aware of the value of baseball memorabilia now, I sure wish I had pilfered it!

This disappointment notwithstanding, I enjoyed my brief dip into pro baseball waters and could not wait to do it again. Frank Howland, a big, strong kid from Amsterdam, NY, got released the same day as I did, and his humor relieved some of my sadness about the pink slip. While waiting for our Greyhound bus headed north, Frank began imitating a ballpark P.A. announcer: "Pitching for Albany (pause) Specs Garbee. And catching (longer pause) the next bus out of Albany—FRANK HOWLAND AND NELSON KING."

I returned to counting nuts and bolts at Bethlehem Steel, but my yearning to return to the pitcher's mound was so strong that I ended up losing my "fallback" job at the warehouse by going out for another try. In July of 1946, I read that Roy Dissinger, a professional baseball scout, was holding a tryout camp just north of Lebanon in Fredricksburg, PA. Roy had left the Cardinals organization and was in the first year of forming his own minor-league operation. He had Class "D" teams in Geneva, AL, and New Iberia, LA, and a Class "B" team in Anderson, SC. His top team was in New Orleans, in the Class "AA," Southern Association.

Unable to resist the siren call of baseball, I called in "sick" to the Bethlehem Steel warehouse on tryout day. With two other players, I hitchhiked ten miles from Lebanon carrying all my gear to the tryout field in Fredricksburg. I don't know what it was about that day, but I was in some kind of zone, pitching with ease and consistently throwing strikes.

Dissinger gave me a piece of advice that day that I used for the rest of my career: "Let every pitch go in front of your belt buckle!" I'd recommend this to pitchers who are having control problems. This tip enabled me to consistently follow through with a smooth delivery and pitches that were "sneakily fast." Although hitting was never one of my talents (as I proved for eleven seasons), I even hit a triple that day. My performance caught Dissinger's attention. To my great surprise and even greater delight, he offered me a contract for $125 a month to report immediately to New Iberia, LA, in the Class "D" Evangeline League. Thinking this might be a dream and I'd wake up counting nuts and bolts at Bethlehem Steel, I signed immediately.

Against the advice of my mother, I quit the job at Bethlehem Steel and headed to New Iberia. I didn't even know where New Iberia, LA, was. To me, it sounded like Siberia in Russia, where the salt mines are. I found out I was going to the bayou country of Louisiana (curiously enough, the largest salt mines in the nation are located nearby in Abbeville). Of greater distinction, New Iberia, located in the heart of

"Cajun Country," is the home of the world-famous McIlheny's Tabasco sauce.

All Aboard the Crescent City Line!

From Lebanon, PA, I caught a Reading Railways train to Washington, DC, where I was to transfer to Southern Railways for the trip to New Orleans, LA. With six hours to kill, I walked outside Union Station for my first view of the Capitol Building and couldn't resist the opportunity to take the guided tour. It was more impressive as the tour director told us the history of this magnificent structure. I viewed it with both delight and anxiety, my eyes constantly on my watch in the naive fear that, if I missed the train to New Orleans, I would have to wait a week to catch another train. I wondered if I had enough money to get back to Lebanon and what would happen to my chances of playing professional baseball. I wasn't about to miss that train!

I arrived in New Orleans late in the evening. I had to take a Greyhound bus to New Iberia, and didn't arrive until the wee hours of the next morning. Unsure of what to do or where to go, I was met by Francis Hecker, a veteran pitcher on the New Iberia team. He was the most gracious person I met in my eleven years in professional baseball. Though he had wanted to join the priesthood, baseball had a stronger tug on Francis' heart. He took me to the home where he and Bill Sutherland, an infielder, were rooming.

Prior to going to bed, I went into the bathroom to clean up. I turned on the light. What a shock! All I could see in the bathtub were hundreds of cockroaches, all quickly scurrying to hide in any dark spot they could find. I wasn't interested where they went, just glad they disappeared. I discovered later that they were not cockroaches, but "water bugs," but

I never spent too much time in that bathroom, taking my showers at the ballpark instead.

The next morning, I got my first daylight view of New Iberia and the bayou country. On the walk downtown to have breakfast, the heat and humidity were already enveloping the town. It was the kind of heat and humidity that indicates the imminent arrival of a thunderstorm, a daily occurrence. That was the why the curbs in the main business section were two to three feet above the street level; they kept heavy rain from overflowing into the businesses.

The rains came nearly every mid-afternoon, but they never washed out a scheduled baseball game. Losing a paying gate in the low budget Class "D" leagues was something not to be considered, no matter how bad the rain. The groundskeeper and the general manager of the team developed a creative method to make the wettest field playable. Gasoline—and I mean plenty of it—did the trick. The groundskeeper and general manager would liberally douse the dirt portion of the infield with gasoline delivered in a large tanker truck. When the infield was sufficiently, they threw a lighted match, and everyone ran like hell. The fire and smoke from the burning gasoline rose well over 100 feet, visible from every spot in the town. This procedure served two purposes. It dried out the infield sufficiently, and it was a "smoke signal" to everyone in town that there would be a game that evening.

Aaron Ward, a second baseman for the New York Yankees during the glory years of Babe Ruth, owned and managed the New Iberia Pelicans. Although he hailed from Booneville, Arkansas, after ten years in the "Big Apple," he and his wife had adopted the big-city lifestyle and fashions of New York. As manager, Aaron never suited up in a baseball uniform. Instead, he wore a multi-colored sport coat, an equally eye-catching tie, bright pants, and white shoes, and topped it off with a white Panama straw hat. His style was so out of place in New Iberia, and definitely out of place in any dugout I had seen then or since.

I lasted just two weeks at New Iberia and pitched one inning. During that time, I had only two conversations with Ward. The first was when I arrived and he had me sign a contract for $125 a month. The second was when he told me I was being released. But in that short period of time, I witnessed things I had never seen before. For instance, the field we played on was a high school football field. Like the New York Giants' Polo Grounds, this gave the baseball park extreme and unusual dimensions. As usual, the majority of good seats were located directly behind home plate, near what would be about the 50-yard line for football. But the dimensions at New Iberia were the opposite of the Polo Grounds. It was 475 feet to left field, 475 feet to right field, and a mere 310 feet to centerfield. As a result, you pitched everyone inside, hoping they would pull the ball.

The league was very fast, given a phalanx of much older and seasoned players anxious to renew baseball careers interrupted by World War II. Likewise, fans were renewing their desire for entertainment, and minor-league baseball provided it with a 140-game schedule. New Iberia Pelican fans made a spontaneous and unusual display of approval when a hometown player hit a home run. A fan would take off his hat, drop in a dollar and pass the hat through the crowd for other fans to contribute money. Hitters could make as much or more than they made on their monthly contract, just from hitting a home run. Unfortunately, pitchers were not so well rewarded. They could go nine innings, throw a shutout and get nothing. Fans and owners always liked home-run hitters and still do.

One of my strongest memories about New Iberia was the fan reaction when a hometown player won the game with a "walk-off" home run in the ninth inning. There wasn't time to pass a hat, but as the fans were leaving the stands, dollar bills or change would be stuffed through the screen behind home plate. The batboys, like trained monkeys, would climb ten or fifteen feet up the screen, collecting and stuffing money into their shirts, and always received a good tip for their work.

After two weeks, I knew I was too young and over my head playing in the Evangeline League. The brief stint in New Iberia included one road trip to Natchez, Mississippi, in the searing and humid heat of July. Hotels were not air-conditioned in those days. With only an overhead fan to move the air, you never really cooled off. We would take bed sheets, soak them in ice water, and cover ourselves, hoping to get some sleep.

It was during this trip that I made my first professional baseball appearance in Natchez, Mississippi. I came in to pitch in the late innings of a losing game and got two outs to end the inning. I was the leadoff hitter in the top of the eighth and swung late on a fastball that landed just inside the right field foul line for a double. So, I went one for one, and that was the end of my career in the Evangeline League for 1946. I was released when we got back to New Iberia. I still tell people that I led the Evangeline League in hitting for 1946. (In 95 games and 23 at bats in the major leagues, a decade later, I never had a hit.)

Returning home to Lebanon, the job at Bethlehem Steel was gone, and I had no idea what to do. I played semi-pro baseball for the Fredricksburg Chix during the summer, but still had no paying job. My brother-in-law was tired of feeding and housing me, and my guilt became heavy. In desperation, I found a job at a factory where they made silk stockings. It was boring as hell, and called for finger dexterity, something I later found out I lacked in abundance. After being discharged from the Army in 1952, I took an aptitude test. One portion of the test was for finger dexterity. I had to pick up thin metal pieces, similar to needles, with tweezers, place them in small holes in a square wooden box. During the 10-minute test, I think I put only one where it was supposed to go. The guy giving the test said, "I've been giving tests for ten years and you are absolutely the worst I have seen. Don't ever apply for a job that requires finger dexterity!" I told him I wished I had taken the test years earlier.

Returning to factory work was the lowest moment of my young life. I was miserable doing this job, and I had to work the 3 to 11 PM shift. If you have ever had to work that shift, you know what I'm saying. Forget all about your social life, there is none. I prayed every evening to find something I loved to do.

My agony was relieved and my prayers answered when Roy Dissinger came into my life for the second time. He was passing through Lebanon in the off-season. After talking with "Tiny" Parry, the sports editor of the *Lebanon Daily News*, Dissinger contacted me to see if I wanted to give baseball another try. Mr. Parry's suggestion that I was a baseball prospect gave me an opportunity to play professional baseball again. I signed a contract for $125 a month to play at Geneva, Alabama, in the Class "D" Alabama State League and was to report for spring training in mid-March, 1947 at Anderson, SC. I did not know it then, but the most defining moment in my life was about to happen.

I arrived in Anderson, SC in mid-March, and the organization had arranged to rent homes from the citizens of the town. I was bunking with four other prospects. The weather was not quite baseball temperature; in fact, it was damn cold. The house had no central heating system, and we quickly discovered that the fireplaces in each bedroom were useless, since there was no gas line to the fireplace and no wood. All we had were thin blankets so we quickly realized they were not enough to keep us warm. After one night of freezing, we learned that, if you slept with another person, you could stay warm. So we "shacked up" together, slept well, and nobody had any homophobic fears or gave a damn about it.

We never overslept. We couldn't wait to get to a warm restaurant for breakfast. I had my first cup of hot coffee in South Carolina.

I can't remember much about that spring except for the first time being on a field with a former major leaguer: Mace Brown, who served as a pitching coach for the camp. He had pitched eight years in the big leagues, seven of them with the Pittsburgh Pirates. Mace's pitching record in the majors was 76-57, but fans still remember him only for one of those losses. It occurred on September 28, 1938 in Chicago. The Pirates had a 5 ½ game lead by mid-August over the Giants and 8 over the Cubs. Anticipating being in the World Series, the Pirates began building an enlarged press level on the roof at Forbes Field. However, the Pirates stumbled down the stretch, while the Cubs got hot. The Bucs' lead on September 27 dwindled to just 1-½ games as they came into Chicago for a three-game series that would determine the league championship.

Dizzy Dean beat them 2-1 in the first game to cut the lead to half a game. The next game was fatal for the Pirates. With the Pirates leading 5-4 in the bottom of the eighth, the Cubs tied the score. Mace Brown came on in relief to end the rally and keep the game tied at five. The Pirates failed to score in the top of the ninth. Darkness was falling; this would be the last inning. In the bottom of the ninth, Brown got two quick outs. Gabby Hartnett, the manager and catcher for the Cubs, came to bat. Mace got two strikes on him, but the next pitch left the park for 6-5 Cubs win. It was called a "Homer in the Gloamin'" in the Chicago sports pages and this 1938 game is known and remains the most memorable and dramatic game in Cubs history. Unfortunately, that game and that one pitch to Gabby Hartnett defined Mace Brown in baseball history. The Pirates never recovered, while the Cubs won 10-1 the next day and finished 21-4 in the month of September, ending two games in front of the Pirates to win the pennant.

I had little or no contact with Mace or Jimmy Francoline, the manager of the Geneva Redbirds. They had their eyes on more talented prospects. Looking back, I can't recall having a personal conversation with either man. I was too involved in having fun and finding personal satisfaction playing baseball. I didn't even think about cut-down day until, as it always does, it arrived. I was about to experience the major defining moment in my life that final day of spring training in 1947.

Roy Dissinger, the boss, came in the final day to make decisions on the players who would fill the rosters for his minor-league teams. He stood behind the pitching mound as he viewed the talents, or lack of them, of pitchers and hitters. My name was called, and it was time for me to make my audition. I can't recall being anxious and I was too young to "choke." As I took the mound, Roy said "I just want to see you pitch. Don't worry about getting three outs, just keep pitching and facing hitters until I tell you to stop." I began by getting the first batter out, and then gave up a single, then a double. I got another out, and then gave up another single. I was not feeling optimistic, but Roy told me to keep pitching. After I gave up a double and retired a batter, he finally said, "That's enough. I've seen all I want."

Certain my performance was not very good, I can still visualize the long walk to the clubhouse. I had to walk up a steep hill to the football field, where the locker rooms were located. With my head down, I walked the final 100 yards to the end zone and the locker rooms. I was surprised that the room was empty. I was all alone. I started to undress, sat down on the bench with my head in my hands, and began to cry; sure I was going to be released. I then said a silent prayer: "If it's God's will that I don't make the Geneva team, I will accept it." But I also hoped it wouldn't be so. After that prayer, I felt a quiet peace.

I showered and dressed as the other players began coming into the locker room. We were notified to report to the baseball field, where Roy

Dissinger would make known the roster for each team. With the entire camp joined on the field, I waited anxiously to hear his decisions. I knew I wouldn't have to wait too long, as he began with the Geneva team. He called out five or six names, and I couldn't tell who they were. All I knew was that my name was not called. Then I head him say, "KING." God, I felt such joy and relief!

However, that joy was interrupted by an annoying feeling—the awareness you have when you are in a group, but don't yet have their approval. When Dissinger called my name, it seemed as if all the players on that field turned around to look at me, thinking, *"HIM? You chose HIM?"* That feeling was palpable on the team bus during the long trip to Geneva. I can't recall anyone talking to me. I felt like an outsider, unwanted, which tapped into subconscious feelings of rejection from my childhood. But this time, my reaction was positive. I never felt more determined in my life and told myself, "Screw them, I'll show these SOBs I can pitch!"

I'm not sure if there is a heaven, but if there is one, it could not be more enchanting and delightful than that late afternoon of 1947 in Anderson, SC. After two releases and failures, this time I wasn't going back home. I was on my way to realizing my dream of playing in the major leagues.

I often wondered what Roy Dissinger saw in me that final day of spring training in Anderson, SC. As my years in professional baseball progressed, I gradually understood what he liked about me. I threw strikes! I never walked anyone that day. Despite giving up hits, I was never afraid to throw the ball over the plate. Scouts and managers search for players who are very consistent in what they do. My talent was being able to throw strikes, and I cultivated it each year I played. My talent reached its zenith in 1954, when I was pitching for Danny Murtaugh at New Orleans in the "AA" Southern Association. I went 56 consecutive innings without walking a batter. In eleven years of pitching and 1,357 innings, I averaged less than two walks per nine innings.

Geneva was a small, tranquil rural town with a population of only 2,500, located just north of the state line separating Alabama and Florida. The town, homes, and people were right out of the movie, *To Kill a Mockingbird*. A good portion of the population was Black, but with segregation then the rule in the South, they were rarely visible, except at the ballpark, which was segregated. Only Geneva's main street and the one parallel to it were paved and bordered by sidewalks. The downtown, or what there was of it, was limited to a short-order restaurant, a pharmacy, a cinema, bank, a few dry goods stores, and a loan office.

Other than the baseball games, Geneva had little or no nightlife. I wondered why and was told that Geneva was in a "dry" county. In my innocence, I actually thought it meant that they didn't get much rain. I found out fast that "dry" indicated the absence of alcoholic beverages. None were sold—legally, that is—in Geneva.

After the long bus ride from Anderson, I arrived in Geneva late in the evening. With two other players, I stayed one night in the only hotel in town. Making only $125 a month, I couldn't afford the prices for an entire season. The team had arranged for us to rent rooms at local homes that cost us only $10.00 a week. After checking out of the hotel, three of us walked to what we hoped was to be home for the summer—a wood frame house with a large front porch, both in need of painting, which was located on a dirt street only five minutes from downtown and the ball park.

The lady of the house, Doshia Milton, was a kind and hard-working woman. She was responsible for taking care of a very ill husband, two daughters, a five year-old son, her grandmother, a milk cow and numerous chickens. As we approached the home, the grandmother was sitting peacefully in a rocking chair on the porch. I saw her lean forward and, while holding two fingers to her lips in a very professional manner, expectorate a distance that nearly reached the street. She was enjoying a pinch of snuff! Most people in southern Alabama did. A town just a few miles from Geneva was known as the "Snuff Capital." It was said that they were always pleased to get rain, since it was the only way to wash the brown snuff stains from the sidewalks.

We were shown our room, which had two large double beds. This meant that two of us would again be sharing one bed. After getting settled, we were introduced to the remainder of the family. Mr. Milton had been a supervisor on the county highway department but was constantly bedridden now. We were told that the group he supervised had purchased some homemade still whiskey. The whiskey was almost pure alcohol and destroyed a good part of his stomach. Mrs. Milton was now saddled with the heavy burden of taking care of him. I can't recall her ever having a moment of rest and peace, though; she remained a kind and optimistic lady.

The two daughters were tall and beautiful young women whose names were normal for southern families, Jimmy Ruth and Carle Dean. However, as a baseball junkie, I thought they combined some of the best names in baseball history. Jimmy Ruth, the oldest, was worldly wise as she had worked in New York City for two years. Her experiences in the Big Apple took away the innocence that was so visible in her younger sister. She seemed to view baseball players as the type of people with whom you should not develop a close relationship. She made that clear by her attitude toward me.

Carle Dean was a high school senior, but looked older. She was tall, with a strong body, and her blond hair and blue eyes gave her a Nordic type of beauty. Unlike her sister, Carle Dean was friendly, outgoing, trusting, and easy to talk with. We would become friendlier during that summer of 1947.

The Geneva Redbirds were owned and administered by three businessmen. The president was George Calliteau, an outgoing and friendly man who owned the pharmacy. One of the other owners was Spurgeon Brown, who had a loan agency and a bus company. He provided the transportation for the team, in the form of a light blue school bus with straight back seats. Needless to say, it was not luxurious. The other owner was a banker.

Baseball Economics

When I began my professional baseball journey at Geneva, there were only sixteen major-league franchises, all east of St. Louis and the Mississippi River. With only 400 jobs available and over 8,000 minor-league players vying for one of those rare major-league slots, it was an owner's market. Branch Rickey, who originated the farm system for developing talent for the major league, noted, "Where there is quantity, you will find quality." The success of his operations at St. Louis and Brooklyn was proof of that formula.

The reserve clause then in effect held players in servitude to the owners who had signed them or owned their contract. This meant that players had no opportunity to test their talent on the open market at any level of the game. This stands in stark contrast to the economics of the game today. There is a clamor now for setting "salary limits," as if they were something new in professional baseball. Salary limits were already in effect, however, not at the highest level of the game, but at the lower levels of the minor leagues when I began my career.

In *Connie Mack's Baseball Book*, Mack explains how and why the "salary cap" made it possible to run such large minor-league operations. There were fifty-one minor leagues in operation in the late 1940s. Each league usually had eight teams, with limits on roster size and the total monthly salary that could be paid during the season. Mack's book provides an outline of the classifications, the number of roster players and the total monthly salaries allowed for minor-league teams in the years following World War II.

In the Class "D" league, such as the Evangeline or Alabama leagues where I began my career, the total monthly salary for an entire roster was $2600. Only at the highest levels of minor-league play, Class "AAA" and Class "AA," had no salary limits. Despite these stark salary limits in the lower minor leagues, the situation created an opportunity for young players like me to learn my trade.

The Importance of Mentors

Without a doubt, one of the true benefits of my first season in Geneva was playing on a team with older players. Minor-league teams were loaded with experienced players returning to the game after the war. They had a wealth of baseball wisdom and were eager to share it with younger players. I have listened to Hall of Fame members Ted Williams and Bill Mazeroski remark that playing on teams with older players hastened their advancement to the major leagues. Mazeroski, who came up when he was only 20 years old, began playing on fast semi-pro teams near Wheeling, WV when he was 15. In discussions I had with him later during my career as a broadcaster, he credited his quick rise to the majors to learning from older players.

I was fortunate to record a lengthy conversation between Ted Williams and Bill Virdon on the topic of hitting. Williams recalled his first season with San Diego in the Pacific Coast League, when he was a cocky 19-year-old who thought he knew everything about hitting. During an early season game he popped up in the infield for the final out of the inning. When he walked out to his position in left field, swearing and kicking his glove, one of the old pitchers in the bullpen asked him what was wrong. Williams replied, "I can turn any pitcher's fast ball around, but they keep throwing me that off-speed crap." The veteran pitcher quietly said, "Kid, until you can prove you can hit that crap, they'll show you a fastball, but they won't let you hit it."

As Williams told Virdon, "It was like a light bulb was just turned on in my mind. I thought, 'these old pitchers make a living getting guys like me out. They must know something about hitting that I should be listening to!'" He finished by saying, "Every time I knew I wasn't going to bat in the next inning, instead of going back to the bench, I sat in the bullpen listening to these old pitchers describe how they set up hitters to get them out. I spent the rest of that year talking to those old pitchers—on trains, in hotel lobbies—learning about hitting. I milked their brains dry."

Had it not been for "Cotton" Bosarge, a veteran second baseman from Mobile, AL, I never would have made it to the major leagues. Bosarge had fiery red hair and a competitive temperament to match. Having served in the U.S. Navy during the war, married and the father of one child, he wanted to see if he could renew his baseball career. Second basemen and shortstops see the battle between pitcher and hitter better than anyone else except the catcher.

"Cotton" approached me one day in Geneva with an observation about my pitching. "I get a good view of how you pitch batters, he began. "You throw strikes consistently and keep the ball down low in the strike zone, but your fastball has no movement on it." He then asked me how I held my fastball. I showed him, holding it with my two fingers across the seams. He asked me why I did this, and I told him that I'd read Bob Feller held his fastball that way. He said, "Hell, you can't throw as hard as Bob Feller! Why don't you try holding the ball with the seams? I think you'll get movement on your fastball." I took his advice and developed a mean sinking fastball. "Cotton" Bosarge's interest and advice that day transformed me from an ordinary pitcher into one who would eventually make it to the major leagues. His kindness remains so vivid to this day.

The Redbirds' ballpark, which was within walking distance from every place in town, did not have one blade of grass on the entire playing field; it was all sand. But this turned out to be very advantageous, as the rains drained easily from the field. In the entire season, I could not recall any game being rained out. That meant no doubleheaders and, most important to the owners of the team, no lost revenue.

Another benefit of a grassless field was the ability to keep baseballs in play longer. Baseballs are the big expense for minor-league teams. Dew falls in the evening in Alabama; when balls were fouled out of the park and into the tall grass, they got wet. To get them back, the owners offered anyone who returned a baseball a ticket to a game and ten cents. That got a lot of them back, but it presented another problem.

When the balls were returned, they were wet from the dew. Alabamans had developed an unusual solution to this problem. Peanuts, a leading product of the state, were and still are a popular treat at baseball parks. In Geneva, you could get your peanuts roasted or "biled," which in Alabama talk meant "boiled." My catcher was Clyde MacAllister, a big guy from Belton, SC, who had just served a four-year tour as an MP in the European theatre. Much older than me, and aware of my youthful naiveté, he took me under his wing and guided me on and off the field through my first season.

"Mac," as he was known, had a great sense of humor and a broad smile to go with it. One night when I was pitching, I noticed him walking toward the mound with a new baseball he had just gotten from the home plate umpire. He was shifting it from his bare hand to his glove like it was a hot potato. I asked him what was wrong.

He replied, "Don't you know what they do with the wet balls they get back when they are fouled out of the park? They put them in the peanut roasting machine to dry the balls. They left this one in too damn long!"

Budgeted on peanuts, the Alabama State League was strictly a "Bus League." We never stayed in a hotel for the entire 140-game schedule but had to ride home after each game. The towns in the league—Dothan, Brewton, Greenville, Ozark, Enterprise, Troy and Andalusia—were all within two or three hours of Geneva. The owners saved money on hotel expenses and also on meal money. We got $1.00 for meals on night games and a whopping $1.50 on Sunday afternoon games. The reasoning was we had to eat two meals on Sunday. White Tower hamburgers, at 12 cents each with a side of chili, got a lot of play.

I have found that you will never have enough money to live on in your lifetime, but you can always live on what you're making. Bob Mentzer, a Ford dealer and advertising client of mine during my radio years in Greensburg, PA, once asked me: "How much money do you think you need to live on?" I told him that I had played baseball for $100-$200 a month and even $9,500 a year (in the major leagues in 1957) and was at the time making about $15,000, but I couldn't really give him a precise answer to his question. When I shrugged, he replied, "Nellie, it's always $2,500 more than you're making."

The clubhouses in the Alabama State League were representative of the quality of the facilities in Class "D" baseball. Enterprise, a new team in the league in 1947, was growing fast with a U.S. Army base located nearby; it had to construct a new ballpark quickly. They did not overspend on the clubhouse. It was so small that only six players could fit into it at a time. We dressed and showered in shifts when we played there. Our own park in Geneva continually had problems with water in the visiting locker rooms. It was not unusual after games for visiting teams to be soaped up just when the showers dried up. Talk about a long bus ride in baseball uniforms and soapsuds. The top-flight teams and parks were at Dothan, Greenville, Brewton, and Andalusia. What made them top-flight? They had grass infields and outfields, and everyone could dress in the locker rooms at the same time.

Geneva had three teams each month: One team was playing, one team was just leaving, and one was preparing to come. Jimmy Francoline was listed as a player-manager on the Geneva roster. This allowed the team to have an "extra" player, but he'd better be a damn good player. Unfortunately Francoline didn't hit or manage very well and he was among the first to be released. Francis Hecker, a veteran pitcher, took over as manager when Francoline got the hook. I had met him the year before during my brief stay at New Iberia. As I mentioned earlier, he was a wonderful person who had at one time considered a career in the priesthood. His devotion to God and to baseball was strong, and he beat up on himself when we were losing, which was often that year.

During one losing streak, while waiting to load up the team bus, Francis was sitting in the front right seat (why that became the manager's seat I don't know, but it is that way with all sports teams that travel by bus), emotionally down, he was holding his head in his hands. Spurgeon Brown, the owner and driver of the bus, noticed his depressed mood, put his hand on Francis' arm, and said, "Skip, you can't make chicken salad out of chicken shit." That pretty much described the Geneva Redbirds in 1947. By the end of the season, I was the only player remaining from the group that arrived on the bus from Anderson that spring.

The final trip for our bus, the "Blue Goose," was to a game at Ozark. I was sitting in the second seat from the front on the left side. We were approaching a "T" intersection facing a huge Coca-Cola sign with black and white diagonal warning stripes on the bottom. I could see a huge gas tanker approaching on the main highway from our right. Spurgeon Brown hit the brakes, but we didn't stop. We had no brakes. He quickly tried to gear it down, and I heard and saw something come through the floorboard like shrapnel. Evidently, the clutch blew out. Somehow, he was able to maneuver the bus, miss the gas tanker, and make a left turn with only the two right tires touching the road. We were about to turn over, but miraculously didn't. The bus remained upright off the side of the highway. Relieved that we hadn't hit the tanker or flipped over, I said "shit!" Clyde MacAllister, the veteran catcher and my mentor, scolded me: "Careful with your language. Pretty soon you'll be chewing tobacco and spitting on the sidewalk!"

The near-fatal event prompted Spurgeon Brown to find someone else to take over the travel responsibilities. I don't know where he found the guy, but he seemed to be right out of central casting for "The Grand Ole Opry" or the "Andy Griffith Show," complete with bib overalls. He had evidently bought the cab and then built the bed for the school bus himself. The seating, what there was of it, comprised two planks, running the length of the cab, one on the left and one on the right. The floor was all wood with no chairs between the two side planks. I know it was designed for grade school youngsters, as we had to all but crawl to get into the bus. The seating was just high enough so your head wouldn't hit the roof when you sat down. For safety purposes as a school bus, the owner had installed a "governor" on the motor so it would not go over

35 miles per hour--on the straightaway. Going uphill, you could get out and walk alongside that bus.

Most amusing was the way our driver hailed the Greyhound Bus drivers as they approached him. Compared to our school bus, they looked like huge ocean liners. He would lean forward, look up and out the front windshield to see the bus driver, and then give him the hand-waving recognition all bus drivers give. He was now a professional, just like them!

With no seats in the middle of the bus, players would plop down and try to catch some shuteye lying on the wooden floor. During one trip, we began to smell smoke. A cigarette ember, fed by the flow of air underneath the cab, had burst into fire. The biggest damage was not to the floorboards, but to the catcher's chest protector. It had caught fire, and we had to borrow one from the home team when we arrived for the game.

In those days before portable radios, cell phones, and television, you had to find ways of entertaining yourself on trips. We did it by singing songs or making conversation. Ezra Embler, an outfielder with great running speed, appeared to have the talent to climb to higher-classification ball. Evidently, though, he didn't hit well enough, as I never heard of him after that year at Geneva. Watching workers in the fields on those long bus rides, Ezra would holler one-liners like, "Get out of that there 'tater' patch and pull up your drawers, don't you know those 'taters' got eyes?" Or, "Get away from that wheelbarrow Buford, you don't know nothin' 'bout machinery." Or, "Get out of that wheat field. Don't you know you're running against the grain?" There are occasions when I wonder what Ezra Embler did for the rest of his life.

Having been raised in an all-boy school at Hershey, the only females I had any "hands on" relationships with were those Holstein cows. I was a rookie in baseball, but even less informed in the ways of male-female relationships. Having gradually gotten to know Carle Dean Milton, I bravely asked her for a date to go to the movies. You remember the lyrics of the song, "How About You?" *Holding hands in the movie show, when all the lights are low, may not be new, but I love it. How about you?* They describe perfectly my feelings on my date with Carle Dean. I was to experience the joy of "falling in love" for the first time. I recall reaching for her hand, and she reciprocated. Wow! It got only as far as kisses and hugs, but for a rookie in love, it was exciting as hell. I was so young and inexperienced that I wouldn't have known how to go any further. Besides, Carle Dean was involved in the local Baptist church, and we neither of us were ready to handle that kind of guilt.

The next spring, prior to spring training in Bartow, FL, I stopped by to see her. Absence had not made her heart grow fonder. She'd found a local beau, and they married a year or so later. I'll always treasure the sweet innocence of my "first love."

The 1947 season at Geneva ended on Labor Day, and I was called up to Class "B," Spartanburg, SC, to assist in their final week of the season. Thanks to "Cotton" Bosarge and the newly found sinking fastball, I had pitched in 36 games and 194 innings to finish with a 3.06 ERA and an 8-11 record. Despite being with a last-place team, I had finally made a mark, small as it was, in professional baseball. My dream of making it to the majors was still alive.

The low salaries for playing professional ball in those days made it necessary to find off-season employment. I was fortunate to get work at the Bethlehem Steel plant in Lebanon, where the raw iron ore from the mines was processed and refined. The mines were located in Cornwall, PA, a short distance by rail from the plant. Cornwall's mines provided the iron ore for the cannons and rifles for George Washington's Revolutionary Army. My first job with the "labor gang" was pick and shovel work, and exceedingly dirty. "Joshko," an elderly Polish man who handed out the equipment for the labor gang, described this job best: "Hard work ain't easy!" After a winter on the labor gang, baseball spring training was a vacation!

CHAPTER THREE

Joining the Pittsburgh Pirates

Following the 1947 season, the Pittsburgh Pirates purchased Roy Dissinger's small minor league farm system. I was among the group of players who assembled at their minor-league spring training camp at Bartow, Florida. Originally used as an airport for training World War II fighter pilots, the Pirates organization transformed Bartow into four baseball fields, and we lived in the barracks and ate at the mess hall. It was an ideal site for spring training. There was little or no nightlife, which, I'm sure, was intentional. We were there strictly for baseball.

I was signed to a contract for $175 a month with New Iberia, Louisiana, in the Class "D" Evangeline League, where I'd been released in 1946. One of the owners reportedly questioned my appearance on the roster, wanting to know what the hell I was doing there, since they'd dumped me two years ago and he was certain I couldn't pitch in this league. I was ready to prove him, and others, wrong. My sinking fastball, a better curve ball, and improved control and confidence caught the attention of Pirates' scouts working the camp at Bartow. With the open, flat ground in Florida, the direction of the wind can have major effects on the movement of a thrown or batted ball. So it was that first day in spring training, as the wind blew from the first-base side toward left field. I ate up right-handed hitters with my sinker. I was stinging hands and breaking bats. One of those hitters was a big, strong right-hander named Frank Thomas, who was in his rookie season and at the start of what would be a long and successful major-league career.

As a high school hitter, Frank had evidently never encountered that kind of movement on a ball. I recall him innocently saying, "Do you know your fastball keeps moving in on my hands?" I replied, "Yeah. That's what I want it to do."

That day, I noticed scouts beginning to fill in the area behind the screen and home plate. The word got around that they should take a look at the movement this kid had on his sinker. Ted McGrew, one of the senior scouts, was so interested he took time to talk with me personally after the game. He said, "I let Ewell Blackwell get away from me a few years ago and I don't want to lose you." For an unknown kid at age 20 to be compared with Ewell Blackwell blew me away. I had the same physique, tall and lanky, threw from third base with a wicked moving sinker, but not with Blackwell's velocity. But to be compared with him was an honor that boosted my confidence further, guaranteeing that this was to be my breakthrough season.

The only nightlife I can remember that spring was hitchhiking with another player from Bartow to Lakeland to see the Tommy Dorsey Orchestra. The Dorseys, Tommy and Jimmy, were born and raised in my hometown, Shenandoah, PA, where their dad was the high school band director. Frank Sinatra, who was the male singer with Tommy Dorsey's band in his early years, credited Tommy's trombone styling for influencing the distinctive phrasing that set him apart from all the other singers of his era. It was a night I still treasure and became more memorable in 1955, after meeting Sinatra on the set of MGM, when I was pitching for the Hollywood Stars of the Pacific Coast League. I don't know how we made it to Lakeland and back hitchhiking, but in those years we were more trusting of others and people were eager to give strangers a ride.

When spring training ended, I left Bartow for New Iberia without any of the fears, doubts, or uncertainties that I'd experienced a year earlier at cut-down in Anderson, SC. I was now established as a qualified pitcher—and ready to prove it in faster competition. When we arrived in New Iberia I shared an apartment with Joe Kaczowka, a small, stylish, left-handed hitting and fielding first baseman from Massachusetts. He had played briefly at Geneva early in the 1947 season before being sent to New Iberia. Joe was one of many players who had returned from combat action in World War II. He had been an infantry rifleman during the heavy fighting at Anzio, Italy, but like most survivors of such carnage, he never spoke of the war. A quiet, friendly and generous person, Joe had found the girl of his life in New Iberia during his stay the previous year. They tied the knot that season before a standing-room-only crowd prior to a game. Joe wore his New Iberia Pelicans uniform and Audrey was radiant in a beautiful wedding dress.

More than any other sport, baseball is a "one-on-one" game. Offensively, the competition pits the pitcher against the hitter; defensively, the heart of the game is between the player and the ball. No matter where you sit for a baseball game, you always leave knowing who played well and who didn't. You or the managers don't need to watch video replays to make those judgments.

Unlike most team sports, baseball is not a game you learn by practice. You learn by playing daily under intense, live game competition. The best proof of that was my 1948 season at New Iberia. In a 140-game schedule, I started 34 games, completed 27, pitched 284 innings and walked only 83, winding up with a record of 20-13 for a sixth-place team. I especially relish the memory of receiving a $100 bonus for winning 20 games from the owner who had said, "He can't pitch in this league." The joy and satisfaction I knew that season in New Iberia created an inward peace and contentment that I had never experienced before. Sure of what I was doing with my talents and life, I was growing physically, mentally, and spiritually. I was working and playing; the two were fused perfectly for me. It was during this season I experienced the "Peak Experience" I described earlier.

My growth as a player and person that season came from the relationships I developed with two players, George Kinnamon and Pete McGarry. They were two very different people, coming from opposite ends of the age, baseball and life-experience spectrums. Even so, both were catchers, and no relationship between players is more personal than that between a pitcher and his catcher. In those days pitches were never called from the manager or anyone in the dugout. It would have been considered insulting to a catcher if they had.

George Kinnamon, a recent graduate of the University of Tennessee, was the first teammate I knew who had acquired a college degree. Lacking his educational history, I was fascinated by his intelligence, inquiring mind, and eagerness to engage in conversations on life and baseball. In his first season of professional baseball, his naiveté about life as a professional baseball player was visible and, at times, embarrassing for him. My relative familiarity with and love of the professional game was something he appreciated. The desires and needs we shared created an instant bond and a friendship that has lasted a lifetime. We made those long, boring bus trips tolerable, and even interesting, by exchanging stories and opinions.

George's career as a player was not as successful as he'd hoped it would be. Branch Rickey took over in 1950 as general manager of the

Pirates and because of George's educational background he signed him to manage in the Pirates' minor-league organization. After a few years, baseball finally lost its hold on George, and he retired to begin a more fruitful life, running a Dale Carnegie speaking enterprise in North Carolina and finally becoming a Lutheran minister. I feel cheated to this day that I was never able to hear one of his sermons. Like Branch Rickey's inspiring talks, I know they had depth and challenged the social conscience of his congregation.

At the other end of the spectrum was Pete McGarry, a red-haired Irishman from Providence, Rhode Island. He began his career at age 17 in the huge St. Louis Cardinal Farm system. Three years later, in 1941, Pete's eye-opening throwing arm made him a prime major-league prospect playing at Rochester, NY, in the "AAA" International League. Had it not been for five years of combat action during World War II, he would have made it the big leagues. Sadly, the scars of the war and the interruption of what might have been a successful baseball career had taken their toll when I met him in 1948. Now at age 27, he was playing in the lowest classification in the minors, Class "D" at New Iberia. He loved the game, but knew the future had passed him by, and tried to find some solace in alcohol.

I had just turned 20 that spring and was fortunate to have an experienced 27 year-old veteran as my catcher. Pete was the epitome of what a catcher should be. He had a fiery Irish temper, a competitive nature, and a tremendous throwing arm that he demonstrated to pitchers if they didn't throw strikes. Pete would step ten feet in front of home plate, drill the ball at you like he was throwing to second base and holler, "Throw the god damn ball over the plate!" He caught my attention and kept it. Pete also bruised the hell out of my left hand. Today, when I think of Pete McGarry, I instinctively rub my thumb over the bone at the base of my left index finger to see if it still hurts.

Early in the season, pitching at home against Alexandria (our ball park, a high school football field, was 475 feet down both lines and only 310 feet to center), I faced a right-handed hitter named Hunneycut, who had just joined them from the Southern Association. I had no book on him, so I went to my best pitch, a good sinker, inside and tight, right where I wanted it for a strike. I figured I'd go back inside again, but he had opened his stance and gotten the fat part of the bat on the ball for a home run to deep left-center. On Hunneycut's second time up, my competitive nature said, "Damn-it, get the ball really inside on the hands this time." I did, and he again opened his stance and hit another home run.

I was really angry as Pete came out to the mound, but he was calm, not upset as I expected. He said, "Did you learn anything?" I said, "Yeah, I got to get the damn ball inside better next time." His response was, "No, dammit, he's looking for the pitch inside. Go away on him!" I did, and I struck him out the last two times. Branch Rickey always said, "Pitching is the art of deception." That night in New Iberia, I learned how to set up hitters. The satisfaction I felt never left me and it was a stepping-stone in my pitching career.

Hitters can also deceive pitchers, of course. Elroy Face, a Pirate teammate regarded among the best relief pitchers in the game, shared the same opinion as Pete McGarry on the location of hitters in the batters box. If a hitter crowds the plate, he wants the ball inside. If he is off the plate, he wants the ball outside. It appears to be the opposite of what it should be, but it isn't. You can show him the pitch he wants, but don't throw it for a strike that he can hit. Make him hit your pitch, not his!

Playing baseball in the hot, humid weather of the Louisiana Bayou country changed my thirst-quenching habits. Iced tea and soda just didn't do the job. I never had a taste for beer until that season at New

Iberia. The popular brands then in the bayou country were Falstaff, Dixie, and Griesedieck. Following home games, I would always join Pete at his favorite watering hole, a small local bar not far from the ballpark. The social lubrication of alcohol never unlocked his thoughts of the war or of what might have been for his baseball career. Instead, it opened a book of wisdom on pitching and baseball that made me an eager listener.

As I've mentioned, Pete tried to find solace in alcohol, which eased his battle to find sleep every night. I was frightened when I went to see him one afternoon at his one-room rental. The room was unkempt, and the mattress, with no sheets, was patterned with so many cigarette burns. Today, I feel sad that I had no understanding of how to help him with his misery and addiction. Pete McGarry's knowledge of pitching had as big an effect on my career as Cotton Bosarge's input the year before at Geneva, Alabama. That season was the only association I had with Pete McGarry. I'd love to have the chance to sit down at some quiet bar for one more conversation with him.

Not only did I learn more about drinking that summer of 1948 at New Iberia, but I also encountered another vice. Gambling was and probably still is a part of life in the Bayou country. Young and naive about the dangers of gambling, I spent a lot of my daytime hours in the downtown pool hall. The owner, Tom Spiros, invited all the players to use the pool tables "on the house." Along with the pool tables, were constant poker games being played for high stakes. The index finger of Tom's right hand was amputated halfway to the knuckle. I never asked how or why, but it was no handicap to him. I took interest in watching him play poker, particularly the method he had for counting silver dollars. Using the stub of the partially amputated right index finger, he would stack 5 silver dollars exactly, picking them up with his thumb and middle finger. He never was questioned by anyone at the table.

The pool hall's main attraction for me was a Western Union ticker tape that kept an up-to-date score of every major-league baseball game being played on a given day. In addition, a blackboard recorded the complete scoreboard of all major-league games. With many games played in daytime then, I took delight in following the scores and, on occasion, posting them on the board as they came in on the wire. It was an entertaining place to spend the daytime hours. I never saw or knew of any players getting involved in gambling at the pool hall. The stakes were too high for players who were earning from $125 to $200 a month. However, as the years went by, I began to understand why Tom Spiros was so willing to have us frequent his place. The conversations at the pool hall usually got around to the New Iberia game of the night before and the one to be played that evening. Their interest was not strictly that of a fan. Gamblers are always looking for a slight advantage and naively we were providing it by talking casually about our team, its strengths and weaknesses, and its strategies.

The fans in the Bayou Country and particularly at New Iberia loved to wager. They bet not only on the outcome of the game, but on whether a pitch would be a ball or strike, which created animosity against the umpires that resulted in foolish fan retaliation. The most drastic reprisal I recall was when disgruntled fans poured sand into the gas tank of an umpire's car. And in Houma, one of the towns in the Evangeline League, two players on the team that 1948 season got into trouble for stealing money from a bookie joint that took wagers on horse racing. They managed to develop a friendly relationship with the bookie and then worked a scam for making winning bets. According to the story, one player would distract the bookie; the other would turn the bookie's clock back ten or fifteen minutes. With a direct line to the track where the races were being run, they would get the winner then place their bet with the bookie. Trusting and unaware of the scam, the bookie took the bet and paid off.

This went on for a while before someone got wise. The players were barred from baseball. They were lucky some guys with flat noses from Chicago didn't come to visit them. If this betting on horses warranted expulsion from baseball, there really is no defense for any player who bets on baseball games. Warnings against this violation were posted on every clubhouse door, from Class "D" to the major leagues. Pete Rose saw them every day, knew the rules, and still failed to abide by them. He paid the price. The Black Sox Scandal in the 1919 World Series nearly destroyed fans' loyalty to the game and ushered in the first strong commissioner of baseball, Judge Kennesaw Mountain Landis.

The addiction to gambling is much worse than alcohol, as I learned from the experience of Tom Lee, who ran a semi-pro team in Elkton, Maryland. Lee's team was part of the strong semi-pro Susquehanna Baseball League on the Eastern Shore of Maryland. During my two years in the Army (1950-52) at Fort Dix, New Jersey, I pitched for Lee's team on weekends. Tom's father owned the first Buick dealership in the Eastern Shore of Maryland. As a young man, Tom spent much of the "Roaring Twenties" in New York City. He enjoyed the speakeasies and met prominent Broadway celebrities. He also developed an addiction to alcohol, which caused him serious and long-lasting physical and emotional problems.

Living in the fast lane, Tom soon found gambling entertaining and addictive. He told me, "There were times following a day at the races when I would come back to my hotel room and throw winnings of $35,000 on the bed." After he started losing he began doubling his bets, which incurred a growing debt to his bookie. So enormous was his tab that a guy from Chicago was sent to erase him. He pleaded for and got time to pay off the entire debt. Of the two, alcohol and gambling, Tom said, "Gambling is the worst. Every alcoholic knows they're not going to get better tomorrow. But for gamblers, tomorrow is always the day they're going to get well."

Gamblers who bet on horses can't have the same relationship they do with baseball players. Horses don't talk. Following the final game of the 1948 season in New Iberia, Pete McGarry and I retired to our usual bar. As I was about to leave, I expressed my thanks to the bartender for the many memorable evenings spent there. I was amazed when he said, "You know, you cost me a lot of money this year." With my "social lubricant" working, I loudly inquired of him, "I won 20 and lost only 13, and you're blaming *me* for costing *you* money?" As a parting shot, I said, "You gotta be the dumbest-assed gambler in town."

My first season in the Pittsburgh Pirates' organization at New Iberia had been a break-through year for me. My 20-win season, with 280 innings pitched and only 83 walks given up, earned me a contract with the New Orleans Pelicans of the "AA" Southern Association. Vince Rizzo, the GM of the Pelicans, sent me a contract for $250 a month if I made the New Orleans team. If I was optioned out to a lower classification, I was to receive only $200 a month. Knowing my chances of making the jump from Class "D" to "AA" in one year were slim, I argued for a bigger monthly raise if I was optioned out. After a 20-win season, I knew I deserved more than a $25 monthly raise. My pleas fell on deaf ears. Knowing the laws of supply and demand, I signed the contract.

The only time I had been to New Orleans was when I was passing through on my trips to and from New Iberia in 1946 and 1948. This time, at least, I knew it would be a longer visit. In early March, I took the Reading Railway from Lebanon, PA, to Washington, DC, and then the Southern Railways sleeper to New Orleans. I arrived the day before spring training and resided with four other players at a private home the team had arranged. Located on Palmyra Avenue, just off Carrolton, it was within walking distance of Pelican Stadium. Mrs. Wiley, the elderly landlady, was a kind and pleasant woman who became a second Mom to me.

George Kinnamon, my catcher at New Iberia, had a girlfriend, Lorraine, living in New Orleans. He said to contact her when I got to the city, which I did the first afternoon I arrived. She lived only three blocks from Mrs. Wiley's place and invited me over for dinner with her family. Like all baseball players looking to save on meal money, I eagerly accepted the invitation. Well-dressed in a new gray gabardine jacket and appropriate slacks, I walked to Lorraine's home, where we shared a great meal and conversation about New Orleans and her beau, George.

Checking my watch, I realized it was time to get back to Mrs. Wiley's house as spring training began the next morning. After walking two blocks, I noticed a car using a spotlight as if searching for numbers on the houses facing the street. I continued walking. The spotlight now seemed to be following me. I turned to get a closer look and noticed it was a New Orleans police car. The officer stopped and asked me who I was and where I was going. I answered his first question, but having just arrived that afternoon, I knew the street but could not recall the house number. Unsure of the exact location, I could only tell him that it was "somewhere near here," which aroused his suspicions. He asked what I was doing and where I had been. I told him I was a member of the New Orleans Pelican baseball team and had just had dinner at a friend's house down the street. The officer then said, "Okay, you can go." I began crossing the street when the police car made a sharp U-turn and approached me. The driver said, "Get in the car!" I couldn't understand what was going on, but I knew it wasn't good.

The police drove to Canal Street and stopped in front of a hamburger and ice cream shop. One of the two officers in the cruiser went into the restaurant while the other stayed with me in the car. When the officer returned, he was accompanied by one of the workers. The officer said, "Can you identify this guy?" It took over 30 seconds for the worker, which seemed to like an eternity to me, before replying, "No, but he sure looks a lot like the guy who robbed the place." Holy Hell! I thought how close I was to being jailed, held overnight and having my face in the headline, "Pelican Pitcher Held in Robbery," on the front page of the *Times-Picayune*.

The police were kind enough to take me back to Mrs. Wiley's home. The first thing I did before going into the house was to get the house number. What an introduction to New Orleans! A few days later, after practice the players with whom I roomed stopped at a local restaurant-bar for a draft and a sandwich. I looked around and noticed the guy from the ice cream shop was at the bar. I quickly approached him, but before I could say anything he said, "Why the hell did they pick you up? I told the police the guy looked and dressed like a bum." I replied, "It sure took you a hell of long time to say, 'He's not the guy.'"

Spring training in New Orleans was heaven compared to Anderson, SC, and Bartow, FL. We shared Pelican Stadium with Indianapolis, the Pirates' "AAA" team in the American Association, managed by Al Lopez.

A pitcher on their team, John Hutchings, was the most entertaining player I had met. At 6'4" and 265 pounds, he resembled "Humphrey Pennyworth," then a popular comic-strip character. John combined the humor of Max Patkin and the uncanny ability of Jackie Price, two of the best baseball entertainers who traveled the minor leagues after World War II. Hutchings had an amazing ability to handle a fungo bat hitting fly balls to the outfielders. Standing in foul territory along the first or third baseline, he would face the crowd as if to hit a ball into the stands, toss the ball up, and swing. The people, as you'd expect, would duck, and yet the ball would have such power and backspin that it carried all the way for an outfielder to shag it. Amazingly, he never hit one into the stands, but spectators always kept ducking!

Evidently, my spring appearances did not amuse or impress the New Orleans brass as, prior to the start of the season, I was informed that I was being optioned to York, PA, in the Class "B" Inter-State League. I would be playing close to where I was born and raised, but my salary would be cut from $275 to $200 a month. York and Lancaster, neighboring cities and close rival in the Inter-State League, were appropriately named: The York White Roses and the Lancaster Red Roses. It was a saner sequel to the "War of the Roses."

I knew I was definitely moving up the baseball ladder. The ballparks were well lighted, all had grass infields, and we stayed at good motels/ hotels. The Inter-State League was another "bus league," but the cities were more centrally located. Teams included central Pennsylvania cities such as Allentown, Harrisburg, Lancaster, Sunbury, and York. Out-of-state teams were Hagerstown, MD, Trenton, NJ, and Wilmington, DE.

As you move up the baseball ladder, you encounter increasing levels of talent. Many noteworthy major leaguers played in the Class "B" Inter-State League. The most identifiable when I entered the league was Robin Roberts, who pitched for Wilmington in 1948. So dominant was Roberts in his first minor-league season that he pitched in only 11 games before he went directly to the majors with the Philadelphia Phillies. Willie Mays, then only 18 years of age, began his minor-league career in 1950 with the New York Giants farm team at Trenton in the Inter-State League. His talent was so obvious that he played in 83 games at Trenton before the Giants moved him to Minneapolis. The following year, he became a star in the major leagues as the New York Giants beat the Brooklyn Dodgers on Bobby Thomson's "Home Run Heard

Round the World" to win the National League Pennant. Both Roberts and Mays are in the Baseball Hall of Fame.

The filtering process for players working their way from Class "D" to the major leagues was exceedingly fine. So rare was the honor of playing in the major leagues that it has been stated you could place everyone who ever played in the major leagues into a stadium and not fill the lower deck. During my first two years in Class "D" ball, I was one of only two players who made that entire journey. The other was Mel Clark, an outfielder who played in the Evangeline League at Baton Rouge and made it to the Phillies in 1951.

Another sign of advancement in the game in Class "B" baseball at York was the team trainer. Baseball trainers then rarely had an acquaintance with medical or physical therapies, and our trainer, "Buddy" Knight, was no exception. Then in his mid-50s, he was showing the effects of his earlier career as a professional lightweight boxer. Damage to the head is a common injury among boxers, and it was noticeable in Buddy, whose nose was flat and memory was weakening. Along with his training duties, Buddy acted as a travel secretary, handling hotel reservations and driving the team bus. Fortunately, the Inter-State League was geographically arranged to accommodate short trips, and York, being centrally located, made it more favorable for travel. Knight had only one bad night driving. It wasn't serious, but with all the hours he put in, he apparently dozed off as we entered York in the wee hours of the morning, scraping six parked cars on the right side of the bus. It sounded like large, empty metal drums rolling down the street that awakened not only Buddy, but also the whole damn team.

The manager of the York White Roses was Frank Oceak. Frank began his playing career in 1932 in the New York Yankees' farm system as a journeyman middle-infielder and spent his entire career in the minor leagues. If you check the history of successful baseball managers, middle-infielders and catchers will dominate the list. They see and understand the game better than other position players, and Frank Oceak was proof of that. He began managing while still an active player at Lafayette, LA and remained a playing manager when he joined the Pirates' farm system at Oil City, PA, in 1942. Sixteen years later, in 1958, Oceak's dedicated labor in the minor league vineyards of the Pirates system was justly rewarded when Danny Murtaugh took over as Pirates manager and named him to be his third base coach. Frank proudly displayed a pair of World Series Championship rings won when he coached the 1960 and 1971 Pirate teams.

Optioned to York by New Orleans at the end of spring training in 1949, I began what was to be a longer relationship than anyone could have anticipated with both Oceak and the Pirates. Frank Oceak was a no-nonsense manager, which he made clear prior to the start of the season during a team meeting when he informed us the only thing we had to do was, "Keep your eyes, ears, and bowels open, your mouth shut, and we'll get along fine." I use that line now during speaking engagements, with the affirmation that only once was I able to do all four. It was in 1955 when I pitched winter baseball at Mazatlan, Mexico. I couldn't speak the language, and I developed a serious case of dysentery.

At York, I had another successful season, winning 16 and losing 15 for a sixth-place team. I led the league in ERA with 2.25 and again pitched in 36 games and 212 innings. Even though I did keep my mouth shut, I still managed to get into Frank Osceak's doghouse. I was rooming with Bill Plate, a first baseman who had been on the York team since the previous year. Bill had developed a friendship with a middle-aged couple who were big fans of the York team. They invited us to join them for a Saturday dinner at their home. Always eager for a good home-cooked meal and save on meal money, we eagerly accepted.

Unless it was Sunday, we always played night games, which meant that we had different meal times than ordinary citizens. Baseball players slept late in the morning, had a late breakfast, then a light meal before a game, and looked for something heartier afterward. When playing at home, we had to be at the park at least two hours prior to game time for batting practice. This Saturday dinner was scheduled for 3:30 PM. We arrived in time for a bit of conversation prior to dinner and there was something cooking that had a familiar smell. I inquired what it was, and the hostess said, "Swiss steak and gravy." That's all I had to hear, as it was the best meal my mother prepared, and I always had second helpings. The Swiss steak was delightful — too delightful. I couldn't resist having two and perhaps "a bit more if you please" helpings of the Swiss steak. By the time we left for the ballpark, I was belching from overeating.

I took batting practice, belching, began warming up, belching, and continued belching as the game began. Facing the first batter, I failed to cover first base in time to retire the runner. The next hitter sacrificed, and I threw the ball too late to get the out at second. With two runners on and no outs, I walked the next batter to load the bases. When Oceak came out to talk to me, I belched again. I knew he was aware of my gluttonous pre-game meal. Still, he kept me in the game, I promptly got in front 0-2 on the next batter, and then hit him in the ass to force in a run and leave the bases full. Oceak quickly came to the mound and angrily said, "Give me the god damn ball. I guess you had too much to eat." Well, did he hit a nerve with that comment! I knew he was right, but in my anger, instead of giving him the ball, I tossed it 15 feet into the air and began walking off the mound. I had taken only about two steps when I when I heard Oceak say, "If that ball comes down, it'll cost you ten dollars, big boy." It did come down, and I did owe him ten dollars, which then was 5% of my monthly pay. I never overate before a game or showed up a manager again. But I still enjoy a Swiss steak dinner and always think of Frank Osceak when I do.

My tall and thin physique garnered less than complimentary comments from opposing benches and fans. In Class "B" baseball, we had no coaches, only a manager. Oceak handled the third base coaching chores, and the pitcher who was not working the game wound up as the first base coach. While performing that duty during a road game at Allentown, a fan in the box seats was kidding me about my physique. He compared me to "Ichabod Crane," the main character in Washington Irving's story, "The Legend of Sleepy Hollow." We began having a friendly running conversation, which the fans were enjoying. He caught my attention with a witty comment: "Hey King, don't you get meal money like the other players? You look like you could use a good meal."

After the game, he took time to introduce himself and invited me to have lunch with him when we returned to Allentown. I took him up on the offer, and we always dined on what he thought would be a fattening meal for me at a local German-style restaurant. I also visited his home and became aware of his hobby, raising purebred Weimaraners. In 1949, he was one of the first in the country to raise that now-popular breed.

The final game I won at York was also the final game of the 1949 season. It was the longest game I had ever seen or participated in. Appropriately it was played on Labor Day, when York was playing at Hagerstown, MD. It was a meaningless game, as neither team finished in the first division or eligible for post-season playoffs. I had made what I'd been certain was my final start two days earlier. Knowing or thinking my season was over, I decided to retire to the bullpen to catch a season-ending tan. During the late innings, Ed Katalinas, who had played semi-pro ball with my brother Paul and was now scouting for the Detroit Tigers, stopped by to say hello. He planned to hang around until the game ended, which we were sure was going to be the ninth inning. However, as hard as either team tried to win or lose it, the game went into extra innings.

This type of game always seems to occur during contests where winning or losing has no importance to league standings. One Easter Sunday at West Palm Beach, FL, Bob Prince and I broadcast a spring training game that went into extra innings. Managers, players, fans, and broadcasters, all eager to get back home for Easter Sunday dinner, wanted to see it end in nine innings, but it went into 16 innings. Elroy Face came on in relief for the Pirates in extra innings. Eager to bring the game to an end, Elroy began verbally telling hitters what he was going to throw, but they still could not score.

The Labor Day game at Hagerstown lasted even longer. It continued tied into the 14th, 15th, and 16th inning with no scoring, when Ed Katalinas said to me, "You're going to get into this game before it ends." I said, "No way. I had my final start two days ago." He was right as I entered the game in the 18th inning and pitched six scoreless innings, winding up the winning pitcher after 24 innings. It is the longest game I was ever involved in as a pitcher, broadcaster, or spectator, and except for a footnote in the *Sporting News*, it didn't mean a damn thing.

CHAPTER FOUR

Bidding Wars, Bloopers, and Beaches

In the spring of 1950 New Orleans witnessed the appearance of Paul Pettit, an 18 year-old left-handed pitcher from California whom the Pirates had signed for a jaw-dropping $100,000 bonus. That kind of money was unheard of then for star-quality major-league players, and unbelievable for a player just out of high school. Despite his age Pettit, at 6'2" and 200 pounds, was a physically overpowering player. Seeing him for the first time it was easy to understand why he dominated high school hitters and why the Pirates had waged a bidding war to sign him.

Eager to protect such a huge investment, the Pirates hired Ben Tincup as a pitching coach to work strictly with Pettit. As a Native American, Tincup was a rarity in baseball. He pitched in the major leagues in the early 1900s. With all of the hype and pressure on a young player, however, it was difficult for Pettit to perform as expected.

One game indicated how profoundly the pressure affected Paul. The Pirates were scheduled to play an exhibition game in New Orleans against the Pelicans on barnstorming trip back north prior to the start of the major league season. That spring, there was reported low morale among players on the Pirates' roster regarding the bonus paid to Pettit and their inability to get increases in their contracts. With that as the background, it was announced that Paul Pettit would start for the Pelicans in this end-of-training game and make his debut against big-league hitters. It helped draw a larger-than-usual crowd for a spring training game in Pelican Stadium.

It was obvious that the pressure on Pettit was intense as the fans and players wanted to see how he would perform against major-league competition. Clyde MacAllister, my catcher at Geneva in 1947, was on the New Orleans roster and was chosen to handle Paul for this game. Mac had spent four years in Europe during World War II—so he knew what real pressure was—and the Pirates knew that his age and playing experience would benefit Paul in his debut. Mac also knew the difference between minor- and major-league talents.

As the game was about to begin, Mac walked out to the mound to talk with Paul. Later, he recalled that he told the rookie pitcher, "Paul, if there's anything I can do to help you, let me know now. Because when I get behind home plate and a guy with a bat gets between me and you—you're screwed." Mac observed that these words did anything but relieve Paul's anxiety: "Paul's jaw dropped, his eyes widened and he didn't say anything."

Unfortunately, things didn't work out well for Paul Pettit or the Pirates. It was rumored that an arm injury he had suffered just after high school ended his pitching career. He never did throw as well as he did in high school and pitched only briefly for the Pirates in 1951 and 1953. His complete major-league totals were: 12 games, 5 starts, 31 innings, 35 hits, 21 walks, 14 strikeouts and a 7.22 ERA. Pettit did, however, continue to play ten seasons in the Pirates' farm system, not as a pitcher, but as a first baseman. Our paths would cross briefly again as teammates at Hollywood in the Pacific Coast League in the summer of 1955. When I suffered my own injury in 1956, I understood the pain, frustration, and disappointment pitchers deal with after an arm injury.

I made the New Orleans roster to start the 1950 Southern Association season, but failed to impress in the limited opportunities I had. After pitching in only three games and eight innings, I was optioned to Charleston, SC, in the Class "A" South Atlantic ("Sally") League. The manager of the Rebels was a former major-league All-Star pitcher, Truett "Rip" Sewell. He had played 12 years with the Pirates (1938-1949) and was making his debut as a manager that season. Strong of character and mind, Sewell was not afraid of going against his teammates when some of the Pirates threatened to form their own association to deal with the owners. Showing his strong, independent nature, Rip sided with the owners and was successful in preventing the Pirates from voting to strike. Commissioner Happy Chandler showed his appreciation for Rip's efforts, presenting him with an engraved gold watch. It was also rumored that Chandler promised him a job in the game after his retirement from play. But, Sewell never got any major-league positions, and I'm sure the managing position in the Class "A" Sally League at Charleston was not part of that promise.

Rip Sewell had gained nationwide attention as a pitcher with the Pirates when he began throwing an unusual pitch termed by writers as the "Eephus Pitch." It later became more acceptably known as the "Blooper."

Pitchers awe fans and batters by the velocity with which they throw a baseball. Rip Sewell was the exception. He confounded batters with an off-speed pitch that resembled the delivery used by pitchers in slow-pitch softball. He threw it overhand with a high trajectory similar to a basketball shot from 3-point territory. The pitch was so slow the ball seemed to float down, like a falling leaf, into the strike zone. Visually, it appeared so easy to hit that players laughed when viewing it for the first time. As umpires became able to consistently judge when it was in the strike zone, Rip began to use it more. Rip and the "Blooper" fascinated writers and fans, but frustrated hitters. One batter, Whitey Kurowski of the Cardinals, detested the pitch so much that he not only wouldn't swing at it – he SPIT on it as it descended into the strike zone.

Sewell was the only pitcher with whom the "Blooper" was identified. Rarely has the pitch been seen since. The most remembered "Blooper" thrown by Sewell was in the 1946 All-Star game at Boston, which attracted national and worldwide coverage. With the National League trailing 8-0 going into the last of the eighth inning, fan interest was waning until Rip Sewell was called on to pitch. Despite the one-sided score, the appearance of Rip and his "Blooper" brought fans' interest back into the game, which reached a peak when Ted Williams, the game's acknowledged greatest hitter, stepped into the batter's box. Williams, who had returned to the game following three years of active duty in WWII as a USMC fighter pilot, responded to the challenge. He drove Rip Sewell's "Blooper" for a home run. Reportedly, it was the only "Blooper" Sewell had ever thrown for a homer. However, there would be another blooper hit for a home run and I was a witness to the event. It was not in front of a major-league audience, nor did it generate national attention. It occurred during the 1950 season at Charleston, SC. At the request of the Charleston general manager, Rip agreed to make his first and only start that year on a Saturday night home game. As you can imagine, the game was highly publicized, drawing a sell-out crowd at Rebel Park as Charleston played Greenville, SC, a Brooklyn Dodger farm team. Rip went through the Greenville line-up the first time with little trouble. The second time around, while facing a strong right-handed hitter named Omar Tolson, Rip flipped the "Blooper," and Omar hit it as far as any ball I saw hit that year in Charleston. It left the park well over the 410-foot sign in left-center field. As Omar rounded the bases, the fans were standing and cheering. Aware of the disconcerting effect home runs have on pitchers, I could see Rip impatiently waiting and demanding a new baseball as the blood began to rise on the back of his neck. Having a "Blooper" hit for a home run by Ted Williams in a Major League All-Star Game was annoying. But throwing a "Blooper" home run to an unknown minor leaguer named Omar Tolson truly pissed him off. That was the last time I saw Rip Sewell pitch.

Rip Sewell's competitive attitude was evident when he pitched for the Pirates and manager Billy Meyer during Sewell's final two seasons in 1948-49. I became more aware of that in 1954 when I pitched for the New Orleans Pelicans. Billy Meyer was then employed by the Pirates as a scout and evaluator of the playing talent in the Southern Association when I had the pleasure of talking with him in the lobby of an Atlanta hotel. We had a lengthy conversation about the 1948 Pirates' team that was in the race for the National League pennant going into the last month of the season.

The 1948 season at New Iberia, LA, was my first season in the Pirates' organization, so I naturally had a personal interest in the major-league team. I was so interested that I made a special trip in September to Shibe Park to see the Pirates play the Phillies in a doubleheader as part of the five-game series. The 1948 Phillies went with a youth movement that later become identified as the "Whiz Kids" and included Richie Ashburn, Granny Hamner, Putsy Caballero, Robin Roberts, and Curt Simmons; in September, they called up Willie "Puddin' Head" Jones, Stan Lopata, Jackie Mayo, and a few others.

The Pirates dropped the first three games as these unknown rookies pounded Pirates' pitching. As Billy Meyer recalled when we discussed that season, Rip Sewell reacted to these defeats by asking Meyer to give him a start in the first game of the Sunday doubleheader. He told Meyer, "I'll get those damned Eastern Shore bush leaguers out!" Rip did get a start, but he never got out of the first inning. The Phillies had already scored 6 runs when Meyer decided to yank him. Rip came into the dugout throwing his glove and screaming, "Those god damn punk Eastern Shore rookies!" Meyer said, "I sat down next to Rip and told him, hell, Rip those rookies probably don't who the hell you are, they're just swinging and hitting that slow stuff you were throwing up there." The moral of the story was that pitchers don't get hitters out on their reputation in any league and certainly not in the majors.

Rip Sewell hated to lose in baseball and life. It was apparent during the years following his retirement from the game. Suffering from diabetes, he lost one leg and finally both, but still played golf and continued an active life until his death at age 82 in 1989.

At Charleston in 1950, I roomed with three players in a home that was only two blocks from the baseball park and adjacent to The Citadel, a well-known military college. My roommates were Larry Dorton, a catcher and college graduate who went on to become a dentist; Jack McKeon, a left-handed hitting third baseman from California; and Cal Hogue, a right-handed pitcher who had outstanding stuff, including a sharp curve ball that was equal to the best in the majors. Cal had the best chance of the four of us to play in the majors. He did make it, but his inability to throw strikes, walking 96 batters in 114 innings, limited him to only brief stays with the Pirates in 1951 and 1954.

Charleston is a beautiful and historic Southern city, near inviting Atlantic Ocean beaches. It is also a very hot city in the summer, and with no air conditioning in those years, we spent most of the daytime hours at Folly Beach. We'd arise early, have breakfast at the beach, then spend four hours riding the waves and catching some sun before returning for a brief nap prior to going to the park. I kept a diary in those days, and it provided a worthwhile document on why I had a less-than-rewarding season. For one thing, I spent too many daytime hours at Folly Beach. Charleston also had a US Naval Base and nightlife, which, I was to discover, go together. A group of sailors frequented our games and sitting near our dugout they would harass us with some friendly banter. As I did with the fan in Allentown, I got to know and developed a friendship with them. Sailors know how to have fun and I enjoyed too many evenings with them that lasted well past a self-imposed baseball curfew.

I started 19 games and completed 14 that season at Charleston, but failed to pitch as well as in the previous few seasons. I won 9 and lost 10 with an ERA of 3.41; most embarrassingly, in 143 innings, I gave up 153 hits, had only 67 strikeouts and 28 walks. When paging through my daily diary later, it was obvious that an overactive social life at the beach — with my naval buddies and with a young lady to whom I became attracted — was the paramount reason for these dismal statistics.

The only games I pitched that season that I can truly recall were played at Macon, GA. The first one was a complete disaster. I started and didn't get past the first inning, giving up 8 runs. I showered, dressed and had a Coke and hot dog before the second inning ended. In the other game, I went nine innings for a win, but what I remember the most were the "bench jockey" comments directed to me from the Macon dugout.

Being tall and thin (6'6", 180 lbs.) always made me a target for the usual comments — "Do your legs swell up like that every summer?" or "Don't drink any cherry soda, you'll look like a thermometer by the fourth inning." The most original remark I heard in my eleven seasons of baseball occurred in that second game at Macon, GA, in 1950. Half a century later, I still can still hear the comment and see the hitter who uttered the remark. The hitter's name was Phelps, a left-handed hitting outfielder. I went the distance for the win, making up for my less-than-overpowering velocity with control and a good moving sinker. Phelps went 0-4 in the game, and following each out, his frustration and anger grew. In the first at-bat, he grounded out to second base on an outside sinker. From the dugout, I heard him holler, "Is that as hard as you can throw skinny?" The next time up, he popped up to first base. From the dugout, I heard: "How the hell did you ever get into this league throwing that crap?" This line of attack continued after he flied to right field in his third time at bat. On his final at bat in the ninth, he grounded to first base, and as I covered the bag for the out, I expected to hear his comment up-close. But surprisingly, he quietly returned to the dugout. I thought, well, he's done for the day, and was looking in to get the sign from my catcher when I heard Phelps bark out, "You tall skinny sonofabitch! What the hell do you do in the off season — clean the insides of rainspouts?" I laughed like hell, as it was the first and only original comment I'd heard from a "bench jockey."

In baseball, most of the verbal abuse coming from dugouts or coaches, other than that directed at umpires is focused on pitchers. The reason is simple: Pitchers control the flow of the game. If you can break their concentration, you can affect their performance, and therefore change the flow of the game. The baseball term for these vocal pests is "bench jockeys." To be effective, they need an audience, and pitchers who respond to their taunts become known as "rabbit ears," since they hear everything.

During my 11-year professional career, I found ample support for my belief that bench jockeys' vocabularies were equal to their batting averages. After all, why else would they be sitting on the bench, not playing? A pitcher's ability to tune out bench jockeys is always related to the number of years he's spent in the game. I recall how, when I was 17 and pitching in my first year of semi-pro ball, I listened to one third-base coach ride me constantly. I had rabbit ears, and he knew it. Late in the game, with a runner at third, he suddenly went quiet and then gently asked me, "Hey kid, let me see the ball." I was about to throw it to him when a veteran teammate loudly informed me that that wouldn't be a wise thing to do.

Over the years, talking with hitters, I've found that the one thing they agree on is their respect for pitchers with outstanding velocity or, as they call it, "heat." When hitters return to the dugout after an unsuccessful at bat and other hitters quiz them on how well the pitcher is throwing, they reply, "Damn, he's got great stuff." After facing a pitcher like me, with below average velocity, hitter's response usually is, "Hell, he doesn't have shit," or "I don't know how he gets anyone out with that crap he's throwing."

It annoys the hell out of hitters when a pitcher uses control and guile to get them out. As Branch Rickey said, "Pitching is the art of deception." Even so, everyone who pitched with limited velocity would have loved to experience, if only for one inning, what it was like to throw as fast as Bob Gibson. We'd all say, "To hell with deception!" The closest I would come to experiencing anything close to that happened in 1953, while pitching with the Denver Bears in the Western League. But, before that, I had to answer Uncle Sam's draft call. The Korean War had begun in June 1950, and many men of my generation were facing challenges that made bench jockeys' taunts seem minor in comparison.

CHAPTER FIVE

Army Interlude

I was twenty-two years old, pitching for the Charleston (SC) Rebels, in the Class "A" Sally League, when the Korean War broke out on June 25, 1950. I was ripe for the military draft. Within a month my draft board in Lebanon, PA informed me I had to report for my physical exam. Unable to travel home during the season it was arranged for me to take my physical at Columbia, SC. The baseball season ended on Labor Day and on September 28, 1950 I was inducted into the Army at Fort Dix, NJ. It was to be another of those defining moments in my life.

After thirteen weeks of infantry basic training I learned to fire every small arms weapon used by a rifleman. I also did a lot of close order marching drills and embarrassingly learned why we did them. It came while standing inspection as an orderly for the 60th Infantry Regimental Commander. The Lt. Colonel came up into my face and asked, "Soldier, why do we do close-order marching drills?" Drawing on my baseball team play experience, I replied, "Sir, we do it so we can learn to work together as a unit." He loudly responded, "No soldier, you do it to learn to take orders. When we tell you to turn left, goddamnit, you turn left. When we tell you to turn right, goddamnit, you turn right. You don't ask questions—you take orders in the Army!"

After basic training I entered a Leadership Training program to prepare me to be an infantry rifle squad leader, a position not associated with longevity. As a cadre I was pushing troops and also served on the BAR (Browning Automatic Rifle) Committee, headed by Lt. Constantine Thomas, a veteran of WWII who was wounded in the early months of the Korean War.

One of my talents, of which the Army was not yet aware, was typing. After a day of training, Lt. Thomas remarked he needed a lesson plan typed and was concerned that nobody at Battalion Headquarters would be available to do the job. I innocently informed him I could type and he immediately took me to Battalion Headquarters and sat me down behind a Royal typewriter. I began to type the lesson plan, when I suddenly sensed someone was standing behind me. It was Major Jackson, the Battalion Commander. He said, "Soldier, you look like a pretty damn good typist." I replied, "Yes, sir, I can type about 70 words a minute." He uttered the words that changed my Army career, "We need a clerk typist at Battalion Headquarters."

Thus ended my days as an infantryman. I spent the remainder of my two years behind a typewriter, not an M-1 rifle. No KP, no guard duty, no bivouac. I highly recommend learning typing. It's the most under-rated job in the Army.

During those two years I was able to play baseball on the 60th Infantry Regiment baseball team. Also on the team were then unknown minor league players, Frank Torre, Don McMahon, and Arnold Portocarrera. There were only two players, both young pitchers, who had played in the major leagues—Erv Palica, with the Brooklyn Dodgers pitched for the 60th Infantry, and Harvey Haddix of the St. Louis Cardinals was on the 39th Infantry team. The commanding officers of both regiments were baseball fans, which heightened the rivalry of the games.

The most important and gratifying aspect of my defining moment at Fort Dix occurred during the summer of 1951. Eddie Earl, a semi-pro infielder from Newark, NJ who played on the 60th Infantry team, arranged a weekend blind date in Newark for me and two other players. My blind date turned out to be his youngest sister, Bernadette. We were introduced for the first time when I stepped off the train at the Pennsylvania Station in Newark. Bernadette was only 5' 4" tall, and the disparity in height between us was dramatic. At age 23, I was five years her senior.

The pairing seemed less than ideal until we met again later that evening. She appeared in high heels, wearing an attractive, bright red dress that made me do a double take. I looked into what were then, and to this day remain, the most beautiful brown eyes I have ever seen. Two years later on December 18, 1952, I presented her with an engagement ring on my knee in the living room of her family home. We have shared the last 55 years together.

I was to be discharged from the Army on September 28, 1952. In early September of that year I received a letter from Branch Rickey, the GM for the Pirates. Mr. Rickey, always ahead of the curve in scouting talent, wanted to take a look at the young players from the Pirates farm system that were about to be discharged from service. He asked if I could make it to Ebbets Field when the Pirates would be playing the Dodgers. Could I? Hell, I'd walk all the way to Brooklyn if I had to! With two other players on the 60th Regiment team, we drove to Ebbets Field early enough to await the arrival of the Pirates' team bus. When it arrived I introduced myself to Bob Rice, the Pirates' traveling secretary, and showed him Mr. Rickey's letter. He was unaware of the workout and took me to the clubhouse to meet manager Billy Meyer.

Surprisingly, Billy Meyer didn't know anything about the workout, but told "Doc" Jorgensen, the team trainer, to get me a uniform. I put on a major league uniform and stepped onto a major league field for the first time that day in September 1952 at Ebbets Field.

The only players on the '52 Pirates I had played with in the minors were Frank Thomas, Cal Hogue, and Dick Smith. Prior to batting practice I got into a "pepper game" and figured one of the coaches would inform me when they wanted me to work out. I heard nothing. As batting practice began I headed out to the outfield to shag fly balls. When the pitchers began to do their running, I thought, "I might as well join them."

When batting practice ended, I anxiously wondered when someone would take a look at my pitching skills. I went back to the dugout and when nobody approached me, I joined in the infield practice, handling relays from the outfielders. I went back to the dugout when I noticed the starting pitchers were beginning their warm ups. Having played six years in the minor leagues, I knew I wasn't going to do any throwing for anyone, so I headed back to the visiting team clubhouse.

The clubhouse radio was on and Red Barber and Vince Scully, who were doing the Dodger broadcast, went over the starting lineups. I began to undress and noticed the only player remaining in the clubhouse was pitcher Murry Dickson, who was then in the twelfth year of a twenty-year major league career. He had tasted champagne with the St. Louis Cardinal Championship teams in the 1940s and won 20 games in 1951 on a Pirates' team that won only 64 games. He was the only truly qualified major league pitcher on the 1952 Pirates' team that lost a record 112 games. I had been a huge Cardinal fan as a youngster and to be in the same clubhouse with Murry Dickson was a treasured moment.

Murry Dickson was listening to the broadcast in the fist inning, with two out and Frank Thomas at bat for the Pirates. Thomas hit a low line drive to center field, which Frank thought Duke Snider had caught on the fly, but actually was trapped by Snider. I still recall the description of the play by Red Barber: "Thomas' line drive was trapped by Snider in center field and he relays it quickly to Jackie Robinson at second base." Excitedly, Barber continued, "Now Thomas is heading into center field and Robinson is chasing him and tags him for the final out in shallow center field."

Dickson, who had seen a lot of ugly baseball that season, said "They ought to send some of these guys so far into the minor leagues that the *Sporting News* couldn't reach them." That 1952 Pirates' team won only 42 and lost 112, but Frank Thomas, Bob Friend, Dick Groat, Gus Bell, Bobby DelGreco, and Dick Hall all went on to have long and successful major league careers.

After two years in the Army, eager to renew my professional baseball career, I was assigned to join the New Orleans Pelicans again for spring training. Two years away from most professions isn't considered a long absence, but missing two years in a short career such as professional baseball is equivalent to losing ten years. In baseball, if you're in your mid-20s and haven't made it to the majors, you are close to being considered a suspect, not a prospect. Baseball players prefer to remain in denial and don't want to face the reality that they are nearing the end of their careers. For me denial was no longer acceptable. It was six years since I began my baseball career at Geneva, AL and I had not gotten past Class "A" ball. At age 25 and engaged to Bernadette, with a wedding set for October 10, 1953, I knew I had to have a break-through season or consider looking for work in another occupation.

Chapter Six

Returning to Baseball, Denver 1953

Times were about to change dramatically in the game of baseball. In 1953 the Boston Braves moved to Milwaukee, ending a string of fifty consecutive seasons of franchise continuity in major league baseball. The Braves were lured by a new TV market and most important, a new baseball stadium. Prior to the Braves' move, every team had owned, operated, and paid property taxes on their baseball park. Like a small crack in a dam, this change soon became a flood. New and growing metropolitan cities began bidding for franchises, and the expenses of building and operating major league baseball parks were transferred to the taxpayers. At the start of the 21st century, only Wrigley Field, Fenway Park, Yankee Stadium, and Dodger Stadium remained of the original 16 franchises that owned, operated, and were paying property taxes on their baseball parks.

Although television now provided added revenue for major league teams, it had a negative effect on the minor league. With major league telecasts now available in many of those locations, attendance for minor league games dropped quickly along with the number of leagues and players.

I became more aware of the time remaining for me in pro ball when I met the manager of the New Orleans Pelicans, Danny Murtaugh. He was the second baseman for the Phillies that summer day in 1941 when I saw my first major league game at Shibe Park. Now, twelve years later, I was on the same field with him.

I had little personal contact with Murtaugh that spring, until "cut-down" day arrived. I was shagging fly balls during batting practice when I noticed Danny walking in the outfield. He would stop to have private conversations with various players. In a comforting way, he would drape his arm around the player as he continued the conversation. A veteran of too many spring training "cut-down" days, I knew what was taking place. Danny finally worked his way to my side of the field, put his arm around me, and before he could say anything, I asked, "Where am I going Danny?" He laughed and said, "It's either Charleston, SC or Denver." I replied, "How about Denver. I've already seen Charleston."

To ease my disappointment he took me aside privately to inform me how difficult it was for him returning to baseball after three years in the army during WWII. In 1946 he was in spring training with the Phillies but was optioned to Milwaukee, then a minor league team in the American Association. He told me to be patient as it took him a month or more before he began to play with the confidence and consistency he had before the war. He was right on target, as I would experience the symptoms he described in the early months of the season at Denver in 1953. I left New Orleans along with Harry Pritts, a left-handed pitcher from Connellsville, PA and Whitey Reis, a native of St. Louis, MO, who were also optioned to Denver.

The Denver team was "busing" back to Denver, with exhibition games scheduled at Lubbock, TX and Albuquerque, NM, but Harry owned a new 1953 Chevrolet that we used for the entire three-day journey. Harry, like most left-handed pitchers, never allowed trivial things to worry him and displayed a devilish sense of humor. We would share an apartment (and some very bad cooking) in Denver for the entire season. Whitey had played American Legion baseball in St. Louis with Earl Weaver, and like Weaver, was a very competitive player. He was also very clever, and could have been a professional stand-up comedian given his talent for impersonating celebrities. Later that season Whitey and I would join up with an act that earned us extra money performing in ballparks at Wichita and Lincoln.

Having lived and played near oceans and rivers, I was about to experience for the first time the effects of playing baseball in higher elevations. Pitchers do running exercises daily all season (100 yard sprints) for about 20 to 30 minutes to keep the aerobic system and legs in good condition. At only 180 pounds, I thought I was in excellent shape after spring training. As I began my running exercise that day in Albuquerque, I couldn't understand what was happening. My lungs burned as if they were congested, I had trouble breathing and I couldn't complete my exercises. Aware of these effects and recalling that Denver was known as the "Mile High City," I began to question my quick decision to go west. If I was going to experience this agony for an entire season, I wasn't going to be in Denver or "Class A" baseball very long. After a week in Denver, though, I became acclimated to running and pitching in the higher elevation.

In 1953, Denver had a population of just 200,000 and no pollution. With clear blue skies, the distant snow-capped mountains were always on display. Most noticeable in Denver was the overall cleanliness of the city and the pride property owners took in their well-kept lawns. Water was plentiful and sprinkler systems kept the grass a lush and brilliant green. Harry Pritts and I rented an apartment near Chessman Park. We later discovered we were just two blocks away from the home of First Lady Mamie Dowd Eisenhower. The area buzzed with excitement when she and the president came for a visit that summer.

I was amazed when I had my first view of Bears Stadium. Built following WWII, it seated 16,000 and was the largest baseball park I played in during my minor league days. Baseball parks built in the early 1900's were always located near railroad or trolley lines, then the convenient mode of transportation. There were few or no parking lots available and you had to find on-street parking. At Shibe Park in Philadelphia, if you were fortunate to locate such an open spot, a person would inquire, "Do you want me to watch your car during the game?" If you agreed and gave him the right amount of money he'd guarantee no damage would be done to your car. If you didn't, you understood there probably would be, so you paid the guy what he wanted.

Bob Howsam, owner of the Denver Bears, had the foresight to see the significance of the change from rail to automobiles. The suburbs were growing rapidly following WWII and automobiles were more of a necessity than in metropolitan areas. Bears Stadium provided large parking areas for automobiles. With no major league team in the area and few minor league teams west or north of Denver, the Denver Bears attracted fans from a wide area, including Nebraska, Wyoming and Utah. The marketing people working with organizations from small towns created unique promotional campaigns that increased attendance and gave identity to those little known towns.

The small town of Yuma, CO (population 2000), located 160 miles east of Denver, had the most original and creative marketing ploy. Known for the jackrabbits that populated the area, they brought 20 or more of the caged varmints to "Yuma Day" at Bears Stadium. They tied bills around their necks in amounts ranging from $10 to $100. After the game the rabbits were turned loose on the baseball field as players attempted to grab the money. It was a riotous affair. I never saw any player outrun a jackrabbit and none did that night. I didn't stay around to see how Yuma fans got the rabbits back in the cages, or if they did. I suppose the jackrabbits that weren't caught were the great, great, grandparents of jackrabbits running around Denver today.

After two seasons away from the game, I saw a noticeable change in the makeup of the 1953 Denver roster. Jackie Robinson had broken the "color line" in the major leagues in 1947, with the Brooklyn Dodgers. But the color barrier was still in effect below the Mason-Dixon Line. In every previous minor league season (except 1949 at York, PA) I had played in the south, segregation was evident in all areas of life. Black fans had separate sections at the ball parks—"White Only" signs on drinking fountains, restaurants, and rest rooms were daily evidence of the public discrimination. No blacks played on teams in southern cities. Denver was the first team I played on that had black and Latin-American players—and also a Jewish manager.

I thought baseball and travel had given me an excellent liberal education, but that season in Denver I earned a Masters degree. We had five Latin-American players—three from Panama (outfielder Bobby Prescott, catcher Marcos Cobos, pitcher Alberto Orsorio); one from Puerto Rico (Chico Salgado, pitcher); one from Cuba (Rocky Contreras, pitcher); and three black American players (Andy Anderson, outfielder; Butch McCord, first baseman; and second baseman Curt Roberts). Curt would become the first black player to play with the Pittsburgh Pirates the following spring.

Despite this sudden mixture of various cultures, language, and colors, we developed a relaxed relationship—though it rarely went beyond the clubhouse. Unfortunately, there were very few occasions when we shared social time with players of different race or cultures. One of the benefits of minor league play was the time we shared traveling long distances by bus, and at Denver, occasionally by train. You had the time and chance to hold conversations that opened doors, allowing the winds of change to clear out the pre-conceived opinions we had of each other.

Latin American players were more isolated at the beginning of the season because of the language barrier. Rocky Contreras, a native of Cuba, entertained himself and serenaded us (or he thought he did) with vocal renditions in his native tongue. Unable to follow the lyrics, I assumed they were popular Cuban songs until I heard him singing the popular American melody, "Tenderly," or as he sang in Spanish, "Tiernamenta." Every time I hear that song I am reminded of Rocky Contreras. There have been a number of successful Latin American players named Contreras in the major leagues in recent years, and I always wonder if they are related to the Contreras I knew that season in Denver.

Because of generations of discrimination blacks had to deal with, they seemed less open and trusting. It was most noticeable with Curt Roberts, a diminutive 5'7" second baseman, who was raised in the Watts section of Los Angeles. A very competitive player, he backed off from no one. As a second baseman, he made one defensive play better than anyone I ever saw play that position. On a slow-hit ball to the right side of the infield that just eluded the pitcher, he moved so quickly, I can't recall him ever failing to get the out at first base. His play during the 1953 season at Denver earned him a spot on the Pirates' major league roster in 1954. He played in 134 games that season batting only .232 and dropped from the major leagues after the 1956 season. Curt died in an auto accident in Oakland, CA in 1969. He was only 40 years old.

The Denver manager, Andy Cohen, was a 1925 graduate of the University of Alabama, where he played both baseball and basketball. As a Jew, Andy's personal understanding of discrimination and prejudice made him an ideal choice to handle a team with such a diverse mix of color, language, and culture. An accomplished professional baseball player, Andy joined the New York Giants in 1926 as a second baseman to become one of the first Jewish players to play in the Major Leagues. He played in only 32 games his first season. In 1928, after a full season in the minor leagues, Andy returned to the Giants as the starting second baseman on opening day at the Polo Grounds. Replacing Rogers Hornsby, one of the all-time greats of baseball who was traded in the off-season to Boston of the National League, he was under scrutiny by the media. Andy told me of that memorable day and his unbelievable joy. With the game tied in the bottom of the ninth inning, he delivered the game-winning hit. The Giant fans carried him off the field and Andy became a sudden celebrity, especially among the large Jewish population of New York City. As he described it, "I never lacked invitations for dinner!"

Everyone took pride in, and wanted to bask in, his star status. At only 23 years of age, it was a heady experience, but as Andy sadly informed me, "I didn't handle it well." He found out he didn't have as many "friends" as he thought. He described it best saying, "When you're going good, everyone wants to take you to dinner and pick up the check. When things change and you're on the way out, you can't find anybody who wants to take you to dinner."

Cohen's major league career was short, lasting only three seasons. Despite hitting for a .274 average in 1928 and .294 in 1929, he never again played in a major league game. He remained in the game as a manager working in the minors for many seasons with some success. He made it back to the major league as a coach for one season with the Philadelphia Phillies in 1960. He also had the unique experience of managing in the majors, but only for one game that season and finished with a perfect record: 1 win, 0 losses.

Andy retired from professional baseball to spend the remainder of his life in El Paso, TX, where for 17 seasons he was the baseball coach of the University of Texas at El Paso team. In 1988 he was inducted in the El Paso Baseball Hall of Fame and the baseball stadium bears his name, Cohen Stadium. He died at age 84 on October 29, 1988.

As a manager, Andy displayed the competitive attitude that must have been evident when he played. He had the speed and quick feet similar to a point guard in basketball, a sport he played at the University of Alabama, and so important for a second baseman. He had an identifiable style of running, with short choppy steps, visible only when he hustled to the mound for a conversation or to confront an umpire. Andy also had a nervous habit when having a conversation with a pitcher on the mound. Talking rapidly, he would move the index finger of his right hand under his nose in quick movements over his upper lip. To this day, when I think of Andy Cohen I robotically imitate that motion. I also remember his favorite saying: *"I guaran-damn-tee you,"* which erased any doubts about what he was saying.

One of the benefits of having returned from army service was that I could remain on the Denver roster as an extra player. It removed the early season pressure to prove I could play at this level. It also gave Andy the patience to determine how best to use my talents. Having been a starting pitcher in each of my previous four minor league seasons, Andy decided to use me as a reliever. It turned out to be a wise decision, even though we weren't certain early in the season. In my first four appearances I didn't impress anyone, giving up 7 hits and 5 runs in ten innings for an ERA of 4.50. Those statistics would normally cause any manager to consider sending me down to a lower classification. The only positive stats I compiled were; 7 strikeouts and 0 walk.

April in Denver is not ideal for baseball. We had to deal with very cold and snowy weather. Three games were snowed out and during night games the temperature hovered in the mid 30-degrees. After the less than encouraging start, the weather and I both improved. I felt more relaxed and began pitching with confidence, confirming the advice Danny Murtaugh gave me the final day of spring training in New Orleans. By mid-August my stats were proof of my success. I had a perfect 13-0 record, appeared in 43 games, 78 innings, had 72 strikeouts, and issued only 12 walks, 4 of them intentional, for an ERA of 1.66.

After a full season in the rarefied air in Denver I developed creditable opinions on pitching. One of the fallacies was that you couldn't throw a good curve ball. I know the movement on a thrown baseball, fastball, curve or any other pitch, is not affected in the high elevation in Denver. I had the best curve ball in my career and my sinker moved equally well. I also agree heartily that a batted ball will travel farther. With this knowledge I found out my style of pitching was ideal for Denver. Never a power pitcher, I developed the ability to throw strikes consistently with a good moving sinker. I kept it low in the strike zone and always stayed ahead in the count on hitters.

Rarely was I forced to throw the "cripple pitches" hitters look for from pitchers who continually work behind in the count. This is major problem for pitchers whose only strength is velocity. They begin aiming the ball, which affects not only the velocity, but also the movement of each pitch. Batters love to hit fastballs that have no movement! If you hang around the batting cage you'll find few hitters asking the batting practice pitcher for curve balls – they love to hit fastballs. It is the pitch they use to determine how long they can wait.

Branch Rickey's theory that "pitching is the art of deception" is disappearing from the game, and I believe the primary reason is the use of the "radar gun" to time the velocity of each pitch. It is the dominant attribute scouts and managers use to judge pitchers. I am mystified why the scoreboard displays the velocity of each pitch. You don't acquire wins by velocity totals. It's how many runs are scored that counts.

Particularly laughable is when announcers will say, "He's into the seventh inning and is still throwing in the mid 90's." They fail to mention he is also losing by three runs. It was jokingly said of Dodger pitcher Preacher Roe, "You could time his fast ball with an egg-timer." Preacher Roe sure didn't overpower hitters, but he knew how to get them out. It is still possible to do so, but teams can't wait that long for pitchers to acquire the necessary pitching knowledge and skills before coming to the major leagues. We have become so fascinated with speed we can't wait for anything today. We all seem to be hurrying—to get to the next red light. Throw away the radar gun! Find pitchers who can throw strikes, keep the ball in the park and get hitters out. Who cares what the damn "radar gun" says!

The most embarrassing moments in my professional baseball experience came in my seventh season in professional baseball after I had acquired some wisdom about pitching and the game. I was enjoying my finest season, leading the league in ERA with 2.00. I had won 15 and lost only 3 and saved 17 games while appearing in 50 games, 48 of them in relief. The first starting assignments came late in the season at Omaha. In a tight pennant race, Andy Cohen picked me to start the short seven-inning game as part of a doubleheader.

I carried a one run lead against the Omaha Cardinals going into the sixth inning with two outs and runners at first and third. With seven years of experience and aware of the Cardinal's use of the double steal in such situations, I knew how to prevent this. All a pitcher has to do is watch the runner at first and when he breaks to second, step off the rubber, check the runner at third and if he breaks, you run directly at him or the runner at first to get them in a rundown and the inning is over.

I was inwardly smiling as I took my stretch and came to the stop in my motion, taking a longer than usual pause while awaiting him to run. He failed to run, and after the long delay I made my delivery to the plate for a called strike. The catcher returned the ball and I was now cockily confident they would use the double steal. I took my stretch and this time took an even longer pause awaiting the runner on first to break for second.

I was suddenly detracted from my concentration on the runner at first base. I heard an increasingly loud noise coming from the crowd and shouting from my infielders. I looked toward home plate and witnessed the most embarrassing moment in my pitching career. The runner from third was only eight or ten feet from home plate. While I was cunningly waiting to fool them, the runner at third had stolen home and tied the game! If I could have opened the rosin bag and crawled into it I would have done so to escape my humiliation. We scored in the top of the seventh and I wound up winning the game, but I am proud to say I learned a lesson on humility. I laugh now at that event and think how excruciatingly embarrassing my mistake would have looked in a major league or World Series game. It sure as hell would have made the ESPN Baseball Highlights!

George Kissell, the manager and third base coach for the Omaha Cardinals had more experience, knowledge, and wisdom than I did. It took only one pitch for him to be aware of my singular focus on the runner at first base. Kissell, who signed with the St. Louis Cardinals in 1940, has remained with the organization for over six decades serving as a minor league player and manager. George served as the Field Coordinator for Player Development until his untimely death in an auto accident the summer of 2008.

Omaha was the scene of another one of my less than stellar pitching performances. Barney Schultz (who later pitched and coached for St.

Louis) was a starting pitcher for the Denver Bears and took a tie game into the ninth inning. He gave up a triple to the first batter in the bottom of the inning, which brought Andy Cohen to the mound. He quickly made the decision to bring me into the game to replace Barney and had me walk the first two batters to load the bases. It was a mistake.

The one thing a relief pitcher wants to do when he takes his warm-up throws is to get familiar with the strike zone and location of his pitches to gain confidence in throwing strikes. I did that when I threw my eight pitches, but then had to throw eight more pitches out of the strike zone to intentionally walk the next two batters to load the bases. You guessed what happened. I went to 3-2 on the batter and the first and only time in my professional career I walked in the winning run. I haven't visited Omaha since.

During my minor league seasons I developed a "Max" Patkin style comedy bit. Imitating a supposed "pitching prospect" with my cap pulled down tight, my pants up high above the waist and knees, my glove hooked onto my belt. At 6' 6" and only 175 pounds I was not a pretty sight, but it was funny. I would begin the act by skipping from the dugout toward the mound and while crossing the baseline I would trip myself. My pitching delivery, similar to how girls used to throw, began with me throwing off the wrong foot. The catcher's return throw was caught with my glove way out in front of me, with my head turned away in fear of the ball. If I dropped the ball, which was often, I then tried to pick it up, but with my foot I would kick the ball before I could complete the task. I would do that two-three time—then crawl on the ground sneaking up on the ball, and with my cap in my right hand, capture it! When I got back on the mound I would go into a position holding a runner in first base—with my head down I then went into a fake dead sleep, before someone would holler to awaken me.

The wrap-up to the performance was a throw to the catcher, which instead of landing on my front foot, I would throw the leg under me and fall hard on my stomach and face and lie unconscious on the mound. I would not move for 20 seconds when a player would come out with a bucket of water and pour it on my head to revive me, which it didn't. I did not move for another 15 seconds when the catcher would came out to the mound, remove his shoe and put it under my nose and the smell quickly revived me. That was the end.

During the season in Denver I worked a comedy bit with "Whitey" Reis. He wrote his own witty skits for entertaining us on road trips and in the clubhouse with imitations of Harry Truman, Bela Lugosi, and other popular personalities. I enjoyed his act so much that 50 years later I can repeat his shtick verbatim.

He began with the deep, accent of Lugosi, "I have come to collect de rent." Then in a falsetto voice he would reply, "But I don't have the rent, I'm in a family way!" To which he would reply, "You're in evvvreybooooddy's god-dam vay!" Then in falsetto he pleaded, "But I'm in bed with arthritis." Lugosi replied, "Is dat god-damn Greek here again? You know the penalty if you don't pay the rent—I'll lock you in the closet and give you nothing but X-lax…" The falsetto response was, "But I'll die!"…and the Lugosi voice replied, "YOU'LL SHIT!"

We combined our act during the season for fun, but when word got around to players on other teams of our skit, we were asked to do it at Wichita and Lincoln. Whitey had much keener entrepreneurial skills than I did; he arranged to have a hat passed around the stands for a donation after our performance. We would split the money. As I recall the most we got was $300—the amount of my monthly salary!

The only other time I performed this act was during an unusual incident at Forbes Field during the 1956 season. We were in the fourth inning of a game with the Chicago Cubs when the lights went out.

There was just enough light to see the playing field, but certainly not enough for hitters to face "Sad Sam" Jones who was pitching for the Cubs that night. The delay was lengthy and the fans were getting restless when some of the Pirates' players egged me on to do my act and I agreed. The skit was cheered, and fans who witnessed my antics that night tell me that it remains a treasured part of their Forbes Field memories.

"Pepper" Martin, a coach for the Chicago Cubs, was a well known and entertaining player on the old St. Louis Cardinal "Gas House Gang" days in the 1930s. He followed my act with one of the best spontaneous performances I've ever witnessed. With the limited amount of lighting, using a fungo bat and no baseball, he and five infielders held a pantomime-fielding act. Each player would improvise making either a spectacular or horrible play or throw. The spontaneity of the performance enchanted not only the fans but also the players on both teams. I never viewed anything like it before, but was later informed that Al Schacht, the original "Clown Prince of Baseball," performed a similar act as part of his routine. It was a shame the act was not saved on film; like the Abbott and Costello comedy skit, "Who's on First?," it deserved a place in the baseball archives.

Whitey Reis was also a good storyteller. He spun one tale about how all teams in the Western League wore uniforms that were designed to identify the strike zone during the previous season of 1952. The areas from the armpits, or the letters on the jersey down to the knees were one solid color as an assist for umpires in being consistent when calling high or low pitches. Whitey was at bat in a night game at Lincoln, Nebraska and took the first pitch for what he thought was low, but the umpire called it a strike. Reis turned around to inform the umpire it was below the area designed as the strike zone. The second pitch was in a similar location near the knees and taken by Whitey, but again called a strike.

Whitey annoyed with the call again informed the umpire it was low, in fact lower than the first pitch.

The third pitch followed the same routine: Whitey took the pitch, sure it was below the strike zone and the umpire called him out on what he thought were three low pitches. Annoyed, Whitey got into the face of the umpire inquiring whether he even knew where the strike zone was. The umpire listened and then advised Whitey, "Son, if you're going to make it to the major leagues, you're going to have to learn to hit that pitch!" Whitey wittily replied, "Hell, if you learn to call it, we'll both make it to the major leagues."

The top defensive infielder at Denver was shortstop Gus Gregory. I had played against him in the Sally League in 1950 when he played for Macon, GA. Gus had the soft hands of a surgeon and the quickness of a magician in getting rid of the ball. He was so consistent in handling routine plays that it was rare for him to make an error. Gus also had a voracious appetite for literature, and a special love for the writing and poetry of Robert Service. A deep thinker off the field, with a strong social conscience, Gus did not play the game with that same level of introspection.

Pat Haggerty, a utility player at Denver, eager to learn more about playing shortstop, approached Gus Gregory during a pre-game infield practice session. So fascinated with Gregory's quick release and accuracy, he inquired how Gus held the ball before making a throw. In particular he wanted to know if he felt for four seams or two seams in preparation for the throw. Gus informed him that he never really thought about it, he just threw the ball. This inquiry bothered Gus so much that the next day he angrily told Haggerty, "God dammit, don't ask me questions like that. I stayed awake all night thinking about it and never got to sleep."

I lost touch with Gus Gregory after leaving baseball and often wondered where and what he was doing. Through Joe Marovich, my tax accountant in Pittsburgh, I was introduced to Pete Gregory, one of Gus' brothers. Pete informed me Gus went on to earn a college degree in education and spent the remainder of his life teaching in the inner-city schools of Chicago.

I had also lost touch with Pat Haggerty after my playing days until one Sunday while viewing a NFL game on television. I didn't know who the game officials were, but I saw this one official who had a style of walking and running that caught my attention. I remarked to my wife, "That guy runs like Pat Haggerty." The announcers finally identified him by name and it *was* Pat Haggerty, who later worked a number of Super Bowl games and became regarded as one of the top referees in the NFL.

My pitching consistency at Denver caught the attention of Branch Rickey, who came to view my talents in a private audition in late August. Mr. Rickey liked what he saw, and admiring my league-leading pitching statistics for 1953, he signed me to a Pirates' contract on October 11, 1953.

I was married on October 10, 1953 to Bernadette Earl in Newark, New Jersey at St. Joseph's Catholic Church. The best wedding gift I received came a day after the wedding, while on our honeymoon in the Poconos. I bought the *New York Times* Sunday edition and while reading the sports page under the heading of "Baseball Transactions," I read: "The Pirates purchased the contract of pitcher Nelson King from New Orleans." I told Bernadette, "I should have married you sooner. I'd have made it to the major leagues much faster!"

CHAPTER SEVEN

My First Major League Spring Training and the Inimitable

Branch Rickey

Bernadette and I began our married life in a home we rented in the Vailsburg section of Newark, near Seton Hall University. She kept her job as a nurse for Dr. Edgar Cardwell, a respected ear, nose, and throat surgeon whose clients included some of the most prominent personalities on Broadway. I found an off-season job with Liberty Mutual Insurance in Newark. Our total weekly family income was $60.00, of which Bernadette made $35.00, so she was the main "bread winner." I would assume that title in March with my first major league contract for $5000—not a month, but a year. When people ask me when I played in the big leagues, I tell them it was 1954 B.C. —*before* cash!!

After each season I detached from the game physically and mentally. I took a recess from the daily preparation and tension of seven straight months of professional baseball. Following the holidays I was eager to get back to preparing for the upcoming season. I had a daily schedule of walking and running at the YMCA, or, depending on the weather, running outdoors through the streets and parks near Seton Hall University. The running craze was not as popular then and no one ever asked what I was running from, and thankfully no one tried to stop me.

Bernadette was unable to join me when I reported to the Pirates' spring training site at Fort Pierce, FL in late February 1954 because there were not enough rooms at the Holiday Inn where the team was quartered. Rookie players were not allowed to bring their wives, but two weeks later that rule was rescinded and Bernadette joined me in Fort Pierce. During those two weeks of separation she experienced for the first time the loneliness that baseball wives face every summer.

Living alone in Newark, she now had the responsibility of all the chores, one of which was operating the coal-fired, hot water furnace. That meant shoveling coal, removing the ashes, and operating the furnace. She handled this task well until one Sunday. Prior to going to Mass with her sister Mary, she opened the draft door to heat up the furnace and warm the house. Upon returning from Mass she had a relaxing breakfast, and then spread the Sunday newspaper on the kitchen floor. While kneeling down reading the paper she suddenly felt the kitchen floor begin to heave up and down. Terrified, she suddenly remembered she had forgotten to lower the draft door on the furnace and quickly ran downstairs to see what was happening.

The sight was terrifying! The entire surface of the furnace was now a bright, glowing red and the pressure on the hot water system created an accompanying percussion sound. Recovering from her shock, Berna ran next door to seek help from the neighbor. The husband answered the door and noticing the fear on her face, asked what was wrong. All Bernadette could utter was, "The fur-furnace, the fur-furnace." They speedily ran back to the house, down the cellar steps and when the neighbor saw the red glowing furnace he hollered, "Oh my God!!" Noticing a water hose, he swiftly turned it on and began dousing the glowing furnace. The cold water produced clouds of steam, creating a sight Bernadette described as a "scene from Hell." It all ended well, but it was the first of what would be many not so pleasant experiences for her as a baseball wife.

After the 15-3 season at Denver, I was in great shape physically, and mentally more confident of my pitching than I had ever been. Being in a major league spring training camp for the first time was a moving experience. I was now associating with players I had revered, like Joe Page, Walker Cooper, Sid Gordon, Cal Abrams, Eddie Pellagrini, and Max Surkont. As a fan I knew them only by name, number, and the daily box scores. Now I was sharing time, space and conversations with them.

I thought it was the start of joining a tight knit group of players—a team. How disillusioned I was! The camaraderie I enjoyed playing on winning teams in the minor leagues was absent during that first big league spring training camp. Later, after much introspection, I understood more fully why this was so.

Branch Rickey, the GM of the Pirates, went with a youth movement in 1952 and 1953, and it was disastrous. The 1952 team, known later as the "Rickey Dinks," had won only 42 games and lost a Pirates' team record of 112 to finish 54.5 games behind the National League champion Brooklyn Dodgers. The 1953 team was not much better, winning 50 and losing 104. With such dismal failures the turnstiles at Forbes Field were rusty and Mr. Rickey understood he had to sell tickets. To do so, he had to acquire players with name recognition in the major leagues. These veteran players were well aware they were not playing on a pennant-contending team. Nearing the end of their careers, they were trying to squeeze another season out of what was not then a financially rewarding profession. Rarely were they eager to offer assistance to younger players. We were considered a threat to their spots on the roster.

Fred Haney, the manager of the Pirates, gave me every chance to pitch my way on or off the team. Andy Cohen, my manager at Denver, who was in camp, sat in on staff meetings and kept me informed daily about how the staff rated my pitching. He informed me, "They are really impressed with your pitching and consistency." This was the kind of news I wanted to hear, but then he added a disclaimer, "But they're looking for a reason to send you out."

That reason turned out to be that two bonus players took roster spots. The baseball owners had signed an agreement that any first year player in professional baseball who received a bonus of $5000 or more had to remain on the active major league playing roster for two full seasons. This edict was designed to prevent owners from offering large bonuses when competing for young, untried talent. I did not then consider how this ruling would affect my career and retirement, but it was to do so profoundly.

The 1954 Pirates had two such bonus babies, Nick Koback and Vic Janowicz, both catchers who had little or no ability to play at this level of baseball. Koback, in two full seasons, played in 16 games and had only 33 at bats and more strikeouts—13—than hits, for a batting average of .121. Janowicz, however, was a "name" player, not in baseball, but in college football at Ohio State University. A multi-threat player as a runner, passer, place kicker, punter and safety on defense, he won the 1950 Heisman Trophy Award as the top college player. After college he served a stint in the US Army and the Pirates signed him to a bonus contract for the 1953 season.

John Galbreath, the Pirates' owner and a great Ohio State booster, was instrumental in arranging the bonus for Janowicz. In two seasons with the Pirates, Vic appeared in 83 games, hitting only .214. After the two bonus years with the Pirates he signed a contract to play football for the Washington Redskins. A near-fatal car accident ended his athletic career in 1956.

Despite the limited roster spots open, I continued to impress Fred Haney and his staff. My ability to throw strikes and be consistent in my performance earned a spot on the final roster cut that spring. After eight long seasons in the minor leagues, I was going north with the Pirates and would test my skills where they counted most–during regular season play in the major leagues.

Most memorable about my first major league spring training was getting to know Branch Rickey. He was the most fascinating person I ever met, in or out of baseball. Considered among the great orators of his time, he certainly was by far the most distinguished speaker in the game of baseball. He could have been a world-renowned preacher or a nationally known politician had he chosen either of those professions. He was not a tall man, and although he appeared to be large, he was not obese or corpulent. Physically, he resembled John L. Lewis, the well-known leader of the United Mine Workers, particularly with his bushy eyebrows and his deep commanding voice.

Mr. Rickey spoke in a raspy tone that began in his diaphragm and rattled around in his throat before booming out like a voice from above. Believe me, hearing it attracted immediate attention and his words were never lost on his listeners. Never using profane language, his most common exclamation was "Judas Priest," which he used both to compliment and criticize.

A towering figure in the game of baseball, Mr. Rickey first gained prominence by forming a system of minor league farm teams while he was general manager of the St. Louis Cardinals in the 1930s. He was so successful that his system of developing talent became the foundation for all major league teams, and remains so to this day. Mr. Rickey firmly believed that "where there is quantity, you will find quality." It was the underpinning of the large farm systems he built at St.Louis, Brooklyn, and later, at Pittsburgh. He hired a staff of highly qualified scouts who combed the country and Latin America for promising young talent. These young players were filtered through a minor league system that was ranked from the lowest, Class D minor league level, to Class AAA, the highest level. The constant flow of qualified major league talent provided winning teams for decades in St. Louis, Brooklyn, and Pittsburgh.

Among the first professional baseball players to graduate from college (Ohio Wesleyan College), Rickey brought with him values that were then alien to those then playing the game. His speeches and conversations expressed the value he placed on character, correct social behavior, commitment to married life, and the work ethic. These strong religious and social convictions characterized him as a "do-gooder" and an outsider in the game he loved. An example of this came across in a talk he gave to Pirates' players and their wives in March 1955, during spring training at Fort Myers, FL. At the end of another commanding and wonderful speech, he told of how he was named to replace manager, Bobby Wallace, then a star player and temporary manager of the St. Louis Browns. Mr. Rickey stated he didn't want to manage and never did again, but took the position out of loyalty to the owner. He asked Wallace to get the players together so he could talk to the team. The talk was not about baseball but about the values in which he believed strongly. Unfortunately, the players not only rejected the talk, but more embarrassing, they mocked and humiliated him by making fun of him around the league. I could tell by the tone of his voice that evening in 1955 how that still pained him.

It was during spring training in 1954 at Fort Pierce, FL when I became aware of Mr. Rickey's wisdom and decency. The team was housed at a Holiday Inn, which in those formative years had no special meeting rooms to handle large groups or conventions. Ironically, the only motel room available to handle our large group was the bar and lounge. Every morning prior to leaving for the field we would gather the team together at the lounge for a talk by Mr. Rickey. The first time he welcomed us and declared in his deep, raspy voice, "I'm not used to being in places like this, and certainly not at this hour of the morning, but Judas Priest, this is the only room that we have available." Following are some of my favorite "Branch Rickey Parables."

"Tillie Walker and Ty Cobb"

Branch Rickey had managed the St. Louis Browns from 1913 to 1915 and one of his players was a center fielder named Clarence "Tilly" Walker. Rickey described him as having the speed, arm and ability of Ty Cobb, but never reaching that level of excellence. I knew who Ty Cobb was, but I'd never heard of "Tilly" Walker. The essence of this parable was why Ty Cobb was in the Hall of Fame and Tilly Walker was just another name in the Baseball Encyclopedia. Spellbound, we listened as Mr. Rickey told us the "tale of Tilly Walker."

"We were barnstorming north after spring training," he began, "and were playing somewhere in Texas. Carpenters were putting up a new fence in the outfield with pieces of scantling wood lying on the field and no fence yet in place to keep the ball in the playing field. Tilly Walker came to bat in the ninth inning with two outs and we were down one run. Tilly hit a ball into the gap in left center field and we all jumped up knowing it could be a home run because there was no fence and the ball would continue rolling. Tilly sensed the same thing and began to go into a home run trot as he rounded first base. But the outfielders never gave up on the ball, which miraculously hit one of the pieces of wood and bounced directly back to the center fielder.

"Tilly, seeing what happened began to run faster, the outfielder made a perfect relay to the shortstop, who then relayed it to third base. We knew it was going to be a close play. Tilly slid to the outfield side of third base and the umpire called him out and we lost the game by a run. After the game everyone on the team was patting Tilly on the back telling him what a tough break it was that the ball hit the piece of wood. 'It should have been a home run, it should have been a home run, Tilly,' they said in unison.

"The next morning we had a team meeting and I began by saying 'I want to talk about yesterday's game.' to which Tilly Walker jumped up and said, 'I know what you're going to talk about Branch, that bad break I got when the ball hit that scantling wood.' To which I replied, 'Yes, Tilly, I want to talk about that, but not about the bad break. I want to talk about you! That was not a bad break Tilly, you should have had a home run and you also should have also been safe at third. When you hit the ball, you stood and watched it instead of running hard right away.'

"Tilly said, 'I know I did Branch, but I am getting better at it, I don't do it as much' and I replied 'Yes you are getting better at that, but when you rounded first base, you gave it the skater's turn, instead of cutting the corner sharply.' Tilly responded, 'I know I shouldn't do that Branch.' and I said, 'Judas Priest, Tilly! It's like going to a whorehouse: You know it's wrong, but you still do it!'

"Now you're already twenty feet behind schedule when you go into a home run trot before you reach second base. Then you see the outfielder that never quit on the ball, get the bounce off the scantling wood and you start to run hard. You slide into third base and if you can throw any part of your 160 pounds to the south side of third base you would escape the tag and be safe. But Tilly, you slide to the north side and into the tag and you were out." Branch ended, "It wasn't a bad break, Tilly. Judas Priest, it was you!"

To ensure we understood the meaning of this parable, he then told us the story of Ty Cobb. He began, "I was managing the St. Louis Browns and we played the Tigers in Detroit. With the score tied, we failed to score in the top of the ninth inning and I noticed that Cobb would be the first batter in the last of the ninth for the Tigers. I sat next to my pitcher, a tall, gangling right-hander, to remind him that Cobb was the lead off hitter. I told him, 'Don't walk him! Make him earn his way on base.' I knew I shouldn't have said that, because he walked him on four pitches.

"Cobb was always a threat to steal a base and everyone knew that. The pitcher threw over to first base and Cobb got back safely and the first baseman lobbed a high arching throw back to the pitcher. As soon as Cobb saw that throw, he made a fake move as if to try to steal second base, but he didn't run. I said to the first baseman, "Do it again," and he did. Each time Cobb would fake running on the return high arching throw to the pitcher. The fourth time the pitcher threw over, Cobb was safe again, but as the high arching return throw to the pitcher was being made, Cobb this time took off for second base. I thought, 'now we've got him! All the pitcher has to do is catch it and throw to second base!'"

But the pitcher, seeing Cobb running, took his eye off the ball. All I could see were arms and legs as this tall, right-hander fumbled around trying to make the catch and throw. He finally caught the ball but hurriedly threw wildly over second base. Cobb, I could see was headed to third and I knew; NOW WE'VE GOT HIM!"

"Tilly Walker was playing center field for us and although he was late coming in on the play, I knew he had the best outfield arm I had seen. Tilly's throw was on target at third base and I could see Cobb was going to be out by two feet. But somehow, Cobb slid and as he did he brought up his spikes and kicked the ball out of the third baseman's glove. The ball rolled into foul territory and before we could retrieve it Cobb had headed home and scored the winning run. I ran up to the umpire and hollered, 'Mister Umpire, it was deliberate interference. He kicked the ball away from the third baseman and should have been called out for interference.' I can still hear the umpire's reply. He said, 'Give him credit Branch. *HE MADE HIS OWN BREAKS*.'"

Mr. Rickey's message was simple. Without a hit being made, or a strike being thrown, Ty Cobb's ability and desire to win at all costs won the game. Rickey's team lost because of Tilly Walker's failure to hustle and to fully use his God-given talents.

"True Friends"

Mr. Rickey took great delight in telling this story of the scarcity of "true friends" in your life. It was a lesson he learned early as a freshman at Ohio Wesleyan College. A very promising athlete in many sports, he made the varsity football team as a punt return specialist in his freshman year. As he fondly recalled the event, it occurred on a bright, sunny Homecoming Day game when with the score tied late in the fourth quarter he returned a punt 60 yards for the winning touchdown.

"There were 10,000 fans at the game and as I returned the punt, I could hear them hollering, 'Go Branch go! Go Branch go!' After the game in a wild celebration, they came down and carried me off the field on their shoulders."

He became an instant celebrity. The following day, walking to church on campus, and later in the cafeteria, everyone recognized him and congratulated him on his winning punt. He basked in the glow of such recognition and having so many new friends.

It lasted until his first class Monday morning, a philosophy class. He said, "As I relaxed in my classroom chair, ready to listen to the professor's lecture, savoring Saturday's heroics and basking in the recognition I was receiving, the professor's first comment brought me to an attentive position. 'If you can count all your friends on one hand, you are a very fortunate and blessed person,' remarked the professor."

Branch said he thought to himself, "Why, the man must be crazy! I surely can count many more than that. There were over 10,000 of them at the football game. They carried me off the field on their shoulders and many more knew me the next day on campus. I knew I could count them as friends."

The professor proceeded to describe what he meant by "friends." To him a friend was "someone who in a time of trouble would do anything for you. If you were in jail and needed money to get out, the friend would provide it with no questions asked. If you had serious personal problems, that friend would sit and listen to you. If you were sick, he would be at your side, hold your hand and stay up all night with you. He would place no limit on what he would do for you. That is a true friend and if you can count them on one hand, you are truly fortunate and blessed.'

"After hearing the professor's description of a friend, I began to wonder how many friends I truly had. After a long period of contemplation, I could name only two, my mother and father. It was then I understood what true friends were and how rare and special they were in my life."

Mr. Rickey and Contract Negotiations

A burden Rickey carried was a reputation for being a "penny-pincher" for the wages he paid players. Many writers compared him to a plantation owner, who had no concern about those who worked for him. In the 1930s, at the height of the Depression, he paid the going rate, which wasn't much. He did the same at Brooklyn and Pittsburgh. Rickey never out-lived accusations of being "tightfisted" and "cheap," however. Tales of Mr. Rickey's contract negotiations are many and all ended with him playing the final card and winning. His wisdom and business acumen enhanced his knowledge of the true value of a player in the market place. He also fully understood the power he held as the General Manager at a time when there was no free agent competition to determine objectively the true market value of major league players.

One of the best Branch Rickey contract stories concerned Gus Bell, who in 1950 joined the Pirates' as a 21-year-old rookie. Gus hit .282 his first season on a last-place team. The next season he played in 148 games hit .278 with 16 home runs and 89 runs batted in for a seventh place team. Getting married and raising a family was a virtue Mr. Rickey constantly preached. He called players who did not take that route "matrimonial cowards." Gus Bell had taken the virtuous route and was not only raising a family, but was also on his way to a rewarding major league career, or so he thought, until he received his 1952 Pirates' contract.

Disappointed, Gus quickly sent it back and became a holdout for the first time. In an effort to break the stalemate, Mr. Rickey invited Gus to come to Pittsburgh and talk personally about the contract. According to the story, Gus was getting nowhere describing his statistics and value to the Pirates. In desperation, aware of the value Rickey put on married life and raising a family, Gus decided to play his final card in the negotiations. He said, "Mr. Rickey, you have always implored players to get married and accept the responsibilities of parenthood, which I have done. My wife and I are married with one child and are expecting another baby this summer and I need the raise." Rickey replied, "Son, I'm paying you to play baseball, not to have babies."

So fascinated was I with Mr. Rickey's oratorical style that I developed a very good imitation of him. It made the slow hours in the clubhouse and on bus trips entertaining. I had so much respect for Mr. Rickey, though, that I never wanted him to hear me doing this imitation. However, during spring training in 1955 at Fort Myers, his son, Branch Junior (appropriately nick-named "the Twig"), approached me in the clubhouse. He requested that I go into the trainer's room where his Dad was getting a rubdown and do my impersonations of him. I said, "No, I have too much respect for him to do that!" He pleaded and said his Dad would get a real kick out of it.

Reluctantly, I agreed and walked into the training room where Mr. Rickey was lying on his back on the rubbing table. He was completely covered by a sheet except for his ankles, which the trainer was massaging. Using a low gravely voice that came from my stomach I began my Branch Rickey impersonation; "There is nobody I would rather see at bat in the ninth inning with the bases loaded, two outs and a tie game than NICK KOBACK. BUT NOT FOR MY TEAM."

I could see his response as the sheet over his belly started to move preceding a good laugh. I then continued, "Bob Friend's got more native stuff than any pitcher on our staff. Of course he got most of it THE YEAR WE TRAINED IN CUBA." The sheet continued moving followed by a deep laugh then a pause after which Mr. Rickey inquired, "You know that's a pretty good impersonation. Where did you learn that?" I replied, "Well Mr. Rickey, I've been in the organization for eight years, but I haven't taken any money out of it." He very quickly replied, "NO, AND YOU WON'T"!

Mr. Rickey always had the last word.

CHAPTER EIGHT

My Major League Debut at Ebbets Field

April 15, 1954 was an overcast 40-degree day at Ebbets Field as the Brooklyn Dodgers opened their home season against the Pittsburgh Pirates. The game was in the eighth inning and I was about to make my first pitch in a major league game.

It had taken me eight years, including two outright releases in 1946, plus two years in the Army, to get to this moment at Ebbets Field. I thought of all those inning and games I spent pitching in small, minor league towns such as Geneva, Ozark, Brewton, Troy, Dothan, Greenville, Andalusia, and Enterprise, in the Class "D" Alabama State League during my first season in professional baseball. The contrast between Ebbets Field and those minor league towns and fields magnified the contrasts and the satisfaction I was feeling.

Having viewed Ebbets Field only in black and white photos and on television in World Series games, I was now seeing it up close, in full color and from the center of the picture. In my eighth decade of life, the memory of that moment is so vivid I can still visualize Ebbets Field—the well manicured infield, the colorful ads on the outfield walls, the manually operated scoreboard in right center, the slight angles at the base of the right field wall that created crazy ricochets for outfielders; the zany Dodger fans who, in that intimate park, seemed to be always in your face; Tex Ricard, the public address announcer who, like most major league public address announcers in those days, sat in a folding chair on the playing field adjacent to the Dodger dugout, since he also had the job of providing baseballs for the home plate umpire.

Fred Haney, the Pirates' manager, had me in the bullpen that day. Being in the bullpen for the Pirates in 1954 at Ebbets Field was similar to having a rifleman's MOS in the infantry. You knew you were going to get into the battle, but you weren't sure when. The fans at field level were so close they could reach out and touch you. The wonderful intimacy was great for the Dodgers and their fans, but hell for the visiting team players, since the bullpen was located in foul territory down the left field line.

The Dodgers' roster that opening day in 1954 was loaded with established veteran players. Junior Gilliam, Pee Wee Reese, Duke Snider, Jackie Robinson, Roy Campanella, Gil Hodges, Carl Furillo, and Billy Cox. They didn't waste any time unloading on Pirates' veteran starter Max Surkont. They got to him for eight hits in four innings, including home runs by Gilliam, Robinson, and Campanella for a 7-1 lead. The bullpen phone rang in the fifth inning and Cal Hogue, a rookie right-hander with an outstanding curve ball, got the call. Cal pitched well, allowing only one hit in three innings before leaving for a pinch hitter in the top of the eighth. When the Pirates played in Ebbets Field, the eighth inning was usually the Dodgers last inning at bat. This game was to be no exception.

In the top of the eighth inning, Sam Narron, the Pirates' bullpen coach, answered the bullpen phone and in what sounded like an executioner's voice, said, "King, it's you." With my major league debut moments away, I took off my jacket and began to experience intense anxiety. Throwing right-handed and sidearm, I used the pitching mound nearest the field box seats. As I was making my first warm-up pitch, the fans were leaning so far over the railing nearest the field I thought with my sidearm delivery I was going to hit them. To ease my concern, but mostly to improve my concentration, I moved to the mound nearest the foul line. This put me physically, but not verbally, away the fans, who kept up their one-sided conversation.

There is a decisive moment for a pitcher that can have a positive or negative effect on his attitude. It occurs immediately after picking up a baseball. If it feels small and light in your hand, you begin to feel stronger. That feeling continues on an upward spiral as you step on the pitching rubber and look at the catcher. You think you're a lot closer than the 60.5 feet from which you are throwing. All these positive feeling were with me as I began to warm up.

My anxiety began to dissipate and my confidence increased. As I got further into my warm-ups, I was throwing everything for strikes. My best pitch, a sinker, was really moving and I was keeping it down low in the strike zone where it was most effective. As I was finishing my warm-ups I noticed one final optimistic sign. My catcher, Vic Janowicz, was having trouble handling my pitches, dropping almost every one. Buoyed by this, I put on my jacket as I headed to the Pirates' dugout on the third base side.

The Pirates' eighth inning was lengthy, as we scored three runs to chase Monk Meyer the Dodger starter to make it a 7-4 game. As the inning continued, I found a seat next to my roommate, Vern Law. He asked how I felt about my big league debut. I told him of the positive things I felt. The ball was light, it looked like I was standing right on top of the catcher, my sinker was moving, I kept it low, I was throwing strikes and noted with confidence that "the catcher was dropping almost everything I threw." He stopped me and asked, "Who was catching you?" I replied, "Vic Janowicz." Just as the Pirates' inning was ending Vern's reply to my question was, "Janowicz? Heck he has trouble catching everyone."

I didn't need to hear that! As I took my first step from the dugout to the mound, that psychological upward spiral began a sudden downward movement. I began to think, "Maybe I wasn't throwing that well." Anxiety began to rise and with it, a growing disassociation from where I was. As I got to the mound, facing toward center field, I picked up the Spalding Official National League Baseball for the first time in a Major League game. I turned toward home plate, stepped on the pitching rubber, looked into home plate and couldn't believe what I was seeing. Toby Atwell, my catcher, looked so far, so VERY FAR, away. If you have looked through the wrong end of a pair of binoculars, you have some idea of what I was seeing.

Negative thoughts were quickly destroying any concentration I might have had. I thought this can't be the mound; I must be on second base. I don't think I can throw a ball from here to catcher Toby Atwell without bouncing it.

My warm-up pitches did nothing. The only thing moving the ball was gravity. I thought Atwell was laughing at the lack of movement on my pitches. Atwell had earned the nickname of "Buster", because like the old-time silent film star "Buster" Keaton, he rarely said anything. As I waved my glove to signal the curve ball indicating my final warm-up pitch I knew Atwell wasn't about to come out to offer any encouragement. He didn't.

As the ball was making its ritual movement around the infield, I heard Tex Ricard, the PA announcer proclaim, "Now pitching for the Pittsburgh Pirates, number 29. King! W A Y N E King"! I said to myself, "Hell, Wayne King is an orchestra leader." Ben Wade, a former

Dodger pitcher, informed me later that Tex, who rarely knew the first names of rookie players, would trustingly seek help from the Dodger dugout. The players always gave him any name but the correct one and Tex would gullibly announce it. In 1955, Gene Freese, then in his rookie season with the Pirates, made his first appearance at Ebbets Field when Tex Ricard introduced him as "Augie." To this day Gene Freese, who had a long major league career, still goes by the nickname "Augie."

Hearing my introduction as "Wayne King" and waiting to receive the game ball from third baseman Eddie Pelligrini, I said a silent prayer, "Please God, get me out of here without too much embarrassment." Additional thoughts began going through my mind– "You can't hide a bad performance in New York, there are so many media covering the game; I have to face at least one hitter before they can take me out..." I had been praying for this moment for a long time. As I looked at Duke Snider, I remembered the old adage, "Be careful what you pray for, you may receive it." Here I was, a right-handed, low-ball pitcher facing one of the best left-handed, low-ball, power hitters in the majors—and in a ballpark with a short porch in right field.

Atwell signaled for a sinker on my first pitch. Somehow I got it near home plate on the outside corner and Snider fouled it for a strike. I was now able to breathe, but I still couldn't spit. I threw a curve inside for ball one, and then got a curve ball where I wanted it, low and inside off the plate, and Snider fouled it off for strike two. Atwell signaled for another sinker. As I made the pitch it was like I was seeing it in slow motion—I threw the ball, followed through and for some reason Snider, with two strikes on him, tried to drag a bunt and fouled off the pitch. I suddenly thought, "Damn, he struck out!" If you saw the emotion Johnny Podres displayed in the final game of the 1955 World Series at Ebbets field, you have some idea of how I felt inside. Now I could spit! I got through the inning giving up only one hit and no runs.

After the game when we returned to the Commodore Hotel in Manhattan, I was anxious to get the early edition of the New York Daily News and read Dick Young's story on the game. I saw my name in the box score. The line read, "King, 1 inning, 1 hit, 0 walks, 1 strikeout." That's all I had to see. If I never threw another pitch, this verified I pitched in the major leagues. It was there in the *New York Daily News*!

The next morning I got around to reading the complete story and game notes by Dick Young. In his notes he stated that "Nellie King, a tall, thin right handed, sidearm pitcher, who resembles Ewell Blackwell, pitched the final inning for the Pirates, allowing only one hit." Being compared with Blackwell caught my attention. He was my idol since I began my career in the minors. As I continued to read Young's article, he asked Jackie Robinson, "Does Nellie King resemble Ewell Blackwell?" Robinson's reply was short, but cruelly truthful: "He does, until he lets go of the baseball."

CHAPTER NINE

Back to New Orleans

Andy Cohen's statement during 1954 spring training, "They're looking for a reason to send you down to the minors," remained in my mind at the start of the major league season. After thirty days the roster had to be cut down to 25 players. I had pitched relief in only four games, all losses on the road, at Ebbets Field, Polo Grounds, Wrigley Field and Milwaukee, when I was informed I was being sent down to New Orleans. Disappointed, I inquired why, and was told, "They want you to go where you can pitch every four days." The reasoning didn't sit well with me as I had spent eight years in the minor leagues learning my trade, knew how to pitch and had the statistics for confirmation. Most worrying, however, was a conditional contract that required me to take a salary cut if I was sent down to the minors.

I approached Branch Rickey, Jr., head of scouting and player development for the Pirates, to plead my case against the cut in pay. Unaware of the conditional clause in my contract, he asked me not to discuss this with his dad and that he personally would make sure I received the $5000 major league minimum salary for the year. I left with great respect for the "Twig" and a better mental attitude as I prepared to join the New Orleans Pelicans in the "AA" Southern Association.

Bernadette and I joined Gail Henley, an outfielder, and Bill Hall, a catcher, who were also cut, for the auto trip to New Orleans. Arriving in "the Big Easy" in early May, we rented a one-bedroom apartment above a furniture store on Canal Street, not far from downtown. The apartment was not air-conditioned and the oppressive heat and humidity of the New Orleans summer was not yet upon us. We failed to take into consideration the effect of sunlight reflecting off of a flat metal roof adjoining our apartment would have on our comfort for the rest of the summer. Our only method of cooling off was by taking a cold shower and standing in front of a large portable fan that we dragged from room to room.

We dressed for the temperature, partially or completely nude most of the time, which, as newlyweds, was not a problem. However, it became a temptation for the owner of the apartment when I was away on a road trips with the team. He did small minor repairs and my wife noticed he spent more time than normal working in the hallway fixing a transom window to our apartment. Using a ladder he had a great view of Bernadette's attire or lack thereof. Not one to suffer fools lightly, she loudly informed him to get down of that damn ladder and stop the "repair work," or the New Orleans Police would be making a visit.

I joined the New Orleans team for a road series against the Nashville Vols, who played in an historic park named "Sulphur Dell." Everyone who played minor league baseball in the south was aware of the dimensions and odd shape of Sulphur Dell. It was 334' to left field, 421' to center, but only 262' to right field. It was a park made for left-handed pull hitters. Combined with the short porch in right field was a steep, 45-degree incline that rose 25 feet to a wooden fence topped with a tall screen. Playing in right fielder at Sulphur Dell was a weird experience. The player had a choice of playing at the bottom of the incline, or standing on the uneven incline like a billy goat. If the right fielder played at the bottom of the incline he was standing on a flat surface with less than 100 feet from first and second base. Sharply hit singles to right field could produce a close play and occasionally an out at first base. Playing deeper and on the incline was tougher. To maintain balance on the inclined terrace, players had scratched out (using their spikes) a flat plateau half way up the inclined terrace on which to stand.

Ben Wade, a pitcher on the Pirates' roster, had played at Sulphur Dell in 1948 after a being cut by the Chicago Cubs. Ben described the first game he witnessed at Sulphur Dell and how manager Larry Gilbert dealt with the unusual dimensions of the park. Sal Modica, the Vols top pitcher who started the game, ran into very serious trouble in the first inning. Losing 3-0, Modica had given up 4 hits, had two runners on base, and retired only one batter. Witnessing the situation, Ben turned to the player next to him and questioned why nobody was warming up in the bullpen. Having suffered some hearing loss while serving in the Navy during WWII, his conversations, even his whispers, were louder than normal. Unaware his comments were heard by manager Larry Gilbert, he was embarrassed when he heard him say, "Ben, don't worry, if you can hold them to eight runs in this park and we'll win every time."

Nashville was heavily loaded with left-handed hitters with swings that resembled a laborer using a shovel to toss dirt over his right shoulder. They pulled everything!

Later in the season I pitched in Sulphur Dell and, except for Bob Lennon, a left-handed power hitter who led the league that season with 66 home runs, I kept the ball in the park. I pitched him low and on the outside corner with a sinking fastball that he couldn't pull. Wisely, he began hitting it to left field. I was glad to give him a single to left instead of a home run. I rarely came inside with a pitch Lennon could pull, which annoyed Erv Dusak, a former major leaguer who was a player-coach for New Orleans. Seeing Lennon getting singles to left field, he challenged me, "Damn don't be afraid to come inside on this guy." With a big enough lead I decided to challenge Lennon and threw one inside. He pulled the pitch and hit it so far over the 60' right field screen that it landed on the roof of an ice plant adjoining the park. I told Erv, "I think I'll keep pitching him low and away."

The sizzling hot weather was always a problem in New Orleans, but we learned to deal with it. As a starting pitcher I took about ten minutes to warm up and had to change my sweatshirt before starting the game. By the fourth or fifth inning I had to change shirts again, and by the seventh inning I couldn't find a dry spot on my entire uniform.

Thin pitchers like me hung in longer than the heavier guys. I pitched every four days as a starter and completed 15 of 23 starts. Although I could scarcely afford to, I'd lose 7 to 8 pounds a game. I quickly regained most of it after the game, sitting on the floor of the shower, enjoying the cool water and colder bottle or two of Dixie beer.

One of my most treasured memories that season was pitching the short seven-inning opening game of a doubleheader at Pelican Stadium against Nashville. We won 6-0 and it took only an hour and a half to complete. I just missed a no-hitter. The only hit I gave up was a drag bunt single down the third base line. Phil Johnson, the *New Orleans Item* sportswriter who covered the Pelicans, wrote an article about the game and commented on my physique:

Nellie King is a long, hauntingly hungry looking young man who is built like a war atrocity and has the attitude and destructiveness of a happy tiger. He is loose, like a puppet is loose, dangling jerkily from its strings, this way and that. He gives the impression of so many bones, tied together with wire and thrust into space. He could be typecast as an Ichabod Crane, a vertical column with no width. He looks like he has a PhD in awkwardness, yet is as graceful and well-coordinated as any ballet dancer. We mention all this only because King does not, either, look like the best pitcher in the league—which he is. That he was the best has long been suspected (ever since he owned a 7-0 record just before the All-Star game). Friday night he put on a show that ended all doubt. King threw the short game of the doubleheader and was just two pitches short of perfection. One was the only hit Nashville got, a dinky bunt down the third base line: the other a grounder to short that was booted. Nobody else got close to base and nobody was walked. It was the stingiest Pelican effort since Earl Williams threw the Birds' last no-hitter in 1945.

Typically, King laughed it off as "an effort. I figure to win tonight," he said. "I been eating and sleeping since Monday. Why, almost got fat. Rest, it's wonderful" (This was an obvious reference to King's test in Little Rock, when he relieved on two successive nights and was charged with two straight defeats.)

King is a basically happy man, who remembers the year he won 20 games for New Iberia (1948) with as much relish as he recalls the stint he put in with the Pirates earlier this season. He is intelligent, 26, married to a wife who's a foot-and-a-half shorter than his own 78 inches.

"I just keep the ball low," he said, offering a formula for Friday's near-perfect 6-0 shutout. "It's hard to hit when it's low. And I kinda got a little leverage to make it go faster. When I can keep it low like that, I'm OK.

Larry Gilbert watched his Vols bite miserably at King's low pitches and afterwards pronounced the lean right-hander as the "best pitcher in the league" without any reservation. And Gilbert, of course, owns the No. 1 baseball opinion in the South. "He's got it," said Larry. "He'll go up. Don't know why he isn't up there right now. There can't be ten guys better than him with the Pirates. If there were, they wouldn't be in last place today.

"See how he kept that ball low. That's the secret. If a pitcher could keep the ball low like he did, and have the control that he had, he'd stay in the major leagues for a long time."

I did keep it low, but an arm injury would soon cut short the amount of time that Gilbert had predicted I would play.

Following the 1954 season the Pelicans participated in the post-season championship playoffs. The heat and humidity was still evident in early September when I won a 10-3 decision in the fifth game of the series at home against Birmingham, the Yankees' farm team. During that game I had one of the rare occurrences of throwing an unintended "spitball." With a runner at second, one out and a left-handed hitter, Lou Berberet at bat, Danny Murtaugh signaled for an intentional walk.

Pete Peterson (later the General Manager of the 1979 World Champion Pirates) was my catcher. Pete took off his mask and stepped out to the right side of the plate to accept the four pitches. Having seen pitchers throw lob tosses on these occasions that turned out to be wild pitches, I always used my normal sinkerball delivery. I threw two such pitches successfully, but on the third, the sweat on my hand apparently affected the flight of the baseball. As the ball neared Pete, it took off in an up and away fashion I never saw before or since and hit him square in the face. Pete and the third baseman were unable to keep the ball from rolling in the visiting dugout and the runner from second scored. I tried, but never could deliberately make a ball do what it did that night in Pelican Stadium. As an aside, Pete Peterson never took off his mask again for an intentional walk!

We won the series with Birmingham in six games and then played Atlanta in the championship finals. For the first time that season we went by plane to Atlanta. It is fascinating today to compare the growth of the city of Atlanta in 1954 to today's metropolitan area. The airport in 1954 resembled what today would be a small county air field. Ponce de Leon Park, the home field for the Atlanta Crackers, had an unusual characteristic: a magnolia tree in centerfield some 500 feet from home plate. My first game in Ponce de Leon Park that season I shutout Atlanta 6-0. Later in the season I found out the tree in centerfield came into play when pitcher Dick Donovan hit a home run that interrupted a picnic two fans were having underneath it.

Donovan, a good hitting pitcher, entertained players from both teams during batting practice with an excellent imitation of Babe Ruth. He would put a pillow under his shirt and pants to resemble the Babe's paunchy appearance. When he hit one over the signs in right field he would imitate the Babe's short choppy home run around the bases. Whitlow Wyatt, the manager of the Crackers, had pitched against Babe Ruth during his career in the American League. I always thought Whitlow enjoyed the act and may even have served as an advisor for Donovan's admirable portrayal of the Babe.

We lost the championship round to Atlanta and I wound up with a very successful 16-5 record and led the Southern Association with a 2.25 ERA. I pitched every four days, and sometimes three, and proved to be as equally consistent as a starting pitcher in New Orleans as I had been while pitching in relief at Denver. In two consecutive seasons I had pitched in 81 games, compiled a 31-8 record (.795), had 19 saves, and issued only 51 walks in 283 innings (1.6 per game). I even pitched 56 consecutive innings midway in the season without issuing a walk.

This consistency makes managers and defensive players happy. I kept the ball in play—and did it quickly as most of the games in which I pitched were completed in less than 2 hours. It made me recall "Specs" Garbee's advice my first spring training in 1946 at Albany, GA, "You don't get paid by the hour. Work fast and throw strikes." Some of today's pitchers work so slowly and are constantly behind in the count. I'm reminded of Pirates' announcer Bob Prince's comment, "This guy works so slow it would take him a week to die a sudden death."

At season's end my wife and I rode north with Pete Peterson. His car was packed full and there was little room for my long legs and body. Pete was anxious to get home as his wife Gladys was expecting their first child (Eric "Ricky" Peterson, who later became a well respected major league pitching coach with the New York Mets).

The trip was mercilessly long but ended well in Elkton, MD, where I bought my first car. A large, roomy, four-door, sky blue, eight cylinders Buick Super, with classic side fenders. I bought it from Tom Lee, who had the Buick agency in Elkton and ran the baseball team I pitched for during my last summer in the Army in 1952. I put over 100,000 miles on it before I traded it in, and still think it was the best car I ever bought!

The 1954 season brought a mixture of disappointment and joy, with joy eventually triumphant. I had the best year of my career as a starting pitcher, winning 16, losing 5 and leading the Southern Association with a 2.25 ERA. In two seasons as a reliever and starter on pennant contending teams, I had compiled a record of consistency that got me back to the majors.

On April 24, 1955, I made my first Major League start in the second game of a Sunday doubleheader against the Phillies at Shibe Park. The memories of how far I had come from that day in 1941 when I saw my first big league game overwhelmed me. I was now sitting in the very same dugout where Babe Ruth and Lou Gehrig once sat. Dreams like that rarely come true. It was so mind-blowing I still get "goose bumps" when I think of it.

The pre-game anxiety for starting pitchers is more extreme than a regular player who competes every day. The anxiety accompanies pitchers, and when it doesn't you usually don't perform well. My pre-game nerves were more pronounced because I was pitching the second game of the double-header. I paced up and down the dugout and retreated often to the clubhouse urinal during the first game

Jack Meyer, a rookie right-hander and Philadelphia native who had reason to be keyed up, started for the Phillies. We failed to score in the top of the first and I took my first look at home plate from the mound. Unlike my first game a year earlier in Ebbets Field I didn't think I was standing on second base! Jack Shepard, my teammate at Denver, was my catcher and we seemed to be on the same page, but my adrenalin was flowing and I was working faster than normal. He would signal for the pitch he wanted, and then run through four decoys. I was so impatient that as soon as I got the sign, I began winding up while he was still going through the decoys. He called time and quickly came out to the mound. He told me, "Dammit, slow down! By the time I give you the sign and finish my decoys you've already thrown the ball."

Meyer and I were hooked up in a great game that was scoreless until the Phillies 8th inning. They scored a pair of unearned runs after an error on a double play ball that could have ended the inning. The inning ended with the Phillies leading 2-0 when the umpires called the game. In those days Pennsylvania had a "Blue Law" respecting religious services on Sunday. No sporting event could start before 1:00 PM and no inning could be played after 7:00 PM. The umpires called the game at the end of eight innings, as it was past 7:00 PM. We were informed we would finish the game during the Pirates' next trip into Philadelphia, which was to be in early July. I felt great satisfaction with having pitched so well.

On April 30, 1955, six days later, I would make my second start against the Cincinnati Reds at Forbes Field. I pitched well and left in the 8th inning with the game tied 4-4. Bob Friend came on to relieve and became the winning pitcher when Preston Ward drove in the winning run in the bottom of the ninth inning.

The game was overshadowed by the pre-game ceremonies. On a brilliantly sunny but cool Saturday afternoon in Schenley Plaza, just outside the left field fence at Forbes Field, the Pirates honored Honus Wagner with the unveiling of a classic and beautifully sculptured bronze statue depicting him at the height of his powers. On hand for the ceremony were baseball greats, Cy Young, Pie Traynor, Fred Clarke, Wilbur Cooper, George Gibson, and all the players from the Reds and Pirates. I vividly recall seeing an ageing Honus Wagner, sitting in a convertible automobile, warmly dressed in a Pirates' team jacket.

It was to be the last summer of baseball for Honus, who died eight months later in his hometown of Carnegie. The Honus Wagner statue today is located outside the new and magnificent PNC Park, not far from where Wagner began his Pirates and Hall of Fame career in 1900, at Exposition Park. In my short and undistinguished major league career it was ironic to have been the starting pitcher for that day and later as a Pirates' broadcaster to serve as emcee at the rededication of the Honus Wagner statue when it was moved to Three Rivers Stadium in 1970. To have been a part of both ceremonies is an honor I still treasure.

On May 5, 1955, in my third consecutive start, I won my first game in the major leagues with a 9-4 decision over the Milwaukee Braves. It came thanks to the solid hitting of first baseman Dale Long, who hit three doubles to drive in six runs, and a clutch relief job by Vern Law. Most memorable, was a 7th inning triple play by the Pirates. With an 8-2 lead going into the seventh inning, I gave up two runs, had two on and nobody out when Fred Haney replaced me with Vern Law, who walked Johnny Logan to load the bases. With game now up for grabs, Law had to face Eddie Matthews, a left-handed power-hitter. Matthews ripped a line drive toward the right field line that appeared headed for extra bases, but first baseman Dale Long leaped, caught the line drive, then threw to Dick Groat at second for out number two, who returned it to Long who tagged Logan for a triple play!

Vern Law got three outs on one pitch and it was like hitting the lottery for me. It was the only triple play I saw in my professional career and it got me my first win in the major leagues.

Charlie Grim, the manager of the Milwaukee Braves, was known as "Jolly Cholly" but that day he wasn't too jolly. Frustrated seeing the triple play and losing to the lowly Pirates, Charlie got into an argument with the umpires in the bottom of the seventh inning and was thrown out of the game. Leaving the field he had to exit through the Pirates' dugout. As he approached the dugout, his cap in his hand, and scratching his gray hair he exclaimed, "I'm going into the damn clubhouse to puke!"

I didn't enjoy the satisfaction that should follow winning my first game in the major leagues. With an 8-2 lead in the seventh, starters were expected to finish such games. I personally felt embarrassed that I didn't, but I wasn't ready to follow Charlie Grimm's act, I had an Iron City!

Another historic date in major league baseball was May 12, 1955 at Wrigley Field. I was the starting pitcher for the Pirates that day, and my pitching stunk. For some unknown reason, my arm felt dead. I never had great velocity, but I couldn't have gotten semi-pro hitters out with the crap I was throwing that day. I felt absolutely naked on the mound, and with the temperatures in the low 40s it was not a day for feeling exposed, mentally or physically. In only two innings I had given up 5 hits, 1 walk, and 2 runs. Fred Haney evidently had seen enough, as I never got to bat and he yanked me for a pinch hitter (Felipe Montemayor) in the third inning. By the fourth inning I had showered, grabbed a hot dog and a Coke, and joined the fans in Wrigley Field to view what would become a memorable and exciting game.

This was the day Sad Sam Jones made history by throwing a no-hitter and winning 4-0. The Cubs should have scored in double figures as they had 15 hits and stranded 13 runners.

Going into the ninth inning, Sad Sam hadn't allowed a hit, walked four, and, thanks to a pair of double plays, faced only three batters in seven of the first eight innings. Working on a shutout and a no-hitter, he made the ninth inning more thrilling. He walked the first three Pirates' batters, Gene Freese, pinch-hitter Preston Ward, and Tom Saffel, to load the bases. Now with the tying run at the plate with a 4-0 lead in Wrigley Field, the no-hitter, shutout and win were all up for grabs. Somehow Sad Sam got control of himself and the baseball. Dick Groat took three called strikes for the first out. Roberto Clemente went down swinging on five pitches. Wrigley Field grew quiet as Frank Thomas a long ball power hitter faced Jones. Thomas swung and missed on a big breaking curve ball, then took the next pitch for a ball. Jones got him to swing and miss on a high pitch. With the count 1-2, Jones went to another big curve ball that Thomas took, but home plate umpire Gore called it a strike. The crowd sighed then exploded when they realized Sad Sam Jones had his no hitter. Les Biederman, the sportswriter for the *Pittsburgh Press,* noted that it was the first no hitter against the Pirates since Carl Hubbell did it, on May 8, 1929 in the Polo Grounds. (I was then only 13-months old!) The box score of that historic game listed, as losing pitcher, King (1-1). It was the last game I would start in the major leagues.

After that game in Chicago I was relegated to the bullpen and used in mop-up roles for games that were already lost. It was humbling and confusing, as I did not feel any pain in my throwing arm, it just felt dead. I had never experienced anything like that before or since. My sinker had no movement and the limited velocity.

The only thing I could figured might have caused this problem was the way I was used late in the season the two previous seasons when we were in pennant races at Denver and New Orleans. I was strictly a relief pitcher at Denver, but near the end of the season I was a starter for two seven-inning games. At New Orleans I was a starter, but late in the season was also used in short relief. I remain convinced that pitchers can't do both without causing a dead arm or more serious arm injuries.

A most embarrassing day for me was during a 1955 Sunday afternoon double-header at Forbes Field against the Milwaukee Braves. The day was hot and humid with both games interrupted by showers. I recall warming up three times in the first game, but never saw action. In the second game I was busy warming up three or four more times, before I was called in to pitch in the eighth inning. I took my eight warm up pitches and the first pitch I threw to Eddie Matthews was hit back to me on one hop, but hydroplaned on the wet grass and hit me flush in the mouth. I felt fine with only a fat lip to show for it when Fred Haney came to the mound. Instead of asking how I felt he said, "Gimme the damn ball." I had spent all afternoon throwing in the bullpen to prepare for action and threw only one pitch and was gone.

Branch Rickey meets with Bobby Bragan and the 1956 Pirates' team during spring training.

UNIFORM PLAYER'S CONTRACT

National League of Professional Baseball Clubs

Parties

Between ....PITTSBURGH ATHLETIC COMPANY, INC.....

herein called the Club, and............NELSON JOSEPH KING............

of ...Newark, New Jersey........................., herein called the Player.

Recital

The Club is a member of the National League of Professional Baseball Clubs, a voluntary association of eight member clubs which has subscribed to the Major League Rules with the American League of Professional Baseball Clubs and its constituent clubs and to the Major-Minor League Rules with that League and the National Association of Professional Baseball Leagues. The purpose of those rules is to insure the public wholesome and high-class professional baseball by defining the relations between Club and Player, between club and club, between league and league, and by vesting in a designated Commissioner broad powers of control and discipline, and of decision in case of disputes.

Agreement

In consideration of the facts above recited and of the promises of each to the other, the parties agree as follows:

Employment

1. The Club hereby employs the Player to render, and the Player agrees to render, skilled services as a baseball player during the year .... 195.4. including the Club's training season, the Club's exhibition games, the Club's playing season, and the World Series (or any other official series in which the Club may participate and in any receipts of which the player may be entitled to share).

Payment

2. For performance of the Player's services and promises hereunder the Club will pay the Player the sum of $.5,000.00 (FIVE THOUSAND DOLLARS) for the season..................., as follows:

In semi-monthly installments after the commencement of the playing season covered by this contract, unless the Player is "abroad" with the Club for the purpose of playing games, in which event the amount then due shall be paid on the first week-day after the return "home" of the Club, the terms "home" and "abroad" meaning respectively at and away from the city in which the Club has its baseball field.

If a monthly rate of payment is stipulated above, it shall begin with the commencement of the Club's playing season (or such subsequent date as the Player's services may commence) and end with the termination of the Club's scheduled playing season, and shall be payable in semi-monthly installments as above provided.

If the player is in the service of the Club for part of the playing season only, he shall receive such proportion of the sum above mentioned, as the number of days of his actual employment in the Club's playing season bears to the number of days in said season.

If the rate of payment stipulated above is less than $6,000 per year, the player, nevertheless, shall be paid at the rate of $6,000 per year for each day of his service as a player on a Major League team.

Loyalty

3. (a) The Player agrees to perform his services hereunder diligently and faithfully, to keep himself in first class physical condition and to obey the Club's training rules, and pledges himself to the American public and to the Club to conform to high standards of personal conduct, fair play and good sportsmanship.

Baseball Promotion

(b) In addition to his services in connection with the actual playing of baseball, the Player agrees to cooperate with the Club and participate in any and all promotional activities of the Club and its League, which, in the opinion of the Club, will promote the welfare of the Club or professional baseball, and to observe and comply with all requirements of the Club respecting conduct and service of its teams and its players, at all times whether on or off the field.

Pictures and Public Appearances

(c) The Player agrees that his picture may be taken for still photographs, motion pictures or television at such times as the Club may designate and agrees that all rights in such pictures shall belong to the Club and may be used by the Club for publicity purposes in any manner it desires. The Player further agrees that during the playing season he will not make public appearances, participate in radio or television programs or permit his picture to be taken or write or sponsor newspaper or magazine articles or sponsor commercial products without the written consent of the Club, which shall not be withheld except in the reasonable interests of the Club or professional baseball.

Player Representations

4. (a) The Player represents and agrees that he has exceptional and unique skill and ability as a baseball player; that his services to be rendered hereunder are of a special, unusual and extraordinary character which gives them peculiar value which cannot be reasonably or adequately compensated for in damages at law, and that the Player's breach of this contract will cause the Club great and irreparable injury and damage. The

Ability

Player agrees that, in addition to other remedies, the Club shall be entitled to injunctive and other equitable relief to prevent a breach of this contract by the Player, including, among others, the right to enjoin the Player from playing baseball for any other person or organization during the term of this contract.

Condition

(b) The Player represents that he has no physical or mental defects, known to him, which would prevent or impair performance of his services.

Interest in Club

(c) The Player represents that he does not, directly or indirectly, own stock or have any financial interest in the ownership or earnings of any Major League club, except as hereinafter expressly set forth, and covenants that he will not hereafter, while connected with any Major League club, acquire or hold any such stock or interest except in accordance with Major League Rule 20 (e).

Service

5. (a) The Player agrees that, while under contract, and prior to expiration of the Club's right to renew this contract, he will not play baseball otherwise than for the Club, except that the Player may participate in post-season games under the conditions prescribed in the Major League Rules. Major League Rule 18 (b) is set forth on page 4 hereof.

My first pro baseball contract for $5,000 at Geneva, AL.

Denver Bears 1953 (L-R) Charlie Sipple, Barney Schultz, Harry Pritts, Nellie King

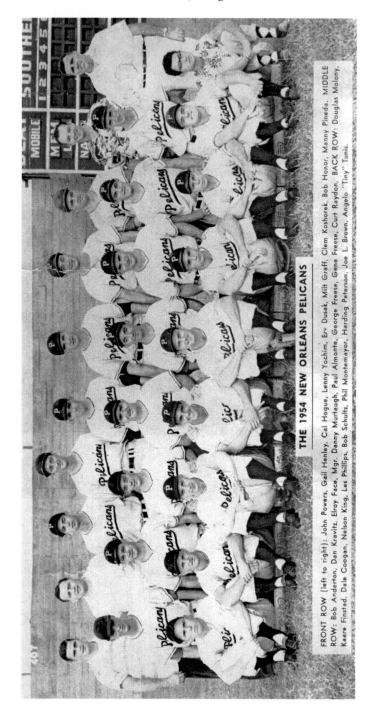

THE 1954 NEW ORLEANS PELICANS

FRONT ROW (left to right): John Powers, Gail Henley, Cal Hogue, Lenny Yochim, Erv Dusak, Milt Graff, Clem Koshorek, Bob Honor, Manny Pineda. MIDDLE ROW: Bob Anderton, Dan Kravitz, Elroy Face, Mgr. Danny Murtaugh, Paul Almonte, George Freese, Curt Raydon. BACK ROW: Douglas Molony, Kaare Finstad, Dale Coogan, Nelson King, Les Phillips, Bob Schultz, Phil Montemayor, Harding Peterson, Joe L. Brown, Angelo "Tiny" Tunis.

1954 New Orleans Pelicans, AA Southern Association

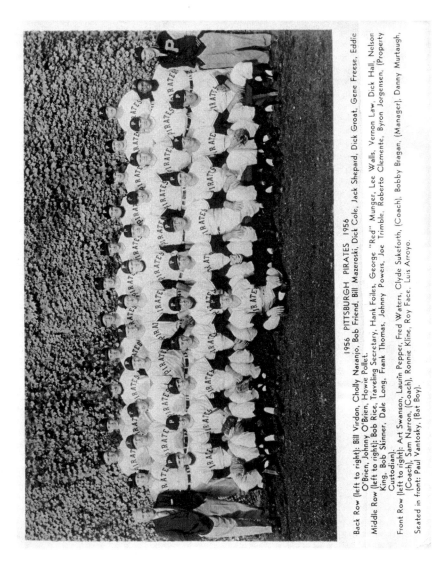

1956 PITTSBURGH PIRATES 1956

Back Row (left to right): Bill Virdon, Cholly Naranjo, Bob Friend, Bill Mazeroski, Dick Cole, Jack Shepard, Dick Groat, Gene Freese, Eddie O'Brien, Johnny O'Brien, Howie Pollet.

Middle Row (left to right): Bob Rice, Traveling Secretary, Hank Foiles, George "Red" Munger, Lee Walls, Vernon Law, Dick Hall, Nelson King, Bob Skinner, Dale Long, Frank Thomas, Johnny Powers, Joe Trimble, Roberto Clemente, Byron Jorgensen, (Property Custodian).

Front Row (left to right): Art Swanson, Laurin Pepper, Fred Waters, Clyde Sukeforth, (Coach), Bobby Bragan, (Manager), Danny Murtaugh, (Coach), Sam Narron, (Coach), Ronnie Kline, Roy Face, Luis Arroyo.

Seated in front: Paul Vantosky, (Bat Boy).

1956 Pittsburgh Pirates team led by Dale Long, whose eight home runs in eight games brought the crowds back to Forbes Field

King Rates Royal Cheers as Ace of Buc Relief Corps

Bull Pen Bulwark

Nelson Gives Up Only One Unearned Tally in First 12⅔ Innings on Mound

By JACK HERNON

MILWAUKEE, Wis.

Nelson King, who stayed around only long enough to sip the proverbial cup of coffee with the Pirates the last two seasons, appears set to enjoy the full major league feast this year.

King's hurling, as the Buccos made a surprisingly speedy start in the National League race, was nearly perfect.

The six-foot, six-inch righthander, whose style strongly resembles that of Ewell Blackwell, yielded only one unearned run in his first 12⅔ innings of relief.

In three of his first four trips to the hill, King faced the world champion Dodgers. Yet, except for an error by a teammate on April 22, Nellie would have blanked the Brooks in nine and two-thirds frames.

King's most brilliant performance of the early race took place on April 29, when the Pirates posted a stunning twin-bill victory over the Dodgers, 10 to 1 and 11 to 3.

Nelson was called from the bull pen to relieve Vernon Law in the fourth inning of the nightcap when the Dodgers showed signs of wiping out the Bucs' six-run lead. Two runs were in, a Dodger was on second and there was only one out when King arrived.

One Slip, a Balk, Then Steadiness

The base-runner, Charley Neal, was then waved to third base on a balk when Nellie slipped and almost fell off the mound while making a pitch.

That was the only slip Nellie made, however, because from then on, he blanked the Brooks on two hits and

Nelson King

ROOKIES

(CONTINUED FROM PAGE 5)

Jack Hernon's Post-Gazette article on my relief work, which helped move the Pirates into first place in mid-June, 1956

Warming up in the bullpen during 1956 spring training

Danny Murtaugh relaxing near his spittoon while reading the lineup for that night's game

Two of the greatest Pirates, Willie Stargell greeting Roberto Clemente after a home run

Bill Mazeroski displaying the consistent defensive skills that put him in the Hall of Fame.

CHAPTER TEN

I Lost a Game in the Grand Canyon!

In late June of 1955 following a game at Wrigley Field, Fred Haney informed me I was being sent down to Hollywood in the Pacific Coast League. I was angered when it was announced the Pirates signed pitcher Paul Martin to a bonus contract and needed a spot on the roster and mine was chosen again.

Disappointed, I phoned my wife with the bad news and grabbed a taxi to the airport in Chicago for my flight back to Pittsburgh. Upon arriving at my gate at Midway Airport, I was amazed to see that Branch Rickey was also on the same flight. My surprise grew when Mr. Rickey inquired what I was doing at the airport. As GM of the Pirates, I thought he would be aware of such decisions. Looking back, either he was being kind, or it was the beginning of the end of his role as GM of the Pirates.

It turned out to be the latter, as the following year he was replaced by Joe L. Brown. After informing Mr. Rickey I was being sent down to Hollywood, with his usual wisdom and simplicity he offered this advice. "You must be disappointed, but you know son, if the manager is going to carry only ten pitchers and he thinks you're number eleven, you ought to go!"

The trip to Hollywood was leisurely and memorable. I was in no hurry to go back to the minor leagues. It says in the player's contract that the player must report to his assigned club immediately. I found that would be difficult for me to accomplish. I had learned I was being sent down on Friday and didn't arrive in Pittsburgh until later that evening. Aware I couldn't get the utilities shut off in our apartment until Monday I figured we might as well visit Bernadette's family in New Jersey and my mom in Lebanon, PA. We returned to Pittsburgh late Monday to shut off the utilities and close the apartment.

The previous September I had purchased that beautiful, 1954 sky-blue Buick Super. What a car—and what a ride! We drove west on Route 40 the first day before stopping at Terre Haute, Indiana. The next day we caught up with Route 66 in St. Louis and started singing "You go through St. Louis, Joplin, Missouri and Oklahoma City looks mighty pretty." Which reminded me of my brother Charles, who lived in Tulsa, so we stopped in the early afternoon to visit. We lingered longer than planned, leaving after lunch the following day. This leisurely drive to Hollywood was beginning to make me feel uneasy with guilt. I was not exactly "reporting immediately" to my assigned club, so we drove long into the night, stopping around midnight at an isolated motel outside Albuquerque, NM.

The motel had an eeriness about it, kind of like the Bates Motel in Alfred Hitchcock's thriller, "Psycho." As we turned on the light to the room, Bernadette remarked how "uniquely color-coordinated" the room was. It had light brown stucco walls, matching beige colored bedclothes and furniture. Even the bathroom featured a beige colored sink, toilet and bathtub. Turning on the water in the bathroom she quickly discovered the color combinations were not the work of an interior decorator, but rather, the result of dust blown in from the arid surroundings. We spent a restless night analyzing every sound outside and imagining the horrors they might bring.

The next day, with the good intention of covering a lot of miles, we continued on Route 66 until mid-afternoon when we were delayed by road construction near Flagstaff. I got out the map to see exactly where we were when I noticed the Grand Canyon was just north of Flagstaff. I said to Bernadette, "We're never going to get out this way again or have the opportunity to see one of the 'Eight Wonders of the World.' Let's drive there, spend the rest of the day and stay overnight and hit the road after breakfast." She agreed. The desire to see the Canyon pushed aside any guilt I was feeling about the length of time it was taking me to report to Hollywood.

On the short trip north to the Grand Canyon there was another minor construction delay. We noticed the car in front of us was from Texas. While getting out to stretch, we struck up a conversation with the married couple. We found out how proud they were of Texas and they told us how BIG things were there. Quickly, the delay ended and we headed to the Grand Canyon. We had seen the glories of the Canyon only in color photos. Our anticipation grew with each mile. We assumed there would be a gradual visual appearance of such an enormous natural wonder. How surprised and even frightened we were when suddenly we looked down out of the side window and there it was—this huge hole—the Grand Canyon.

What an awesome sight! After that first view I have always thought the first person that came upon the Grand Canyon literally stumbled upon it, fell all the way to the bottom, and never lived to tell about it.

We quickly searched for a spot for a better view of the awe inspiring scene, winding up next to the couple from Texas. As we edged close to the railing, sighing almost simultaneously at the enormity and beauty of it all, I heard the wife from Texas say, "Charlie, did you ever see anything like it?" I turned to Bernadette and whispered, "Ever see anything like it!? Hell, they don't even have anything this big in Texas!"

We enjoyed a fine dinner overlooking the canyon and considered staying another day to take the mule trip to the bottom. But duty called. We awoke early the next day to enjoy the glorious and varying colors created by the rising sun striking the canyon walls. It was magnificent. The early rising time was unusual for me. One thing players can't do without at breakfast is the morning newspaper. Eager to discover how the Pirates were doing without me, I turned to the sports page where I noticed they had lost a double-header in Philadelphia last night. This confused me as they usually played double headers on Sunday or holidays, and July 4th was two days later. Further reading led me to the box score for a more detailed examination of the pitching line for the games.

I was surprised to read that the losing pitcher in the first game was KING. I thought it had to be a typo. Then I recalled the game they completed last night was the game I started in April that was not completed because of the Pennsylvania Blue Laws. I turned to my wife and said, "Berna, you're not going to believe this, but I lost a game in the Grand Canyon last night."

Our trip to Hollywood was now quite behind schedule. My guilt button, like the gas pedal of that 54 Buick Super, was pushed all the way down. We headed west on Route 66 and made Needles, California at high noon, with the temperature hitting 105 degrees. During lunch, my wife, looking at an enticing swimming pool at the motel, and with the wisdom and common sense that the male of the species cannot comprehend, asked, "We're not going to drive across the Mohave Desert at high noon, are we?" At age twenty-seven, with the usual male ego, I was convinced I was invincible. My wife was certain I was crazy and in dangerous denial of the hazards of crossing the Mohave Desert at high noon in July. The denial defeated my wife's wisdom and common sense and we headed out to cross the Mohave Desert.

Bernadette reminded me our car had no air conditioning. I noticed that a gas station at Needles was selling "car air conditioners" for only $15.00. This so-called "air conditioner" was a metal container shaped like a jet engine. I was informed all I had to do was fill it with dry ice and hook it onto the outside of the driver's side window of the car. The desert air would enter through the jet engine opening, go over the dry ice, and circulate cool refreshing air throughout the car. It was useless.

From Needles to the western end of the Mohave Desert we suffered through 110-115 degree heat. The only coolness I felt came from my wife's long periods of icy silence, the kind of silence that only married men know. The silence was broken only when her anger could no longer be contained. The hot Mohave temperatures were nothing compared to her descriptions of my lack of intelligence when she did speak. I'd never heard words like that from my bride of 18 months. After witnessing many overheated cars pulled off to the side of Route 66, the only thing I was watching was the temperature gauge. The trip convinced me of the validity of the Buick advertising slogan, "Buick Makes Fine Cars."

After the tiresome and anxious drive on Route 66, it was a pleasure leaving the Mohave Desert and driving into the blossoming valley of San Bernardino. Green trees and lawns were a pleasant and welcoming sign. The openness of communities in the Los Angeles metro area was in strong contrast to the jammed conurbation of buildings in the metropolitan areas in the east. Despite the large and fast-growing population spread over an enormous area, we were surprised that Los Angeles had no identifiable downtown like Chicago, New York, or Boston. Rege Cordic, the most popular morning radio figure in

Pittsburgh history from the mid 1950's to 1967, moved to LA in 1967 to host a morning drive time program. Comparing LA to the strong community identity in Pittsburgh, Rege remarked that "Los Angeles is like 10,000 Monroevilles (a community near the Pennsylvania Turnpike on Route 22 east of Pittsburgh). There's no 'there' there!"

After searching the newspapers for apartments, Bernadette was fortunate to find an attractive and moderately priced apartment in Toluca Lake, a growing community in the San Fernando Valley. We later discovered that many Hollywood stars resided in Toluca Lake, including Bob Hope. It was reported Toluca Lake was one of the early successful real estate investments Bob Hope made in the fast-growing Los Angeles area.

Exactly one week after being sent down from the Pirates I finally put on a Hollywood Stars uniform at Gilmore Field. The park opened May 2, 1939 and was the most intimate baseball park I'd ever played in. The front row seats along first and third base were just 24 feet from the field and home plate was only 34 feet away. It made for easy conversations between players and fans.

With no major league teams yet located on the west coast, Gilmore Field attracted all the well-known movie stars of that era: Spencer Tracy, Gary Cooper, Milton Berle, Bing Crosby, and many others. Harpo Marx, Groucho's younger brother, who never spoke in the movies, was a Hollywood Stars fan and a constant visitor in our locker room. I confess I never spoke with him and I can't recall that anyone did. Chuck Connor, a former major league player (Brooklyn and Chicago Cubs), was just breaking into the movie business in 1955 and hosted a pre-game TV interview show for the Stars' home games. Chuck went on to enjoy huge success in "The Rifleman" television series.

It was said that more beautiful women attended games at Gilmore Field than any other park in the minor leagues. I recall seeing Elizabeth

Taylor, Jayne Mansfield, and others during the 1955 season at the Stars games. They did not go unnoticed by players, some of whom took a more than passing interest in knowing exactly where they were sitting. During my first game at Gilmore field an unusual ritual amazed me during the "seventh inning stretch." A number of players hurriedly left the dugout to go under the stands. When they returned I noticed they all were brushing peanut shells and popcorn off their uniforms. Veteran pitcher Ben Wade informed me the players crawled under the stands to look up under the ladies' dresses to see if they were or were not wearing panties.

Jack Cummings, who won an Oscar for the best picture of 1955 as the producer of "Seven Brides for Seven Brothers," was a big Hollywood Stars fan. Late in the season he took Lee Walls, Bobby Del Greco, George O'Donnell, my wife, and me on a tour of the MGM Studios. At one point, we entered a studio where a scene for "The Tender Trap," starring Frank Sinatra, was being shot. When we entered the room, DelGreco, a big Sinatra fan, almost collapsed when he saw "old Blue Eyes" relaxing near a piano. Sinatra was so gracious; we had our photo taken with him, and he personally signed it. That photo remains a family treasure.

I met manager Bobby Bragan for the first time in Hollywood, and was captivated by his ability to attract media attention, mainly through his disagreements with umpires, which were frequent. A photo taken at Gilmore Field showed Bragan lying on his back on home plate, knees bent, with his head cradled in his hands, defiantly looking up at the umpire, who had just thrown him out of the game. He resembled a little boy saying, "No, I'm not going to go to bed!"

Bragan had not seen me pitch before and had me throw batting practice the first day. Eager to see how my arm felt after seven days off driving cross-country, I threw for 15 minutes. I figured I would not see any action that night, but I was wrong. Bragan used me in a short relief role. The next day my arm ached so badly I couldn't throw very well. I was relegated as mop-up reliever for the first few weeks.

That was the spot I was called in to pitch in my first game at Gilmore Field against the Los Angeles Angels, who brought on the power hitting Steve Bilko and a scrappy second baseman named Gene Mauch. Before major league teams relocated to the west coast, the Hollywood-Los Angeles rivalry was like the Dodger-Giant face-offs in New York City. These intense games always drew big crowds, and also brought out all the dimensions of Bobby Bragan's personality. Although he was the manager, Bragan regularly inserted himself into the lineup as the catcher.

With an overflow throng at Gilmore Field, Bragan was behind the plate. Bob Garber, a hard throwing right-hander, started for us, while Don Elston, a right-hander, started for the Angels. Garber was having a great year, but not on this night. We fell behind early and never caught up. Earlier in the game, Carlos Bernier, our center fielder, was "beaned" by Don Elston. At the time, the incident didn't create any furor and seemed to be forgotten by everyone— except Bobby Bragan.

We were down something like 8-4 when I was told I would pitch the ninth inning. When I finished my warm-up and came into the dugout, Bragan sat next to me and said, "Elston's the first batter up in the ninth inning and I want him to go down." He then told me the sequence of pitches he would call for. "I don't want you to do it on the first or the second pitch. I want to start with a curve ball out over the plate, for a ball. I want the next pitch to be another curve ball, out over the plate for a ball. I want to make sure he's leaning out over the plate when we do it, and I want him do go down!"

I got the message. I threw the first two curve balls outside for balls. Bragan then gave me the "flip him" sign (the same motion you make with your thumb when shooting marbles). I threw a fastball high and inside to Elston. As he threw up his bat to protect himself the ball hit the bat, came right back to me and I threw him out at first base. I got the next two guys out, which I believe was the first time I had retired three in a row since I reported to Hollywood. After the game I went home feeling more optimistic about my pitching than I had since April, when I took that scoreless game into the eighth inning at Philadelphia in my first major league start. The next day Bragan had a clubhouse meeting and said, "When I call for a knock down pitch, I want to see the hitter go on his ass. I want to see some dirt on his uniform. That'll cost you $10, big guy!"

I always had a difficult time throwing at hitters when asked to do it. I could take the responsibility of throwing at a batter when I wanted to, but not when someone asked me to do it. I would not have made a good "hit-man" for the Corleone or Soprano families!

It is has been said of some pitchers, "He would knock down his own mother if she came to bat in the right situation." These pitchers took great delight and relished the reputation for "knocking down" or "dusting off" hitters. Sal Maglie's reputation for throwing under the hitter's chin during his years with the New York Giants earned him the nickname of "The Barber." Sal, who seldom smiled, always wore a day-old beard, which made him look more menacing than he really was. Not being an overpowering pitcher, he did not frighten hitters as much as those who threw hard, but they respected him. Hitters never knew when it might happen with "The Barber."

One of the most daunting "knock down" pitchers during the few seasons I was in the major leagues was Marv Grissom of the New York Giants. At 6' 3", 205 pounds, his weather-beaten face and physique resembled the "Marlboro Man." Unlike Sal, Grissom not only looked mean, he *was* mean. In Roberto Clemente's 1955 rookie season with the Pirates, every pitch from Grissom was aimed at his head. Roberto inquired of Giant's catcher Ozzie Virgil, "Why does he throw at me every time I come up?" Ozzie said, "He just doesn't like some hitters, and you're one of them."

Stan Williams, who pitched for the Los Angeles Dodgers from 1958 to 1962, had the reputation of "keeping a book" on hitters he wanted to knock down. He would update it regularly depending on how batters were hitting him. He threw hard and was wild, but his attitude magnified the hitters' fears. Bill Mazeroski, who played 17 seasons with the Pirates, had the best comment about Stan Williams. "That guy used to scare me so much; I think the happiest day I had in the National League was when I heard that Stan Williams was traded to the American League!"

Alex Grammas, who coached third base for the Pirates during my early years as a broadcaster, told me an unusual story about a pitcher's desire to "knock down" a hitter. It occurred in 1954 during his rookie season with the St. Louis Cardinals. The Cards were playing the Dodgers at Ebbets Field, and made a comeback in the late innings against Jim Hughes, the Dodger's best relief pitcher. Hughes led the National League with 24 saves that year and had just given up a home run when manager Walter Alston came to the mound to make a pitching change.

Grammas was kneeling in the on-deck circle and in an intimate park like Ebbets Field, he could hear the conversation on the mound between Alston and Hughes. Alston asked Hughes for the ball indicating he was going to make a pitching change. Hughes didn't give him the ball. In fact he argued with Alston to be allowed to pitch to one more hitter. Alston again asked for the ball. Hughes again refused, stating loudly that he wanted to face one more hitter. Finally, Hughes realizing that he was not going to change Alston's mind, looked at

Grammas kneeling in the on deck circle and threw at him, hollering, "Some SOB was going to go down before I got out of here, and you're the only guy on the field wearing a Cardinal uniform!"

Don Drysdale earned a well-deserved reputation as a "knockdown" pitcher. Throwing sidearm he had a wicked sinking fastball that moved in on right-handed hitters. Like most sinkerball pitchers he made sure he always came in very tight on them. However, he did "knock down" hitters and never disputed having that reputation.

I vividly recall a game Drysdale started against the Pirates in 1971 at Dodger Stadium. It was a Sunday afternoon. Roberto Clemente, who usually did not play a day game following a night game, was in the starting lineup. Clemente did not start the game the night before, but entered as a pinch hitter in the eighth inning and got a hit that tied the game. It went 14 innings before the Pirates won the game and Roberto wound up with four hits in four at bats.

Drysdale, aware of Clemente's four-for-four the night before, dusted him early in the count in the first inning. Clemente got up, and in a style described so well by Pittsburgh's poet laureate, Sam Hazo, as "rearing his head back on his neck like a proud horse," stepped back into the batter's box and hit Drysdale's next pitch into the seats in right center field for a home run. Clemente came up again in the third inning. Drysdale again knocked him down. Clemente got up, rolled his head back, stretched his neck, and hit Drysdale's next pitch over the center field fence for another home run. Years later when Don was doing Dodger broadcasts I mentioned those incidents he remarked, "I remember that day. It was the last time I threw at Roberto Clemente."

In the early to mid-1950s, Robin Roberts of the Phillies was the top pitcher in the game. It was said Roberts would allow you to hit the ball, until you got a runner into scoring position. Then he would crank it up a notch and blow hitters away. No pitcher in that era was more consistent than Roberts. For six seasons, from 1950 to 1955, he pitched 300 plus innings and missed seven straight with 297 innings pitched in 1956. From 1952 to 1954 Robin Roberts completed 20 or more games and won 20 or more games, including 28 in 1952.

Despite Roberts' consistency and amazing success, there were some in the game who though he'd be more effective if he threw at hitters more. He rarely did. It wasn't his style. I have found out that pitchers can't intimidate good hitters. Pitchers who try, find out it only makes good hitters into better hitters.

The big change in baseball in the modern era is the stature of starting pitchers. Rarely do they pitch a complete game. A "quality start" is now considered six innings. Except for the few remaining name pitchers, like Roger Clemens, Randy Johnson, Pedro Martinez, and a few others, starters have lost their identity. They don't sell tickets in advance.

In my day, starting pitchers were expected to finish what they began. If they didn't, they were considered soft and felt humiliated. Nothing describes the attitude of starting pitchers in those earlier years better than a story told to me by Don "Ozzie" Osborne, the Pirates' pitching coach in their 1971 Championship season. Ozzie had spent a lifetime pitching in the minor leagues and most of it in the Pacific Coast League as a starting pitcher.

He told me about a game he pitched in Portland in the late 1930s. Winning by a run in the ninth inning, he had two outs and three runners on base. The manager came out to yank him and asked him for the baseball. Ozzie refused. The manager again asked for the ball and annoyingly put out his hand, palm up, and turned his head looking toward the bullpen while shouting, "Gimme the god-damn ball!" The manager felt something drop into his hand and it wasn't a baseball. Ozzie had dropped a wad of chewing tobacco into his hand. The manager angrily dropped the chew and said, "You SOB, you better get this hitter out or we're gonna have the damndest fight in the clubhouse you've ever seen." Ozzie said, "I got him out!" Pitchers today appear all too eager to give the manager the ball.

I overcame the dead, sore arm that had diminished my ability during the 1955 season. At the end of the regular season the Stars and Los Angeles played in a "City Championship" series. It came down to the final game and George "Red" Munger was slated to be the starting pitcher, but he never showed up for the game because of an unfortunate family situation. Bobby Bragan informed me during batting practice that I would be the starting pitcher. His confidence in me gave me the mental lift I needed.

I pitched effectively and had a lead through seven innings when Bragan brought in Joe Trimble, who recovered from arm injuries late in the season. Joe had major league stuff featuring a sharp, breaking overhand curve ball that ate up hitters. He closed the door and the Stars won the city series. With Bobby Bragan's aid my confidence was restored. Little did I know that when Bragan took over as manager of the Pittsburgh Pirates in 1956 he would continue using me as a short reliever. I credit Bragan for giving me the chance to prove I could pitch and win in the major leagues.

At the end of the Hollywood season I approached Branch Rickey, Jr. to tell him my arm felt fine and I wanted to pitch winter ball to increase my chances of returning to pitch in the big leagues. He agreed to my request and arranged for me to play at Mazatlan, Mexico. It would be the first time my wife and I traveled outside the United States.

CHAPTER ELEVEN

An Ugly American

Eager to play winter ball in Mexico, I appreciated my wife's willingness to join me in my first trip "south of the border." Neither of us imagined how profound the cultural differences would be. Making our acclimation worse was the damage done by a typhoon that hit Mazatlan a week before our arrival. Floods had washed out roads and cut off the electricity. My lack of understanding of the culture and anger about the daily inconveniences created by the storm grew each day. Looking back of this experience, I realized I was an "Ugly American."

Our trip began with a flight from Newark, NJ to Tucson, AZ. We traveled by bus to Nogales, Mexico where we found accommodations overnight at a local motel. We left an early wake up call and arrived at the airport with time for clearing customs and having breakfast. Our flight included stops at Hermosillo, Los Mochis, and Culican before arriving at Mazatlan. Before boarding the flight, we had time to view the 30-seat, two-propeller plane. It was not a comforting scene. Two laborers on ladders were working on the propeller engines with what looked like ordinary pliers. When it came time to board, the stewardess showed us to our seats, four rows from the front. A youngster who was crying loudly was creating a disturbance that the stewardess corrected by whacking him on his rear and telling him to be quiet. His mother did not protest. Welcome to Aeronaves de Mexico!

The stewardess went through the ritual of showing us how to fasten our seat belts as the pilot drove the plane to the end of the runway for takeoff. As the plane began to move, I was certain we did not have enough speed to get off the ground. (As an indication of our anxiety level on this flight, while typing this chapter I asked my wife to recall how she felt during that first flight on Aeronaves de Mexico. She answered, "How should I know? I was too busy saying the Rosary.")My observation on the lack of speed for a take-off was correct as the pilot quickly hit the brakes and we were informed we would be returning to the terminal. We got off the plane while the workers returned with their ladders to work on the engines.

After some delay, the pilot decided to give it another try, but this time without passengers. He took the plane to the end of the runway and gathered what he was sure was appropriate speed to take off and returned to the terminal. We were asked to re-board, and despite the anxiety, all passengers returned to the plane. My wife was now heavy into the rosary and I told her, "Don't worry, if the pilot didn't think he could take off, he wouldn't try it." I was right and we had a safe flight.

With three more stops before we got to Mazatlan, there were still sweaty palms on every landing and takeoff. The first two landings and takeoffs at Hermosillo and Los Mochis were on dirt runways, with local peasants squatting alongside to view the landings. We landed at Culican on a concrete runway and were taken to an outside screened facility to have lunch. The accommodations were not ideal for dining, as the tables were still wet with the spray they had used to kill insects.

We finally reached our destination at Mazatlan in the early afternoon and enjoyed our first sight from the air. The view of the crescent shaped shoreline and beach that defined the western limits of the city was marvelous.

Living arrangements overlooking the beach were made for us at the Freeman Apartments. The view of the Pacific Ocean from our apartment was fantastic. Daily we would take delight in watching groups of swordfish and porpoises leaping from the water. The beach was named Olas Altos for the high waves that funneled into the crescent shaped beach. It attracted many swimmers who enjoyed body surfing all day on the big waves.

Bernadette would agree that the name Olas Altos was most appropriate. One day while swimming, a large wave swept her up and turned her over. When she came up for air she had lost her glasses. As she searched for her glasses she was unaware that the wave had loosened the top portion of her swimsuit and she was naked down to the waist. The spectacle quickly caught the attention of the male swimmers. Oblivious to her nakedness, she continued searching for her glasses, when I shouted loudly to inform her to pull up her swimsuit. She never found the glasses. I'm sure a swordfish or dolphin is wearing them today somewhere in the Pacific Ocean.

Pleased with our accommodations, we agreed they were ideal. However, later that evening we discovered because of the typhoon that hit the area a week before, Mazatlan was unable to keep electric generators going for 24 hours. We assumed the generators would be working for the evening hours, but the city turned off the electricity after 6:00 PM and we had to live by candlelight until the next morning when the electricity returned.

A large hotel adjacent to our apartment had lights turned on all evening, which made us question why we didn't. It turned out the hotel had its own generator and did not have to depend on the city's electricity. I still questioned the decision to turn off power during the evening. I thought how dumb these Mexicans were, and expressed my opinions loudly from our apartment.

With no electricity, the refrigerator defrosted at night. The melting ice dripped into a glass bowl we used to store the eggs. When Bernadette opened the door to get eggs for breakfast, the water and the eggs were frozen solid. I made more comments about the stupidity and ignorance of the Mexicans. I was embarrassed by my words when I discovered the electricity was available only during daylight hours so industrial plants and business could continue working, as they provided needed income for the citizens of Mazatlan.

Just as I had during my first journey through the U.S. south in 1946, I became aware of the prevalence and injustice of poverty. Despite their impoverishment and the need to repair the damage done by the typhoon, the people displayed an inner strength and a real joy for life.

The typhoon's impact was evident during our first bus trip to open the season at Los Mochis. We arrived at a wide stream where the flood had washed out a bridge and I wondered how we would be able to continue. We did, thanks to the talent and "can-do" attitude of the Mexican workers. We were transported on a hand-made wooden flatbed barge, similar to the kind depicted in the Tom Sawyer stories. We loaded all of or luggage from the bus onto the barge and two men rowed us across the stream with no problems, delivering us to another bus waiting to complete the trip.

The streets in Los Mochis were unpaved and putrid water lay in the ditches. We were warned not to drink any of the local tap water and after entering my hotel room I knew why. The water from the bathroom tap was grayish and foul smelling. I joined some of the players for dinner at a restaurant not far from the hotel. I can't recall what I ate, but I do not recall drinking the water. I ordered bottled beverages as suggested. The next morning I awoke and had to wash up with the foul smelling tap water. I then made the mistake of brushing my teeth and in two days I had developed a bad case of the "Aztec two-step," which soon developed into dysentery. I was in no shape to play baseball after this, but I persisted.

Games were scheduled on Friday and Saturday with a doubleheader on Sunday. Monday and Tuesday were off days, and Wednesday and Thursday were scheduled for practice. As the "American" pitcher, I had the number one spot in the rotation and was also expected to pitch in relief for the other games. Despite suffering from nausea and dysentery, I felt an obligation to pitch since I was making $700 a month in salary and the team had paid for our plane fare and accommodations.

The baseball field at Los Mochis reminded me of my first season in the minors at Geneva, AL. There was not a blade of grass on the entire field. The contrast from the major league parks was more difficult to handle than it was as a rookie working my way up the baseball ladder. The Los Mochis fans created their own revelry including the ritual of throwing seat pillows at each other. Late in the game they began lighting firecrackers and throwing them into the crowd. I had to deal with the effects of dysentery, but somehow managed to pitch successfully on a hot and sunny day. Between innings I noticed what I thought was a balloon blowing near our dugout. It was not a balloon, but a blown-up pig's intestine with the blood still visible, picking up dust and dirt as it rolled by me. It did nothing to calm my nausea.

I was eager to see the end of the series at Los Mochis and return to the cosmopolitan Mazatlan. As soon as I returned to our apartment, my wife could see I was very ill. She requested the manager to get a doctor to treat me. The doctor showed up the next morning and introduced himself as Dr. Corona-Corona. The double name was unique, but not so much as the fact he wore two pair of glasses. He diagnosed my illness as dysentery and dehydration, prescribed an antibiotic, and gave me intravenous fluids reverse my dehydration. Bedridden for two days, I recovered enough to make practice on Wednesday and Thursday.

I somehow got by with a decent game on Friday. A big factor in my success was the background for the hitters at the Mazatlan Park. It was full of advertisements that made it difficult for hitters to pick up the pitches. The next two days I was feeling the effects of my activity but remained available to pitch in relief. I was called on in relief, and feeling the effects of diarrhea, I got out of the inning and quickly returned the dugout toilet. We were retired quickly, 1-2-3, and the team took the field while I was still on the toilet. This was the first time I remember a game being delayed by dysentery.

I went through the same ritual again, being dehydrated, needing intravenous fluids that kept me bedridden Monday and Tuesday, making practice on Wednesday and Thursday, and pitching the first game on Friday. I saw brief action in relief, but could not return to the park for the Sunday afternoon game. In the wee hours of Monday morning I got up feeling worse and asked Bernadette to call for a doctor. Bernadette, who served as a Red Cross nurse, was aware that this could not go on any longer. I recall her telling me, "If you say we are going home, I'll call for a doctor. If you don't, I'm not going to." I told her we were going home and the doctor arrived and informed me that my condition was serious. I had lost 15 pounds in three weeks. We contacted the Pirates' office to inform Branch Rickey, Jr. of my illness and the need to return home for health reasons. He agreed and we joyously returned to the United States.

My Mexican experiences made me aware of the advantages I took for granted living in the United Stats. I felt then, and still do today, that if a leader offered and provided the benefits and social services people so desperately needed, Mexicans wouldn't care if they were Socialists or Communists—anything had to be better than what they had in 1955. I understand why so many citizens of Mexico are eager to cross our borders. They are simply looking for a better life.

After playing ball at Mazatlan, I recalled manager Frank Oceak's comment at York, PA: *"Keep your eyes, ears and bowels open, and your mouth shut."* Mexico was the only place I was able to do that.

CHAPTER TWELVE

Bobby Bragan, Abner Doubleday, and a Memorable Day

Spring training in 1956 was held at Fort Myers, FL and the change in the Pirates' roster was apparent. Joe L. Brown, who took over as General Manager, immediately put his mark on the team. He chose the young and colorful Bobby Bragan to replace Fred Haney as manager. The veteran players that dominated the 1954-55 rosters were all gone. Brown went with young, talented, but untested players, some of whom would become the nucleus of the 1960 World Series Championship team: Dick Groat, Roberto Clemente, Bob Skinner, Bill Virdon, Gene Freese, Roy Face, Vern Law, and Bob Friend. The success of that 1956 team, however, resulted from the leadership and incredible power hitting of first baseman Dale Long. Dale was hitting near .400 for the first three months of the season and set a then major league record, hitting 8 home runs in 8 consecutive days. We all fed off of his success to become a team that believed we could win in the major leagues.

A prodigy of Branch Rickey during his Brooklyn Dodgers days, Bragan copied Rickey's biblical style of speaking in parables to get his message across. Bragan preached at a clubhouse meeting in 1956 to start a series with the St. Louis Cardinals at Sportsman's Park. We had just completed a series with the Cubs in Wrigley Field, blowing a chance to win the final game. With two out, down by a run, Lee Walls was at second base when Roman Mejias hit a single to right center field to score Walls. On the play to the plate, Mejias moved to second. The game now tied, the Bucs had the potential winning run in scoring position as Dale Long stepped in to hit. We anticipated a win since Long had carried us to so many early season victories in games like this. However, he never got a chance to hit. The Chicago pitcher stepped on the rubber, putting the ball in play, then stepped off and threw to third base for an appeal play. The umpire signaled out. Walls had failed to touch third base, so it was the third out and we lost the game.

As we headed under the stands in Wrigley Field up a long flight of steps to the visiting locker room, I thought, "Bragan is going to blow his top over this one." He said nothing. Our locker room resembled a funeral home. Everyone sat silently at his locker, feeling the pain of the loss. Bragan said nothing as we showered to catch the team bus to the airport. Bragan remained silent on the bus ride to Midway Airport. We arrived in St. Louis, took the bus to the Chase Hotel and I thought, "NOW, he'll have something to say." He didn't.

The next evening we had the usual clubhouse meeting before the start of the series with the Cardinals. It appeared the last play at Chicago was now history. Bragan, with one foot resting on a large trunk, a scorecard in his hand, appeared to be getting ready to go over the lineups and how we would pitch and defense the Cardinals. His first words were, "Eighteen thirty nine." We couldn't figure what he was talking about.

Bragan enlightened us. "In 1839, a man named Doubleday came out of West Point, laid out a field, with four bases, ninety feet apart. It's the same damn game, Walls. You still have to touch them. That'll cost you fifty bucks!" Bragan was probably the only manager who would do research on Abner Doubleday to lay a fine on a player.

The next day we played a bright and sunny Saturday afternoon game with the Cards. Vern Law who started for the Pirates was having some early season trouble and poor luck. With one out and two on, he faced Stan Musial, who hit an easy pop foul that third baseman Dick Cole prepared to catch. However, he was not wearing sunglasses, and lost the ball in the sun for an error and Musial then hit a double to drive in two runs as the Cards went on to win 6-3.

Bragan had nothing to say after the game, but came well prepared for the pre-game meeting on Sunday. Using Branch Rickey's style of telling parables he began, "When you hire a carpenter to come to your house to fix something, he doesn't bring only a hammer does he? No, he brings all the tools. If you get a plumber to repair a problem, he doesn't just bring a plunger does he? No, he brings all the tools. It's the same damn thing in baseball Cole! You have to bring all the tools! That'll cost you $50 bucks!"

I recall watching Bragan's devilishness with a major league umpire. during our first trip to Ebbets Field for a Saturday afternoon game on April 28, 1956. Frank Dascoli, an excellent ball and strike umpire, who was also really naive, was behind home plate. Our pitcher was having difficulty, which prompted Bragan's to visit the mound. As usual, the infielders and the catcher gathered around him. Bragan said, "Just wait, Dascoli will be here soon." No sooner had he gotten the words out than Dascoli appeared, leaned over him and asked, "What are you going to do, Bragan, leave him in or take him out?"

Bragan impishly asked for the opinion of every infielder. Third baseman Dick Cole said to keep him in. Shortstop Dick Groat said to take him out, complaining there wasn't any movement on his fastball.

Second baseman Gene Freese agreed with Groat. First baseman Dale Long said to keep him in, as did catcher Jack Shepard. Bragan then turned around, and asked Dascoli, "What do you think we should do, Frank?" Displaying his naiveté, Dascoli earnestly replied, "You're in the big leagues now, Bragan; you've got to make that decision, not me." Bragan kept the pitcher in, and with a wry smile headed back to the dugout. Mission accomplished: He had pulled the leg of yet another umpire

Bragan was different, but never dull. During his first year in the major league he developed a relationship with a then-unknown New York sports reporter named Howard Cosell. Their strong personalities and desire to be acknowledged were well matched. Howard was always looking for a story and I can't recall ever seeing him without his tape recorder during those early years.

Thanks to Bragan's confidence in my ability to throw strikes, I was proud to be a contributing part of the team's success. It takes time to believe you can play and compete in the major leagues, for me that happened April 25, 1956 at Shibe Park against the Phillies. Leading 6-5 in the 7th inning, Bragan brought me in to relieve Vern Law. For a relief pitcher, this is the toughest job: your team has the lead and you are expected to keep it. I did it for the first time under that pressure by retiring nine straight hitters to earn my first major league save. The confidence and satisfaction I felt following that game was unbelievable. It was the first time I knew I could pitch, contribute, and win at this level of baseball.

Following the game, we took a bus to New York, with an off day on Thursday before starting a weekend series against the Dodgers at Ebbets Field. My wife, who had been staying with her family in Newark, met me at the Newark Airport exit of Jersey Turnpike. After being sent down to the minors twice in the two years we were married, and after our

Mexico experience, it was heart-warming to share my joy and success with Bernadette. We enjoyed the off day in New York City by getting tickets to see the Steve Allen TV Show. We enjoyed the performance of three then-unknown singers—Steve Lawrence, Edie Gorme and Andy Williams. All went on to become national and international stars.

During the Dodger series I stayed at my in-law's home in Newark, took the train from Newark to Manhattan, and then hopped on the subway to Brooklyn and Ebbets Field. We lost the first two games on Friday night and Saturday afternoon at Ebbets Field. With a doubleheader on Sunday, I left Bernadette's home around 9:30 AM to drive to the Pennsylvania Railroad Terminal in Newark, where I parked my car and took the train and subway to Ebbets Field. I arrived at around 11:00AM. Little did I know how long and successful a day it would be. We pounded Dodger pitching and won a doubleheader by scores of 10-1 and 11-3. Bob Friend went the distance in the first game, allowing only 6 hits, one of which was a home run by Jackie Robinson.

Two then-unknown rookie pitchers, Don Drysdale and Sandy Koufax, saw action in the first game for the Dodgers. Drysdale started but was knocked out in the sixth inning, trailing 6-0. Koufax came on in relief in the eighth inning and gave up five hits and four runs in just two-thirds of an inning. As I said, it takes time to believe you can win in the big leagues. Drysdale and Koufax didn't take that long, but that Sunday afternoon in 1956 was part of their initiation into the major leagues. Both went on to prove they could win and did so consistently for years on Championship teams.

The starting pitchers for the second game were Vern Law for the Pirates and Billy Loes for Brooklyn. Neither was around after four innings. Loes, who was having arm problems, gave up home runs to Frank Thomas in the first inning and to Vern Law in the second before leaving the mound with one out and the bases loaded in the second inning. The Pirates cleaned the bases on a single by Clemente and a sacrifice fly by Dale Long for a 6-0 lead. Vern Law ran into trouble giving up one run in the third and two in the fourth when I got the call to replace him with two out and runners at first and second.

On my first pitch I spun completely around as the spikes on the left shoe got stuck in the mound. It was a balk and both runners moved up. Surprisingly, I did not panic, but had to laugh at such an awkward delivery. It loosened me up and I went on to pitch five and one-third innings of shutout ball to get my first win of the season. We won the game 11-3, and the joy of beating the Dodgers and being on TV in the metropolitan area added to my delight as my wife was able to view the game with her family. After the game I accepted my brother-in-law's invitation for a ride back to Newark rather than having to take the subway and train.

I hadn't had anything to eat since breakfast, except for a terrible sandwich provided by the Ebbets Field visiting clubhouse guy between games. I was anxious to join Bernadette for a good dinner and a few drinks to celebrate the exciting day. When I got to her home, I said, "Let's go out to dinner!" and asked her where the car was. She said, "You had it this morning when you left…" I suddenly remembered that I had parked it at the Newark railroad station and realized we had driven right past it on the ride back from Brooklyn. Winning a game and beating the Dodgers in a doubleheader can do things like that to your head!

As a team we rode the amazing offensive production and team leadership of first baseman Dale Long. Long had brief appearances in 1951 with the Pirates and the St. Louis Browns, but failed gain a roster spot. In 1955 Branch Rickey tried to make Dale a catcher. The most difficult part of that decision was acquiring a catcher's glove for the left-handed Long. Mr. Rickey had Rawlings make the first and only left-handed catcher's glove I had ever seen. Branch should have saved the money. Long used it only during spring training when he caught batting practice.

Dale Long won his real claim to fame in 1956, bringing the fans and excitement back to Forbes Field with his record-setting home run hitting. I vividly recall the enlivened media buzz he created during with a record-setting run of hitting 8 home runs in 8 consecutive games. In my three years in the majors, all with the Pirates, I won only seven games and two of them came during Dale Long's record-setting performances. The second of those wins came in a Friday night game, May 25, 1956 at Shibe Park, when Dale homered in his sixth consecutive game to move him to within one game of the record. After the game, members of the national media were crowding the Pirates' locker room for the first time in years. Having picked up the win, I was relishing the media attention Dale Long had attracted.

With an afternoon game scheduled for the next day, I showered quickly and waited on the team bus to return to the Warwick Hotel. The delay was longer than usual when someone inquired, 'What the hell are we waiting for?' Someone replied, "Long, the writers are still talking to him." Then another reply, "Let him grab a cab, let's go." I got up from my seat, walked to the door of the bus, took off my coat and said, "I'm going to lie down in front of the bus and it ain't leaving until Dale Long gets on!" We all enjoyed a good laugh and definitely waited for Dale.

The next day (Saturday, May 26, 1956) brought a flood of writers and photographers, including some from the then-infant national publication, *Sports Illustrated,* to see if Long could tie the record. He did so in dramatic fashion. Hitless in three at bats, he homered over the scoreboard in right center off Phillies reliever Ben Flowers' knuckleball. After that game, Long and the Pirates were the big stories in the newspapers. *Sports Illustrated's* reporter and photographer stuck around for another day to follow the story.

The Sunday game with the Phillies was rained out, setting the stage for Dale Long to set the record at Forbes Field against the World Champion Dodgers. Thanks to a large local and national media presence, the game received the hype it deserved, as the fans jammed Forbes Field for the first time in years. I was in the bullpen that evening and experienced an unusual atmosphere for an early season face-off. It was like a World Series game. Carl Erskine, the Dodgers' starter, retired Long in his first at bat. As Dale stepped in for his second at bat, the crowd's anticipation and hopes grew. They were rewarded when Long hit Erskine's pitch over the screen into the right field lower deck to set a major league record. The standing ovation started immediately and continued for three minutes, and would have gone on longer had it not been for Jack Berger, the Pirates' publicity director, who was in the Pirates dugout that evening waiting for Long to set the record.

Long was not aware of the impact the record setting home run had on the fans, but Berger was. This was a PR guy's dream! Like a wise marketing man, he knew what the fans wanted and he gave it to them. Berger literally shoved Long out of the dugout onto the field. The ovation continued as Dale Long bowed and waved to the crowd. It didn't end until he tipped his cap and disappeared in to the dugout. Branch Rickey, who was in attendance that evening, said, "I have been in major league baseball since 1913 and that is the first time I have ever seen a player called on to make a curtain call."

Curtain calls then were requested only for record-breaking occasions. As more games began to be televised, curtains calls lost their value. Today players take a curtain call for hitting a double in the fourth inning. Fans who attended that first curtain call game at Forbes Field on May 28, 1956 still recall how wonderful the evening and adulation were for Long's triumph.

The 1956 season was the most enjoyable season of my major league career. I was part of the Pirates' team that moved into first place in the National League on June 12, 1956 a game that was particularly memorable. With the Pirates leading 4-3 in the bottom of the ninth inning with one out and runners at first and second, Bobby Bragan again showed his confidence in me when he brought me to relieve Elroy Face. The first batter I faced was Johnny Temple, a player who had played for Columbia SC when I was pitching for the Charleston Rebels in 1950. I jammed Temple on the first pitch with a sinking fastball which he hit on a two hopper to third base for what looked like a certain double play, but Bill Mazeroski was not yet on the Pirates' roster and we failed to turn the game ending double play.

With two out and runners at first and third I had to face Frank Robinson, who in his rookie season was quickly building credibility for a Hall of Fame career. Catcher Hank Foiles came out to the mound to discuss the situation telling me confidently, "We'll start him off low and away." To which I replied, "Hell, Hank if I could start everyone off low and away, I wouldn't be coming in now, I'd be starting." We both laughed and agreed I would try to get ahead using my best pitch, a sinker that he fouled off. The next pitch was a curve ball that Robinson swung on and missed.

Now out in front 0-2, Foiles wanted another curve ball, which I threw just off the outside corner for show and it was taken for a ball. Foiles signaled for another curve ball, which I shook off. During an eight year career in the minors I had mastered the art of deception Branch Rickey said was so necessary for a pitcher's success. I learned how to move the ball in and out on batters and wanted to throw a fastball on the outside corner. My reasoning was that Robinson had seen three pitches, a fastball inside and two curve balls away. I wanted to throw a pitch on outside corner with a fastball and have the pitch move back over the plate for a strike. I placed it as perfectly as I had ever done. I knew I had fooled Robinson who was looking for another curve ball. Pitchers can see the look on the face of hitters when they are fooled; their eyes suddenly open wide and know they have to make a quick decision. That happened to Robinson, who swung late and struck-out.

I felt the pride and joy artists feel when they complete a painting as planned. To make it more rewarding the Pirates moved into first place for the first time in many years. It was a new and exciting feeling for a group of young players. This was the beginning of the success the Pirates would feel in coming years, culminating in the 1960 World Series. They followed it up in 1970 with a NL Division Title and four more, capturing another World Series in 1971. Even though the early 1956 success didn't last through the second half of the season (we finished 7$^{th)}$, it was the first sign that our team could compete and win at this level of baseball.

I was not a member of the Pirates' team that won the 1960 World Series, but I shared the joy and satisfaction of that unforgettable season.

Bragan's Last Game with the Pirates

Bobby Bragan's 1956 early season managerial success ended with the Pirates finishing seventh, six games ahead of Chicago. Late in a dismal 1957 season Bragan, not accustomed to losing, was eager to make trades and expressed his feeling openly in the press. He did not agree with Joe Brown's patience in waiting for the young players to develop as winning players in the major leagues. He described it this way: "When you put down fifty cents for a hot dog the guy doesn't say 'Come back next week.' The fans pay now and want you to win now." It was obvious Bragan was no longer on the same page as General Manager Joe Brown and he was on a short rope.

Not surprisingly, it happened after an incident with the umpires in Milwaukee. I was in the Pirates' dugout on the third base side when Bragan asked for an appeal on a play after Red Schoendienst had scored from second base. He thought Schoendienst failed to touch third base and appealed to Umpire Frank Secory to make the call. Instead of making the call at third base, Secory walked over to the Pirates' dugout looked directly at Bragan, signaled and hollered, "Safe!" It was as though he had said, "Take that Bragan."

That's all Bragan needed to hear. I heard him tell the batboy, "Get a hot dog and an orange drink kid, I'll be back for them." He went out to argue with Secory and was thrown out of the game. Returning to the dugout, he asked for the hot dog and orange drink. The batboy said, "I couldn't get a hot dog, but I got the orange drink with a straw." Bragan headed out to the field with the drink offering every umpire a sip and his opinion of them. It was an embarrassing show and it was to be the last game Bragan managed the Pirates.

The next day we opened a series in Chicago. When we arrived at the Wrigley Field clubhouse, Joe L. Brown was in the clubhouse to inform us that Bobby Bragan was no longer the manager of the Pirates. As he described it, "Bobby Bragan and I are no longer looking down the same road."

With nobody in mind to take over the job permanently, Joe Brown offered the temporary position to veteran coach Clyde Sukeforth, who turned it down. Brown then selected another coach, Danny Murtaugh, as the interim manager. It turned out to be one of the best decisions Brown made in his role as the GM of the Pirates. It would also continue a relationship that began in the early 1950's when Brown was the GM for the Pirates AA New Orleans team in the Southern Association and chose Danny Murtaugh as his manager. The association and friendship would last a lifetime

CHAPTER THIRTEEN

An Eye-Opening MLBPA Meeting

After the 1956 season, my wife Bernadette and I returned to Newark, NJ, where I found work at the Newark *Star Ledger* in the circulation department. In the early fall I received a phone call from Bob Friend, the Pirates' player representative for the Major League Baseball Players Association (MLBPA). I was informed there was a MLBPA meeting in the offices of Norman Lewis on Park Avenue in Manhattan. Given my proximity to New York, he asked me to attend the meeting for him and take notes. I eagerly accepted.

Park Avenue was virgin territory for me. I was impressed with the tall buildings and luxurious surroundings. I went from being impressed to awed when I entered the offices of J. Norman Lewis, then the player's representative, and was introduced to the other team representatives–Robin Roberts (Phillies), Sherman Lollar (White Sox)), Bob Nieman (Baltimore), Early Wynn (Cleveland), Roy Sievers (Washington), and others. With a long history in the game I knew every player in the room. I can't say they had the same knowledge of me, but it was exciting to be in their company and to be a part of their deliberations.

Robin Roberts, with the aid of Norman Lewis, handled the meeting prior to a scheduled visit by Commissioner Ford Frick. Norman Lewis informed us that the commissioner could give us only 30 minutes of his time for the meeting, which raised some eyebrows. We wondered what could make him so busy after the World Series and end of the season. Norman Lewis decided we had better use the limited time wisely by choosing a few topics that were of most importance.

After some discussion we agreed there were two specific subjects we wanted to address. First was the increase in television revenues from the All Star Game and World Series. We desired to have portions of the additional money allocated for funding the players' pension plan. The second item was to include the wives and children as participants in the health care plan that only covered the players. Sure of our decision, we awaited the commissioner.

Ford Frick arrived on time and was introduced by Norman Lewis to all the players. Following the introduction, Robin Roberts began the meeting by expressing our appreciation for the commissioner taking time to meet with us. Aware of the time limit, he informed Ford Frick there were only two items we want to seriously discuss with him.

Robin was very articulate in expressing our desires about the need for additional money to be funded into the pension plan given the increase in television rights and advertising revenue. As he turned to Frick for a comment we were surprised to hear the commissioner say, "Well, you know I can't discuss such a proposal with you. You'll have to take that up with the Owner's Pension Fund committee." That ended further discussion on that topic.

Robin quickly approached the subject of providing health insurance for the wives and children of major league players. Frick shot that down as quickly as he had the pension funding. He stated we would have to take that up with the Owners' Committee. Our two discussion items took up less than five minutes of his time, and both were shot down

The conversation with the commissioner then addressed items so trivial they were embarrassing, but quickly caught the attention of Frick. Bob Nieman informed the commissioner of the background in center field at Baltimore that caused problems for hitters. He said, "There is a house painted in glowing white, located just to the left of center field. When a right-hander is pitching it makes it difficult for batters to pick up the pitch." I noticed the commissioner begin to take notes.

Someone followed with a complaint about the situation in Cleveland to inform us no toilet was available for players in the bullpen. They had to go behind the bullpen, or walk back to the dugout to take care of these bodily functions. Frick continued taking notes.

A similar complaint was made about Kansas City, then a relatively new team in the American League. There was no toilet in the bullpen, but also none in the dugout, so player had to go all the way back into the clubhouse to relieve themselves.

These discussions took up the remainder of the time. The commissioner put the pencil and paper away and before leaving told us how good is was to have a discussion with the players' association. Norman Lewis then escorted Frick out of the office to the elevator. When he returned, his comments were brief but educational. I remember them as if they were uttered today. He said, "Gentlemen, you have just spent thirty minutes discussing your problems with the most powerful man in the game, the Commissioner of Baseball." Pausing briefly, shaking his head in disbelief, he continued, "You know what he's going to do for you? He's going to change the background in Baltimore for hitters. He's going to put a toilet in the bull pen in Cleveland and one in the dugout in Kansas City."

Lewis summed up the futility of our situation, "Gentlemen" he began, "You think you have problems. And you *do* have serious problems: Nobody is listening to you!" Baseball then was a paternalistic system. The owners were the parents and we were the children and each party accepted their role.

Eventually, a man with experience, knowledge, fortitude, and a keen understanding of labor management problems became head of the Major League Baseball Players Association. That man was Marvin Miller, who, along with Curt Flood, changed forever the relationship between owners and players. Players no longer believe they need someone to take care of them when their career is over. Marvin Miller made them believe they had power. The motto became, "Take care of me now and I'll be able to take care of myself later."

CHAPTER FOURTEEN

Danny Murtaugh, an Arm Injury, and Saying Good-Bye to

the Pitcher's Mound

D anny Murtaugh, modest and calm, was the exact opposite
of Bobby Bragan. He had no desire for media attention. His
experience as an infantryman in Europe during World War
II and the years served in the minors as a player and manager left a
strong feeling of appreciation and the understanding of what life was
truly all about.

My conversation with Danny during cut-down day of spring
training at New Orleans in 1953 gave me the first clue of his sensitivity
for players working their way up to the major leagues. Having played for
Murtaugh in 1954 at New Orleans, I knew he spoke only when he had
something important to say. That didn't change when he took over as
manager of the Pirates in August of 1957. He didn't hold his first team
meeting until two weeks after being named manager.

The meeting was brief and to the point. He opened by saying, "I
haven't said much since taking over, but I have been doing a lot of

watching and listening and I don't like what I'm hearing or seeing." He then went on to lay down plain but simple things he expected. Murtaugh's quiet demeanor and ability to remain in the background led some players and media people to think he did not have a great baseball mind.

Murtaugh's first two years managing the Pirates were mildly successful while Joe Brown was putting together the competitive team that would win the World Series in 1960. In 1958, he got reserve infielder Dick Schofield, who would play a major role in the 1960 stretch drive taking over for the injured Dick Groat. In January of 1959, Brown hit the jackpot in a seven-player trade with Cincinnati. In exchange for power hitting outfielder Frank Thomas, RHP Ron Blackburn, substitute outfielders, Johnny Powers and Jim Pendleton, the Pirates acquired Smoky Burgess, Harvey Haddix and Don Hoak. All three were to play major roles in the 1960 Championship season.

Haddix wrote his name in the Pirates' and baseball record books on May 26, 1959 at Milwaukee when he threw a perfect no-hitter for 12 innings, but wound up a 1-0 loser. He also was the winning pitcher in two World Series games, including the final seventh game. Hoak became the on field team leader and Smokey Burgess provided consistent hitting as a starting catcher and pinch hitter. In December 1959 Brown acquired outfielder Gino Cimoli in a trade with the Cardinals. He completed the roster in late May of 1960 getting left-handed pitcher Vinegar Bend Mizell, in exchange for second baseman Julian Javier.

Murtaugh's personal understanding of the struggles the average player faces at the major league level was his strength. He described it well stating, "The longer you sit the more you doubt." Danny never allowed players to doubt. He consistently used them in starting or replacement roles, keeping them sharp and confident. To confirm his opinions on their strengths and weaknesses he spent the last week in

Florida working with the players on game situations. He knew who could bunt successfully with runners on first and second, which pitchers could make the defensive play in this situation, which hitters could provide a sacrifice fly with a runner at third with one or none out. He never put players in situations where they could not perform. The 1960 and 1971 Pirates' Championship teams believed they owned the final three innings of every game they played and proved through the long season and two seven game World Series Championship. Murtaugh played a major role in developing the confident team attitude displayed by both of these teams.

An arm injury I experienced in June 1956 destroyed any chance of me returning to pitching with the confidence or success I had briefly enjoyed at the major league level early that season. The margin of ability between players at that level is very small, but expands quickly when a player suffers an injury. Pitching with an arm injury in the major leagues is like swimming in the ocean while bleeding with sharks circling nearby. The problem is not only physical but also a mental dilemma. Your talent dissipates and your confidence erodes. That's how I felt during the 1957 season.

When you have an injury that is not physically visible, your courage is questioned. Only pitchers understand how frustrating this can be. Joe L. Brown, the GM of the Pirates, a strong backer of me during the time I played for him at New Orleans and the Pirates, implored me to learn to pitch through the pain. He used an analogy that I thought unmerited, stating that in college he occasionally ran the 100-yard dash with a pebble in his shoe, but he finished the race. I told him the comparison was unfair. He only had to deal with the pebble for a few seconds and could remove the pebble at the end of the race. I had no such easy solution. I had to deal with it in every game and on every pitch.

The arm injury forced my retirement at the end of the 1957 season. When pitching against the Cubs at Forbes Field in July of 1956, I was unable to pitch with the success I enjoyed in those early months of the season. I recall vividly the pain I experienced when I threw a curve ball to Gene Baker. I foolishly told my catcher Jack Shepard that I couldn't throw a curve ball and to call only for fastballs. I retired Baker and then had to face Dee Fondy. With the first pitch I threw to him I felt more pain than I ever experienced. It was the beginning of the end of my career as I never was able to pitch with the freedom from pain and confidence I enjoyed prior to the injury.

Despite a visit to a specialist at the renowned Johns Hopkins Hospital in Baltimore, there was nothing surgically they could do for me. The Pirates' team physician, Dr. Joe Finegold, decided to give me cortisone shots to speed my recovery. The pain of those shots was worse than the injury, and ultimately were of no help. Cortisone to me was similar to putting oil on a gate. It worked well when the oil was still there, but when it dissipated, which was quickly, the pain was searing. The Johns Hopkins specialist commented on the unusual strain on the pitching arm. He stated that everything had to move in a smooth sequence for all the joints, tendons, and muscles to work perfectly and if you were tired, or had an injury somewhere, it could affect the coordinated progression and cause an arm injury.

I tried to figure out what I might have done to cause the injury. I came to the conclusion that it occurred when I had to change a tire on my car in mid-June. I had to use more than normal strength to loosen the lugs and experienced pain for the first time. The injury and the pain progressed and I was never able to again throw with the ease and confidence I had enjoyed.

Having been relegated to mop up roles following my arm injury, I saw action in only two games in the month following the injury. On July

25th, I was the winning pitcher in what I think was the most unusual game I ever witnessed between the Pirates and the Cubs at Forbes Field. The Pirates led going into the ninth inning with Elroy Face pitching. In a very rare performance Elroy was unable to close it.

Now trailing 4-7 with two out and two on in the Cubs ninth, Bragan called me in from the bullpen. I took my eight warm up pitches and faced right-handed hitter Eddie Miksis. I threw a curve ball on the first pitch, which he hit on two hops to Dick Groat at shortstop. Groat retired him at first base for the final out of the inning. With a three run lead Turk Lown came on in the bottom of the ninth inning to pitch for the Cubs. He gave up a single and walked two batters to load the bases with no outs.

Stan Hack, the manager of the Cubs, decided to make a pitching change, bringing in right-hander Jim Brosnan to face Roberto Clemente. Brosnan took his eight warm-up pitches and on his first pitch, Clemente hit a line drive off the light tower on the right side of the Forbes Field scoreboard in left field. The ball took a sudden bounce to the right and rolled along the warning track next to the ivy-covered brick wall as three runs scored. With the score now tied, Bragan tried to hold Clemente up at third, but Roberto ignored the sign and on a close play just beat the throw for an inside the park, grand slam, walk-off home run and an 8-7 win.

A finish like that will be remembered by anyone in attendance as I was reminded decades later during a visit to my doctor, Dan Shrager. He described to me the most memorable baseball game he saw was with his Dad and younger brother at Forbes Field. He vividly described how Roberto Clemente hit an inside the park, grand slam, home run in the bottom of the ninth inning for an 8-7 Pirates win. I asked him, "Do you recall who the winning pitcher was for the Pirates in that game." He replied, "No."

I informed him I was, and described another little-known or remembered aspect of that game. As the winning pitcher, I threw only one pitch and the losing pitcher, Jim Brosnan also threw only one pitch. I am sure this was and remains the only game in the history of baseball that was decided by an inside the park walk-off grand slam home run and the winning and losing pitchers throwing only one pitch.

The last game I won in the major leagues was June 27, 1957, in relief at Wrigley Field in 5-4 in ten innings. My confidence was as low as it could be. I was lacking trust in my pitching. For the first time in my career I was afraid to throw strikes. I was "choking" so bad I was having a panic attack and mental breakdown on the mound. I was so unsure of myself I called my catcher Dick Rand to the mound and confessed how tight and anxious I was. Allowing someone to know my agony relaxed me somewhat. I was leading 5-4 with the bases loaded two out in the last of the tenth inning. Bobby Bragan had nobody warming up as he was going to let me to win or lose the game by myself. I was lucky to get the win as Chuck Tanner with two runners on base hit a line drive that went right at Dick Groat for the final out. I felt no pride in getting the win in that game, but it did help me to overcome most of that fear for the remainder of the season.

September 15, 1957 I made my last appearance in the majors in a Sunday afternoon game against the St. Louis Cardinals at Sportsman's Park. The last pitch I threw was a hanging curve ball that Kenny Boyer hit deep into the left field stands for a home run. The ending was in severe contrast to the first hitter I faced in the majors at Ebbets Field in 1954, striking out Duke Snider. A week later I was informed I was not going to make any more road trips with the team. My season and career were over.

The flame of hope had died and with it the love for baseball that had fueled so many satisfying years. In early October of 1957 I received news I didn't want to hear, but it came as no shock to me. The Pirates informed me that my contract would not be renewed and I was now the property the Pirates' farm team at Columbus, OH. Denial that my baseball career had ended was no longer possible.

At age 29, one of only 400 players in the Major Leagues and earning $9,500 a year, I was at the top of my profession and my wife Bernadette and I had became parents of our first child, Laurie, on August 4, 1957. The discontent of having to leave the game at this time in my career and in our family life led to a deep depression. I recall driving alone aimlessly through the South Hills of Pittsburgh, thinking of "what might have been." It was like a death had occurred.

During my seasons in the minor leagues I witnessed too many former major leaguers working their way back down. I didn't want to do that and immediately announced my retirement from the game. I have always listened to my heart to find my treasure, but at that moment I was unable to hear any response.

With the hopes of finding employment in Pittsburgh, Bob Friend a Pirate teammate, approached me to consider joining a sales force he headed with Federated Investors, a fledgling mutual fund firm, started by Jack Donohue and Dick Fisher. With no previous interest, or knowledge of the stock market, Bob sold me on the success I would have in the Pittsburgh market given my identity as a Pirates player.

Federated Investors in 1957 had only two small offices downtown in the Jenkins Arcade; today it has grown to be among the largest firms in the Mutual Fund business. Their success and name is very visible on the Pittsburgh skyline atop the large modern building that bears the Federated Investors name.

I wish I could tell you I was part of that success, but nothing could be farther from the truth. I grew up in the Depression years and all I knew about the stock market was that it crashed in 1929 and that people who lost their life savings were reportedly jumping out of windows on Wall Street. I learned that money doubles in ten years at seven percent, and by investing a certain amount monthly and taking advantage of "Dollar Cost Averaging" you could do it safely with a "Balanced Fund."

With this knowledge and my identity in Pittsburgh, selling funds should have been a slam-dunk for me. It wasn't! I wound up educating many, but selling few. After my childhood experience, I had difficulty handling rejection. I would call 20 people to set up three interviews and was fortunate to get one sale—most of them to family and friends. I discovered you quickly run out of family and friends in sales. Working on a "draw" against commissions, I was paid a flat amount with the agreement I would pay back on the draw against my commissions. After only one year I was discouraged and in debt. To ease my baseball withdrawal pains, I pitched batting practice the summer of 1958. That fall I faced the reality that I had to disassociate myself from baseball and mutual funds, hoping to find something that would give me the satisfaction I had enjoyed in baseball.

I returned to the Newark, NJ, and thanks to the kindness of Bernadette's brother, Walter Earl, we moved into a home he was renting in Chatham, NJ. I began looking for a job but was unable to land anything. Reading the Newark Star Ledger, I noticed an ad for John J. Ryan, Inc., an investment firm that specialized in New Jersey Municipal School Bonds. I answered and acquired an interview with the owner, John J. Ryan, an engaging Irishman with a smile that matched his pleasant personality.

A Notre Dame graduate, Ryan had great affection for baseball. During the interview I became aware he had hired two former players, "Snuffy" Stirnweiss and Bob Sweeney. I had played against Sweeney in 1949 when he pitched in the Brooklyn Dodgers farm team at Lancaster,

(PA) under manager Al Campanis. Stirnweiss, a former Yankee second baseman began working with John J. Ryan following his retirement from the game. He was killed, September 15, 1958 in a tragic train accident in Newark Bay, and that was the position for which I was interviewed and hired.

Learning the Municipal Bond business and being paid $70 a week, I appreciated John Ryan's patience. Although I leaned a lot, I had little success earning commissions on sales. To support my wife and first-born child, I worked on weekends at a liquor store in the winter and caddied in the summer at the nearby Canoe Brook Country Club. Finding little personal or monetary satisfaction from my work, I got down on my knees nightly, praying that I could find something that would again give fulfillment to my life.

My prayers were answered in early January of 1960 when I received a phone call from Jack Berger, the PR Director of the Pittsburgh Pirates. He informed me he received a call from Joel Rosenblum, an owner of three small radio stations located just outside of the Pittsburgh market to inform him he was looking for a former player to do sports for his stations. It sounded like something I would like to consider and I asked Jack what salary was being offered.

When he said $10,000 a year and recalling I made $9,5000 my final season with the Pirates I told Jack I'd be very interested in discussing it with Mr. Rosenblum. My wife, pregnant with our second child, due in late March 1960, understandably was not eager to make another move, but agreed it was worth considering. After visiting with Joel Rosenblum and Warren Koerble, the station manager at WACB in Kittanning and WSHH in Latrobe, I accepted the offer.

Jack Berger later related Rosenblum's baseball naiveté during their phone conversation. Jack incorrectly assumed he was calling about a hiring a former Pirate player. He asked Joel Rosenblum, "Who were you thinking of?" To which Rosenblum replied, "I was thinking of Joe DiMaggio." Startled by the response, Jack told him, "There is no way Joe DiMaggio would leave New York to work in Butler, Kittanning or Latrobe!" To which Rosenblum replied, "Why not? He's not playing baseball anymore." Berger quickly informed him that Joe DiMaggio was making very big money doing commercials in New York City. When asked whom he would recommend, Berger replied, "Nellie King." God works in mysterious ways and that's how I got into radio broadcasting. This was one of the most defining moments of my life as I went on to learn the trade in small stations and advanced to the Pirates' broadcasting team in 1967.

I still treasure Jack Berger's kindness in recommending me to Mr. Rosenblum. It describes a treasured verse on kindness I read daily when awakening and I always think of Jack Berger when I do. "An act of kindness, no matter how small, is never wasted."

CHAPTER FIFTEEN

Early Radio Years – Arnie Palmer

My initial on-air work showed me that I had much to learn about the business. Having spoken at Kiwanis, Lions, and Rotary clubs; churches and large sports banquets, I never used a written script, just ad-libbed stories from a list of notes. It was my first experience in reading copy aloud for listeners. I was embarrassed at the number of errors I made, particularly when doing sponsor commercial copy. I had difficulty reading for more than 10 seconds without erring, but I practiced reading aloud and in time became more proficient.

Doing play-by-play of high school sports was less stressful. I was not working from a script; I was having a relaxed conversation with a listener while describing what was going on in the game. I even had a brief and embarrassing time as a disc jockey. It was before tapes and CD's and everything, including commercials were on 33 1/3 and 45 RPM records. The turntables had gears for each speed, but I continually seemed to play them at the wrong speed. All of my early radio experiences made me appreciate the work professionals do so well. In the spring of 1960 I moved to WSHH in Latrobe. I was blessed that first year by the success of the 1960 Pittsburgh Pirates and Arnie Palmer.

Most are aware of the overwhelming Steelers' appeal during the 2005-06 season and the 2009 NFL Super Bowl Championship. It is difficult for fans today to believe the Pirates in 1960 had that dominance and more, but they did. The communications business in 1960 was not fragmented as it is today. There were only three major TV networks, CBS, NBC and ABC, and no cable or satellite TV networks. There were fewer homes with TV sets, let alone air conditioning, and no computers. People spent the summer evenings sitting on the front porch listening to Pirates' baseball on radio. During the 1960 season you could walk down any street in Western Pennsylvania and not miss a pitch hearing the Pirate broadcast coming from the radios of fans sitting on their front porches. Mike Levine, a popular KDKA newsman, told me the rating for Pirate baseball in August and September of 1960 indicated 60 to 70 percent of the audience was tuned to the games. That kind of dominance is now a thing of the past.

Although my baseball career with the Pirates was brief, it was enough to buttress my identity and credibility on radio. In my first year of broadcasting at a small daytime radio station in Latrobe, PA, I hit a bonanza. The Pirates began the 1960 season with many come-from-behind games that would be a trademark for the entire season. I covered many Pirates' regular season games and I was able to renew old friendships with former teammates. Despite working at a daytime only station, my association with Jack Berger, the Pirates' PR Director was beneficial in me acquiring World Series media credentials

The 1960 Pirates were a group of experienced, mentally tough, hungry, happy, at times crazy, but always-confident players who felt they owned the final three innings of every game. They produced a fantasy season. The fans and media called them the "Battling Bucs." Benny

Benack's Dixieland Band created a loose and fun-filled atmosphere at Forbes Field with a theme song written by an advertising agency for Iron City Beer, that had everyone singing, "The Bucs Are Going All The Way!" Little did the fans realize their trademark of coming from behind to miraculously win games would continue all the way to the final inning of the seventh game of the World Series.

The series was supposed to be a mismatch between the favored New York Yankees and the underestimated Pirates. It was when you added the total runs scored that the Bucs won all the close games. Prior to the Series, I interviewed Pirates' players asking whom they thought would be the star of the Series. Groat, Face, Law, Hoak, Clemente, and Virdon were mentioned often. Harvey Haddix, whom I had played baseball with in the Army, was the only player to pick Bill Mazeroski. I asked him why and with the wisdom of a veteran pitcher he said, "Because the Yankees will pitch to him."

The Series began and ended in Forbes Field and it was as dramatic as you could get. The Bucs won the opener 6-4, but were blown out in two straight embarrassing losses, 16-3 and 10-0. Their confidence shaking, the Bucs won the final two in Yankee Stadium with strong pitching from Law, Haddix and Face, who saved the first three wins. With the Pirates leading 3-2 in the series, back in Forbes Field for the sixth and, if needed, a seventh game, winning the World Series was now a reality for Pittsburgh fans.

However, Whitey Ford for the second time shut out the Bucs 12-0 so there would be a seventh game. *New York Daily News* sportswriter Dick Young best described the situation. His lead line read: "As Mrs. Dionne said to Dr. Dafoe, 'Don't go away. There's more to come'." (Dr. Dafoe was the name of the doctor who delivered the Dionne quintuplets.)

The series now came down to one final game. It was to be the most memorable baseball game ever played in Pittsburgh, and perhaps in World Series, history. Blowing an early 4-0 lead, the Pirates trailed 5-4 following Yogi Berra's three run homer off ace reliever Elroy Face in the sixth. The Yankees appeared to wrap it up with two more in the eighth for a 7-4 lead. But, as Dick Young wrote, there was more to come. Trailing by three, the Pirates' Gino Cimoli pinch hit for Face and singled to right center.

Then the Pirates got a huge break when Virdon's grounder to Tony Kubek appeared to be a sure double play ball, but the ball took a bad hop on the "alabaster plaster" (as Pirates' announcer Bob Prince describe the rock hard infield at Forbes Field), and hit Kubek in the throat putting two on and no outs. The blow forced Kubek to leave the game and Joe DeMaestri replaced him at shortstop.

With nobody out, Groat gave one of many of his clutch hits, with a single to drive in Cimoli. Jim Coates replaced Bobby Shantz, who had earlier pitched four scoreless innings. With runners at first and second, Bob Skinner moved Virdon and Groat to third and second with a perfect sacrifice, but Rocky Nelson's fly ball to right did not allow Virdon to score. With two out and a 7-5 lead, Coates would make the blunder that set the scene for the most exciting finish of a seventh and deciding game in the history of the World Series.

Clemente tapped a slow roller down the first base line, which should have been the final out of the inning, but Coates was late covering at first base and Clemente, hustling as he always did, was safe. Virdon scored, to cut the Yankee lead to one run at 7-6. Hal Smith, who replaced Burgess (who left for a pinch runner in the seventh) hit what then appeared to be the series-winning hit. With the count of 2-2, Smith hit a three run homer to left center that gave the Bucs a 9-7 lead going into the ninth.

Bob Friend, who rarely relieved, was called on to finish the game. Bobby Richardson and pinch hitter Dale Long opened the Yankees' ninth with singles to put the tying runs on base. With the Yankees' left-handed power hitters—Maris, Mantle, and Berra—coming up, Murtaugh had no choice but to go with left-hander Harvey Haddix. Harvey retired Maris on a foul out, but Mantle singled, scoring Richardson to make it 9-8 as Dale Long, the tying run, went to third just ahead of the throw by Clemente with only one out. Casey Stengel, who had erred in allowing Long to stay in the game, finally realized he needed speed and Gil McDougald was inserted to pinch run for Long at third base.

In one of the most unusual plays, Berra hit a line drive to Rocky Nelson, who was holding Mantle on at first base. Nelson trapped the ball, tagged first, which took off the force play at second. As he went to throw to second, Mantle, who probably thought the ball was caught on the fly, or made one of the most intelligent running decisions in series history, (I firmly believe it was the former) slid back into first base ahead of Nelson's tag, as McDougald scored the tying run. I vividly recall watching catcher Hal Smith after this play. His head and shoulders dropped in disbelief. The game was now tied and his three-run homer was just a footnote in the box score. Haddix then retired Bill Skowron to bounce out to end the inning, but the fans' shock and disbelief took them out of the game.

Viewing the game from one of the booths overhanging the first base side at Forbes Field, I recall how eerily silent it was, similar to a wake, as the Pirates came to bat in the bottom of the ninth. Bill Mazeroski stepped in to face Ralph Terry, the fifth New York pitcher. The rest is history. Maz hit what many believe remains the most dramatic home run in baseball history to beat the Yankees 10-9 and capture the 1960 World Series Championship.

How Mazeroski felt during those historic moments remained untold until some forty years later. It came not during a sports interview, but during a post-dinner question and answer session at a Pirates Alumni golf outing at South Hills Country Club in the summer of 2001. A member asked Maz to "Walk us through what was going on in your mind at that time." Maz, in his humble "aw shucks" way, preferred not to respond until everyone, players included, pleaded with him to do so. Roy McHugh, a prominent sports writer for the *Pittsburgh Press* in 1960, witnessed Maz's home run and when I informed him of the question asked by a fan at the dinner he remarked, "What a great question. Nobody thought to ask Maz that question before." As best as I can recall, this is how Maz described that unforgettable event.

"As a kid living in Rayland, Ohio, I was a big Cleveland Indians fan and hated the Yankees." He continued, "I remember thinking as we took the field in the top of the ninth inning with a two run lead, 'here we are, needing only three outs to beat the Yankees to win the World Series.' However, when the inning began to fall apart and they tied the game I started to think, 'The damn Yankees always seem to win the big games!' After the inning ended in a tie, I sat dejected in the Pirates' dugout, feeling the disappointment of losing the lead." He recalled, "Until I heard a coach holler, 'Maz, grab a bat, you're the lead off batter in the inning.' I had completely forgotten I was the batter to open the bottom of the ninth inning."

Maz continued his vivid recollection of that moment, "All I was thinking of was getting a good ball to hit and to hit it hard. The first pitch from Terry was a high fastball that I took for a ball. I remember hearing Johnny Blanchard, who took over the catching duties when Berra moved to left field, holler to Terry, 'Keep the ball down on this guy. He's a good high ball hitter.' The next pitch was another high fastball, but in the strike zone. I knew I hit it good and ran hard, knowing it could be a double and possibly a triple as Berra was going to have trouble fielding the carom off the left center field wall. I got near second base when I noticed the third base umpire raise his hands signaling a home run. That's when I began celebrating, waving my hat, knowing we beat the Yankees. From the time I reached second base and saw the umpire signal home run, until I touched home plate, my feet never touched the ground."

The crowd at Forbes Field, along with people working downtown and everywhere in western Pennsylvania, began a spontaneous and amazingly peaceful revelry. To this day, Pirates' fans that took part in the celebration can tell you where they were and what they were doing when "Maz" hit that home run. Only a year ago a fan told me he was driving on Smithfield Street near Kaufmann's Department Store, listening to the game on radio when "Maz" hit the home run. He jumped out of the car, left the motor running, went into a bar across the street and joined in the festivities. Soon the people in the bar moved out into the street with their drinks, joining in the bigger celebration outside. Confetti was now pouring from office buildings downtown; people were driving with their lights on, yelling, and honking their horns.

I was lucky to witness the Pirates' clubhouse celebration. Players sprayed champagne all over the room as they shared hugs with each other. Bob Skinner and Bill Virdon each grabbed a bottle of champagne and shrewdly hid them in their lockers. When the clubhouse cleared, they sat and enjoyed the memories and the champagne.

Virdon, a strong, quiet man from Missouri, had so much champagne that he made one of the weirdest requests I ever received. He said, "Nellie will you take a shower with me?" With raised eyebrows I replied, "Why the hell should I take a shower with you?" His response was more sober than I anticipated as he said, "I have had too much to drink and I'm afraid if I get into the shower, I'm going to fall on my ass and get hurt. We're having a big party at the Webster Hall Hotel and I sure don't want to miss that!" I joined him for the shower and he then invited my wife and me to the team party.

The Webster Hall was jammed and I had no ticket to enter the party, but was allowed entrance. The only sour note was when Tom Johnson, one of the owners of the team, questioned my presence. He had a reputation for becoming obstinate when drunk, which he was that night, and angrily remarked, "What the hell are you doing here?" I informed him I was invited by Bill Virdon and let it go at that, but it did take some of the glow off the enjoyment for the reminder of the evening.

The only full-time radio station in the Westmoreland County area was WHJB in Greensburg, which was also the only station doing live play-by-play broadcasts of high school football and basketball at night. Fran Fisher, the sports director at WHJB, had developed a strong local following and left to take job at his hometown station in Lewistown, PA. With limited live play-by-play opportunities at Latrobe, I applied for the WHJB position and was hired. It turned out to be a good move for Fran and me.

Fran went on to become the radio voice of the Penn State Nittany Lions football from 1966 to 1982. He returned to PSU football in 1992 to work with George Paterno until his retirement before the 2000 season. I went on to do Pirates' baseball from 1967 to 1975 and have enjoyed a warm relationship with Fran Fisher ever since. In jest, whenever we meet, I remind Fran Fisher of how that decision changed our careers. I tell him, "Nobody has heard of us since."

The experience of doing live play-by-play broadcasts was educational, but often embarrassing. I had the ball on the 52-yard line, or a first down and ten from the 3-yard line and many others I'd like to forget, but I was gaining experience and finding joy and satisfaction doing live play-by-play of football and basketball. Of the two, basketball was easier. You worked inside, had a courtside location, the players were easily visible, and there were only 10 players to identify.

Football was the most difficult; broadcast locations were rarely ideal. In my first year I did a taped broadcast of a Latrobe-Penn Hills football game from an adjacent building, another atop the roof on the stands, and even while sitting in the stands with the fans. With 22 players on the field and an equal number on the bench, player identification was always a problem. That is why broadcasters still depend on spotters to assist them at every level of the game. Working with my WHJB partner Tom Johnson, we had to order the telephone lines for the broadcast, assist in selling advertisements, haul all the broadcast equipment (50 yards of extension cords), and with no PR person or sports information director to provide background and updates, you had to do additional research on team rosters, coaches, and statistics.

Arnie Palmer, a hometown boy from Latrobe, was about to become the biggest name in the game of golf in 1960. He had captured his first major golf championship winning the 1958 Masters. In 1960 he won his second Masters and the U.S. Open, coming seven strokes from behind in the final round of the U.S. Open in 1960. His aggressive style of play made him the nationwide favorite of public links golfers who formed what became "Arnie's Army." Palmer's success in the 1960's made professional golf an attractive TV sporting event enabling the game to reach unforeseen popularity that continues to this day.

National telecasts of golf in 1960 covered only the final two days of major tournaments, and usually only the final four or five holes of play. With two 1960 major wins at the Master and U.S. Open, and the PGA Championship slated at the Firestone County Club in Akron, Ohio, it was obvious to me this was a natural marketing event for the Latrobe radio station. With that in mind I put together a package of eight, 15-minute reports daily, from 12:45 to 7:45 PM, on Palmer's play. I was successful in selling it to Joe Wentling, an avid golfer and successful local businessman, who owned the Wendon Oil Company. Joe Wentling's success in business and his interest in golf were evident as he was among the original members in 1958 to join the exclusive Laurel Valley Golf Club in Ligonier, PA.

The idea of providing listeners with hourly coverage of Palmer's play for four days in three major golf tournaments was so successful it continued until I joined the Pirates' broadcast team in 1967. I wasn't aware at the time that I had applied the most important aspect of marketing with the golf reports on Palmer's play until listening to Tom Snyder's CBS-TV talks show years later. His guests were Colonel Sanders of Kentucky Fried Chicken and Ray Kroc, the founder of McDonald's. The conversation centered on the marketing success of both and Snyder inquired, "Here I am talking to two of the most successful business men in the nation, one of you sells chicken, the other sell hamburgers, neither are innovative or creative items." He then asked, "What's the secret?" To which Ray Kroc replied, "Find out what the people want, and give it to them."

Joining a group of local professionals and businessmen, I covered my first Masters Golf Tournament in 1961. The group from Latrobe included Gabe Monzo, a good friend of Arnie Palmer's who owned the Mission Inn, Moe Loughner, a salesman for Latrobe Brewing (Rolling Rock Beer), Americo Shifra, a local tavern owner, plus Don McMahon, and Jerry Cooper, real estate developers, and attorneys Al Nichols and Pete Lampropolus.

We rented a home in Augusta for the entire week for $400, making the per-person cost for eight of us just $50! Today with popularity of the Masters, unless you know someone who has had tickets for years, you can't find a house or room in Augusta during Masters week.

Gabe Monzo's culinary skills were on display nightly with a home cooked meal and the dining room table was filled with bottles of every drink imaginable. It made for a treasured week of golf, conversation, camaraderie, and memories that have lasted a lifetime.

Although these men were not covering the Masters for the papers, their acquisition of press credentials gave them all the benefits. Included were entrance to the tournament, press area, clubhouse, locker room and dining facilities. Most treasured was the opportunity as members of the media to play the Augusta National course the day after the tournament. We simply had to enter our names on the sheet in the Press Room for tee times starting at 7:00 AM. The only stipulation was we had to be off the course by noon, as former President Eisenhower, who as the Masters week guest of Cliff Roberts, was to play the course. Don McMahon, Jerry Cooper and Al Nichols, who had acquired press badges, joined me in a foursome to play this historic golf course.

Seeing Augusta National has been described as a religious experience and I would agree. The ride up Magnolia Lane to the clubhouse is appealing, but doesn't compare to the overall beauty and lush greenness of the course, which is breathtaking. Playing it is indescribable. The first time I played the course was in 1962, when Arnie Palmer captured his third Masters Championship. Playing the course for the first time and with the same pin locations as on the final day I was operating on adrenalin with the unbelievable excitement and joy of playing at this shrine of golfing.

I birdied the short par-4 third hole and finished the front with a pleasurable 42. It wasn't that way on the back although I found pleasure in hitting the green at #12 for a par three and reaching the green in two at #13 for a par. The adrenalin was gone; after that it was agony. I shot a 51 on the back for a 93. Playing Augusta National gave me the same feeling I had playing baseball on the same fields where the greats played at Shibe Park, Ebbets Field, Sportsman's Park, Crosley Field, Wrigley Field and the Polo Grounds.

I met Bobby Jones during a Wednesday practice round in 1961. He was sitting in a golf cart with Clifford Roberts at the landing area for tee shots on the par 5th and 15th holes. George Bayer, then the longest hitter on the tour, hit a tee shot that carried the top of the hill near Bobby Jones and rolled down the deep slope that left him only 170 yards from the green. I recall Bobby Jones' comment on that drive, "They're playing a game I am not familiar with."

That story had more relevance in 1963 when Jack Nicklaus captured his first green Jacket. During one of the rounds he hit a tee shot on #15 similar to George Bayer's, but longer. In the Press Room he described how he played his second shot. "I got to my ball for my second shot and asked my caddie what club I should hit to the green. He said, 'an 8-iron should do it.' I questioned his selection stating that nobody hits an 8-iron second shot to this hole. I took a 7-iron and hit it over the green, onto the tee area and almost into the water on the par-3, 16th hole." Bobby Jones' comment two years earlier and Nicklaus' drive in 1963 proved how rapidly the game was advancing and the effect it would have on the construction and length of golf courses.

The golf media gave Tony Lema the nickname of "Champagne Tony" as he bought bottles of the bubbly for them when he won a tournament. He enjoyed golf and described his philosophy on life as, "I came into this world naked and I'm probably going out the same way." He didn't spend time worrying. I can't recall the year, but I do remember the hole-by-hole description of his round at Augusta, and in particular how to play the long dogleg left par 4, 5th hole. It is a high risk-high reward shot off the tee. If you can draw the ball and carry it past the large area of trees and bushes at the left corner of the dogleg you're in position for a rare birdie.

As Lema described his thoughts that day he said, "I was one under par after four when I got up on the tee at #5. I viewed the large area of bushes and trees on the left and remembered Jimmy Demaret's advice on how to play the hole. He said, 'You don't want to hit it left here. There's an Eastern Airlines ticket counter down there'."

I saw Arnie Palmer win two Masters Titles in 1962 and 1964. He looked like a certain winner when I covered my first Masters in 1961. The final round was played on Monday that year because of a rainout on Saturday's third round. Palmer was playing in the last pairing and came to the final hole with a one shot lead over Gary Player. He hit a perfect drive on the 18th in the middle of the fairway to set up a 7-iron shot to the green and the usual final round pin position at the lower left side of the green. His second shot was pushed and caught the trap on the right side of the green. Needing to get up and down from there for a par and the title, he bladed his sand shot over the green adjacent to the CBS-TV tower on the left side of the green.

The color went out of Arnie's face. He knew he now had to get up and down in two for a tie. To give him more time to consider his shot, Charlie Coe, who was paired with Palmer, putted out to finish his round. Palmer's chip shot from an uphill lie to a green that ran downhill and to the right, went 20 feet past the pin. He missed the putt and finished with a six to give Player his first Masters win.

Gary Player had never led the Masters until the 1961 third round of play on Sunday. I vividly recall watching him play the difficult par-3 12th water hole. I was viewing the play with binoculars from the 14th fairway and saw his tee shot fly over the green, against the fence that separates the Augusta National from the Augusta Country Club course. As I was viewing the shot a Scotsman, in knickers and a Tam O'Shanter cap, inquired, "Wha hoppened?" I informed him that Player had hit a ball almost on to the Augusta Country Club course. His reply was, "A PRO-fesssional should ne'er hit a shot like that."

The old Scotsman's comments were more memorable when following the round I was in the players lounge in the clubhouse and overheard a conversation between Player and Gene Sarazen. Player was telling Sarazen of that poor shot he hit on #12 and how it occurred. Gary said, "I was sitting on the bench near the 12th tee in front of the huge scoreboard waiting for the green to clear. I suddenly heard a loud roar coming down the 11th fairway and took a quick look at the scoreboard to see what had happened and saw them moving my name to the top of the scoreboard." He continued, "It was the first time I had led the Masters Tournament." He then told Sarazen of the mental pressure he felt as he prepared to play his tee shot to the par 3 hole. "I asked my caddie what I should hit and he handed me a 7-iron. I got over the ball and my bloody knees were shaking so much I couldn't stop them. I took my swing and as soon as I hit the ball my caddie said, "My God, you've hit it on the August Country Club course." Recalling the Scotsman's comment and having faced the pressure of pitching in the big leagues, I was aware that everyone, including the top pro golfers, has a "choke" level they can't ignore. It is rare, but it happens to even the best professionals.

Palmer's failure to win the 1961 Masters was one of those moments. I did an interview with Palmer at his home after the 1961 Masters and inquired how he dealt with that. I wondered if it was similar to a driver who has had a serious accident and slows down when he approaches that location. Palmer's response was "Hell, no I go work on my clubs; I figure it was the golf clubs, not me."

Palmer's relationship with his dad "Deacon" was very close and he kept Arnie close to his roots. I recall the time Arnie won the British Open at Troon, Scotland. I didn't cover the event, but had someone call us on the phone from the course with reports the final day. He gave me the information on Arnie's win and asked, "Arnie's wife is here, would like to talk with her?" I of course said yes and we had a nice conversation about winning another major tournament and the joy she shared with Arnie on this occasion. After taping the conversation I called Arnie's mother at home and told her of the interview with Winnie.

The next day I called her to inquire if she heard the tape and also asked how "Deacon" was taking Arnold's winning the British Open Championship. Her comment was, "Well, you know Deacon, he doesn't get too caught up in all this, but I believe that is changing." She went on describe why, saying, "This morning we were having breakfast and he was reading the *Post-Gazette*. He put the paper down and took off his glasses and said, 'You know Mom, I'm beginning to believe the kid's a pretty good golfer'." Talk about an understatement! Through all of Arnie Palmer's success, Deacon kept Arnie's feet solidly on the ground, enabling him to endear himself to millions of golf fans worldwide for over 50 years.

CHAPTER SIXTEEN

Bob Prince, "The Gunner"

A history of Pirates baseball could not be written without lauding Bob Prince, "The Voice of the Pirates," or as he was also known, "The Gunner." No one dominated Pirates baseball more than this larger-than-life Pittsburgh media personality. The son of a career U.S. Army officer, Bob was widely traveled and worldly wise even in his teen years. He studied law, attending Harvard, Oklahoma, and Stanford with limited success, confessing he loved the social scene too much. Jack Henry, a Pittsburgh raconteur, described Prince's college resume best: "Bob Prince's diploma has more fingerprints on it than Elizabeth Taylor's ass." Everyone will agree that his talents would have been wasted in a courtroom. He was made for radio and baseball. I was fortunate to spend the last nine of those years working beside him. Our relationship, like the roller coaster ride at Kennywood Park, was all ups and downs, but never dull.

Bob Prince did not want an identity—he *needed* it! He gave the word "personality" a distinctiveness rarely matched in those days. Wearing wild, flashy sports coats and a demeanor to match, you always knew when Bob was in a room. During a broadcast you had no problem figuring out whether the Pirates were winning or losing. You either loved him or hated him, but you listened. Prince was well aware of the mixed audience response; as he was leaving the Press Room to begin a broadcast one night he hollered for all to hear, "Gotta go to the radio booth. Twenty thousand listeners are getting ready to turn me off."

Bob started his Pirates broadcasting career in 1948 under the tutelage of Rosey Rowswell, who began doing Pirate broadcasts in 1936. In those early days, baseball radio broadcasts they were not done live since the owners' feared fan attendance (and revenues) would drop. How wrong they were; radio broadcasts actually created more fans. Games were "recreated" in a radio studio by using the information sent from the site of the game over the Western Union ticker tape. By using sound effects, and the listeners' imagination, announcers were able to make it sound as if they were broadcasting the game live from the ballpark. One of the great advantages of not being at the park gave the announcer the freedom to control the flow of the game. They did this by staying a half or a full inning behind the game descriptions coming off the ticker tape. It became obligatory for baseball announcers to fill the slow or dead periods in every game. The good announcers did it by telling stories while still keeping the listener involved in the flow of the game. Rowswell was a wonderful storyteller, on and off the air, and also wrote and published poems. Bob Prince did not write poetry, but was his equal or better as a storyteller and master of ceremonies.

Prince told a memorable story of a game he and Rowswell "recreated" in the WWSW studio the 1948 season. The Pirates were playing in Cincinnati and it was an extra inning game. When doing recreations and staying an inning behind the action it gave announcers a bit more freedom than doing it live. This story describes vividly how Rosey took advantage of that freedom. The game was in the 11th inning of the broadcast, but Rosey already knew what had happened in the 12th inning. As the Reds came to bat in the bottom of the 11th inning Rosey described it this way. "Well the Pirates did not score and Reds are coming to bat in bottom of the eleventh inning in this tie game at Crosley Field." There was a brief pause, when Rosey suddenly proclaimed, " I CAN'T TAKE.… I CAN'T TAKE IT ANYMORE… WESTLAKE HIT A HOME RUN IN THE 12TH INNING AND THE PIRATES WON THE GAME." He wasn't going to sit in the studio for another extra inning, so he ended the game quickly.

I feel the announcers who began broadcasting baseball and doing recreations of the game taken from the Western Union wire were the best announcers in baseball history. They knew how to set a scene verbally when big moments arrived in a game. They quickly described it, and then let the noise of the crowd tell you what had occurred. Prince was in that group. He began his broadcasting career when the style was less analytical, but more conversational.

When tuning in a Pirates' game Bob Prince was broadcasting it didn't take long to know if the Pirates were winning or losing. You could tell by the sound of his voice and descriptions. His love for the home team allowed many to call him a "homer," which he was delighted to accept as a compliment. If the game was a close and exciting contest, he stayed with the game. If it wasn't, as Jim Woods described it "He would drift way out into the ether somewhere," telling stories that had no relationship to the game, but keeping the listeners engaged.

One of the memorable "out in the ether" moments occurred in the early 1960s. I was sitting on my back porch in Greensburg enjoying a beer while listening to Prince and Woods. The game between the Bucs and Cardinals had no importance in the standings, as both teams were out of the race. It was one of those games when Bob really drifted away from the game while telling a story. In the background I heard the voice of Art McKennan, the Forbes Field public address announcer say, "Mungie, Rab Mungie," as Bob continued on with his story. Very shortly Jim Woods interrupted him stating, "Bob, the Cardinals are going to use a pinch hitter, his number is 58, but it's not listed in the game program." To which Prince said, "Well Possum, you know it's that time of the season when they bring up all those kids from the minor leagues. Check the game program again and see if there is a Rab Mungie listed, as I just heard Art McKennan mention his name."

Woods checked the program again but could not find a Rab Mungie listed. Bob returned to the broadcast saying, "Well Rab Mungie, a left-handed batter, will pinch hit for the Cardinals and takes the first pitch for a ball." Woods commented that he looked a lot like Grady Hatton to which Prince agreed stating, "By God Possum, you're right, he does look a lot like Grady Hatton" (and it was Grady Hatton). Prince then continued, "Here's the 0-1 pitch to Mungie, it's a ground ball to Mazeroski at second base who throws him out at first base and Mungie is retired 4-3." In the background I could hear Art McKennan announcing, "Will Rab Mungie from Charleroi please report to the Pirates' office – your son has been found!" Rab Mungie was 0-1 in his major league career. It is a classic Bob Prince story.

Prince had a gift for identifying players with nicknames, and using word descriptions of plays that remain a part of vocabulary of Pirate fans old enough to remember him and even those too young to have heard him. They have been passed down from generation to generation. Nicknames such as: Tiger" (Don Hoak), "Dog" (Bob Skinner), "The Great One" (Roberto Clemente), "Quail" (Bill Virdon), and "Possum" (Jim Woods, his broadcast partner). He created innovative descriptions such as, "a Hoover" (double play), "by a gnats eyelash" (a batted ball that was barely fair or foul), "Chicken on the Hill" (a home run by Willie Stargell), "It would take this guy a week to die a sudden death" (describing a slow working pitcher), or "He pitches like he's double parked" (Pitchers who pitched quickly), and most memorable, his home run call, "YOU CAN KISS IT GOODBYE!" The one that best described his constant optimism for the Pirates, and to this day brings a smile to my face, always followed a Pirates' win that ended a long losing streak ending a very long losing streak. Bob would loudly proclaim, "We may *never* lose another game!"

As vividly as Bob Prince dressed and as loud as his personality was, his charity work was done quietly. He originated many charity golf events and other fund raising affairs and dominated sports banquets with his professional ability as a Master of Ceremonies. His personal charity was less visible and it was personified in his relationship with Rich Golembiewski, better known around town as "Radio Rich." He acquired the nickname because a portable radio held next to his ear was always visible walking downtown or at athletic events. "Radio" never knew his parents. He was found on the doorstep of the Sisters of Charity Catholic Convent. Despite this beginning and his limited mental capabilities (he was slightly retarded), he lived a self-supporting life thanks to his friendship with Bob Prince and Joe Gordon of the Steelers. Radio Rich was visible in the press booth at Pirates and Steelers games thanks to the courtesy—and sometimes to the annoyance—of the Pittsburgh media.

"Radio's" relationship with the Pirates, Bob Prince and baseball was stronger than other teams, due mainly to the length of the season. Prince took care of his medical and other needs and regularly handed out twenty-dollar bills to Rich when he needed money. A classic Radio Rich story Prince loved to tell was when he realized Radio needed false teeth so Bob took care of the costs. A few weeks later he handed Radio Rich the usual twenty-dollar bill and Rich said, "I need more money." To which Bob said, "Hell I just paid for getting you false teeth." Radio replied, "Yeah I know. Now I can eat streak and I need more money for eating."

Radio used to arrange his own transportation for trips to other major league cities when the Bucs were away from Three Rivers Stadium. He never asked for money, but always showed me his bus schedule and where he would be staying. Prince and I became used to this and we always asked, "How much do you need, Radio?" He always got the money without asking. A most memorable Radio Rich moment for me was just before Christmas when he would call me and say, "How you doin'? You know I wear a size 42 coat." It was his way of informing me what he needed.

Radio was a great Duquesne Dukes basketball fan and when I became Sports Information Director at Duquesne he was a constant and welcomed visitor. He called me weekly for conversation and the last phone call from Radio Rich came around 5:00 PM one weekday. We spoke for almost 10 minutes and he never spoke of any personal problems. He just wanted to visit with me on the phone. Unknown to me, he was suffering with cancer and was taking chemotherapy. Unfortunately, he did not know how to discuss his physical illness.

I wish he had, as 45 minutes later I was informed Radio Rich died on the sidewalk outside his apartment on the north side of Pittsburgh. He died as he lived, alone, which was a shame, but thanks to the kindness and caring of Bob Prince and Joe Gordon of the Steelers he enjoyed life and the friendships he made. I served as a pallbearer at his funeral and for a person who had no family it was heart warming to see most of the Pittsburgh media, who came to pay their final respects.

Bob Prince was a natural marketing man for the Pirates at a time when budgets for promotions were not as big as they are today. His first visible and very successful promotion came during the 1966 season. During a broadcast he noticed Danny Whelan, the Pirates' team trainer, waving a green rubber hot dog from the dugout. When Prince inquired what he was doing, he explained the green hot dog had mystical power that cast a spell on the opposing pitcher during a Pirates' rally. He asked Whelan if he could use the green hot dog idea to give to Pirates' fans to wave during games. Whelan agreed, and "The "Green Weenie" was born and remains a hot collector's item.

The second Prince promotion came following the move to the Three Rivers Stadium. Working with Joe O'Toole, a Pirate VP and a native Pittsburgher, they came up with a black and gold headscarf familiar with the many ethnic population of Pittsburgh. Marketed and promoted only by Prince during Pirates' broadcasts he called the promotion "Babushka Night." Despite being marketed for a weekday night game with the Phillies, it was a surprisingly successful promotion. So successful that the walk-up gate sale that the Pirates did not have enough gates open to handle the crowd. The game had to be delayed 20 minutes or more to get the fans into the game. Over 40,000 fans showed up for "Babushka Night" which was then the largest weekday crowd ever at Three Rivers Stadium. "Babushka Night," like "The Green Weenie," remains a memorable part of Pittsburgh Pirate history, thanks to Bob Prince and Joe O'Toole.

The first Pirates' promotion, "Prize Day," was held on the final home game of each season at Forbes Field. Jack Berger, the Pirates' PR Director, acquired a long list of prizes to be given to fans after the game by drawing their game ticket number. Prince, in his inimitable style, handled the drawings and entertained the fans on the PA system at home plate. It lasted more than an hour and he kept the fans amused and interested as everyone waited for the final prize, which was a live pony! You can imagine how Prince handled that unusual gift! He asked, "How do you take a pony home in your car?"

Bob's longtime partner in Pittsburgh was Jim Woods, who in my opinion was the best "second banana" in baseball broadcasting. He had the resume to match this title. During his long and impressive career, Jim worked with many of the top baseball announcers in history. He began doing Atlanta Crackers baseball broadcasts in the mid-1940s, working with Ernie Harwell, who would later become a legend in Detroit. He moved to the major leagues working with another legend, Mel Allen doing New York Yankees games. When Phil Rizzuto moved into the booth, Jim moved across the Hudson River to do New York Giant games with another broadcasting legend, Russ Hodges.

Anyone who heard Hodges' description of Bobby Thompson's home run off Ralph Branca in the bottom of the ninth to capture the 1951 NL Championship can tell you where they were and describe it— "The Giants win the pennant! The Giants win the Pennant. The Giants win the pennant. They're going craaazy"

When the Giants moved to San Francisco in 1958, Jim Woods joined Bob Prince on Pirate broadcasts. After twelve great years with Prince and the Pirates, he joined Jack Buck on the St. Louis Cardinal broadcasts. His stay in St. Louis was brief, as Jim did not enjoy the personal appearance and marketing work required by the Cardinal network. He left St. Louis and joined Len Martin doing Boston Red Sox games.

One of the most interesting, but little known, bit of lore about his broadcasting career was that Jim Woods replaced a fellow named "Dutch" Reagan (Ronald Reagan) as the announcer for the University of Iowa football broadcasts. A very impressive broadcasting resume for a truly fine announcer who never desired to be the "top banana."

CHAPTER SEVENTEEN

Pirates Broadcasts, 1967 to 1975

In 1964 Don Hoak, captain of the Pirates 1960 World Championship team, became the first former player to do Pirates' broadcasts. His personality and knowledge of the game made him an instant and respected member of the broadcast team. Despite Don's success as a broadcaster, he yearned to return to the game as a coach or manager. After three seasons he left the booth to take a job as a coach under Gene Mauch, the manager of the Philadelphia Phillies.

With Don Hoak gone, there was an opening on the Pirates' broadcast team. I had not applied for the position until I read Al Abrams column in the *Pittsburgh Sports Gazette* that I was among the top candidates for the vacant slot. I had a job in radio that I was enjoying and figured, what did I have to lose? So I applied and was given immediate consideration. I made a number of auditions and did well enough to make it to the final audition held in the large KDKA-TV studio. I was given the lineups and information on the players and was told to ad-lib the opening commentary. Just prior to starting the audition, Bob Purkey, who was also going to audition, entered the studio, which broke my concentration. I stumbled, and then stopped. I had spent seven years learning my trade in small stations and wasn't going to blow this opportunity. I quietly asked Bob if he would please leave, as he was a distraction, which he did gracefully.

Relaxed, confident and able to concentrate, I ad-libbed for more than five minutes, before Les Quailey, the Atlantic Richfield producer for Pirates' broadcasts, informed me to get on with the lineups. The people in the booth and I all laughed over the comment and I am sure that audition sold me. I joined Prince and Woods for the 1967 season for a salary of $13,000, which was less than I was making doing on air work and selling radio spots at WHJB in Greensburg.

Working with Bob Prince and Jim Woods, two professional broadcasters, I wanted, or needed, to be accepted by them. However, there was an undercurrent of resentment among major league broadcasters about "jocks" moving into the radio booth. Having been a "former jock," I didn't fit in easily with Prince and Woods in the early years and was the odd man out. Over the years I have come to the strong opinion that three people in a broadcasting booth is like three people in a marriage. It doesn't work.

Bob Prince had a method of keeping score that I copied. He used a two-ended pencil with red and black lead and marked all the scoring plays in red lead that enabled him to easily recap the scoring plays. In my attempt to gain acceptance from Prince and Woods, I made it my duty each game to get the starting lineups and fill out their game scorecards that included lineups, averages, home runs and RBI's. I was most eager to get the starting lineups as early as possible to complete the task, which created one the most memorable errors in the nine seasons I did Pirates' broadcasts.

Because of the pre-game filming of a scene for the movie, "The Odd Couple," starring Jack Lemmon and Walter Matthau, the Pirates had an earlier time for batting practice than usual during an afternoon game in 1967 at Shea Stadium. The scene had the Pirates at bat with the bases loaded and no outs. A Pirates' batter was scripted to hit a ground ball to third base, which would begin an around-the-horn triple play for the Mets. It took longer to get the players involved than it did to actually complete the shot. The director wanted Roberto Clemente to hit into the triple play. Clemente, a very proud man, quickly turned that role down; he wasn't going to hit into a triple play for anyone, for any kind of money.

After Clemente declined, they began their search for another batter. The director's choice was brilliant. Who better to put in such a situation than Bill Mazeroski, who had the most memorable hit in World Series history? Mazeroski remains a very shy person (as became clear during his 2001 Hall of Fame acceptance speech) who does not seek the spotlight. However, his ability to perform under pressure was legendary, and he agreed to take part in the scene. Maz was to hit the first pitch to third base on a routine two or three hopper. He did so perfectly; it took only one pitch and one "take" for the shot!

Now back to the innocent mistake I made and the impact it had on the game that afternoon. Prior to our batting practice, I got the New York Mets lineup off the game scorecard posted in their dugout. No lineup had yet been posted in the Pirates' dugout, so I searched for the manager, Harry Walker. Evidently Harry forgot about the filming and arrived late for batting practice. When he came onto the field I quickly asked him for the Pirates' lineup. As he gave it to me verbally I wrote it down, Alou, Mazeroski, Clemente, Stargell, Clendenon, Alley, Pagan, Pagliaroni, and Fryman. As the Pirates were taking batting practice, Jose Pagan saw me writing down the lineups and inquired, "What spot am I hitting in and who do I follow in the lineup?" I told him he followed Alley and was hitting seventh. I especially remember the alliteration, saying Alley, *Pagan, Pagliaroni,* and Fryman

Having acquired the needed information, I retired to the Mets Press Room to have lunch and fill out the three scorecards. In my first season visit to Shea Stadium, I was not familiar with many of the New York media or Mets personnel. A gentleman in a Mets blue and orange blazer approached me during lunch asking if I had the Pirates' lineup. I told him I received it verbally from the late arriving Harry Walker. He seemed anxious to get the lineup and was thankful I was able to provide the information.

The game went along for three innings without any problems. In the Pirates' fourth inning it all began to unfold. The lineup I acquired verbally from Harry Walker was not the same lineup he presented to the umpire prior the start of the game. Harry had reversed the batting order. Pagan now was hitting in the sixth spot and Alley was hitting seventh. Sheriff Robinson, the Mets first base coach, had the duty of making sure the Pirates were batting in the order listed on the scorecard exchanged by managers and umpires prior to the first pitch.

The first time through the Pirate order, Sheriff Robinson informed manager Wes Westrum that Pagan and Alley were batting out of order. Westrum did not protest as they failed to reach base. In the fourth inning Pagan hit a shallow fly ball down the left field line that just dropped into fair territory in front of Cleon Jones, for a double that scored a run. Quickly, Westrum ran onto the field to file his complaint with home plate umpire Augie Donatelli. Augie, thinking he wanted to argue on a fair or foul ball, said, "It was a fair ball all the way, Wes." To which Westrum replied, "I don't want to talk about a fair or foul ball. I want to talk about the Pirates' batting out of order!" That quickly had the Pirates and umpires checking their lineup cards. They agreed the

Pirates were hitting out of order from the start of the game and Pagan was ruled out and the run did not count.

In the broadcasting booth we thought the lineups were correct. We were more convinced when the lineups were identical to the lineup listed on the big scoreboard in right center field. It read Alley, Pagan, Pagliaroni, and Fryman as the last four numbers and names of the board. I began to wonder how this occurred. It turned out that the gentleman to whom I gave the Pirates' lineup in the pressroom was Jack Lightcap. Unknown to me, he turned out to be the public address announcer at Shea Stadium whose duty it was to call the scoreboard operator to make sure they had the lineup posted on the board. He gave them the lineup I had acquired verbally from Harry Walker; not the one Walker had given to the umpires. The other oddity was more unusual. Jose Pagan was the only player who, prior to taking batting practice, asked me who he followed in the lineup.

Alley and Pagan failed to check the official scorecard posted in the dugout. They confirmed their order in the lineup by checking the Shea Stadium scoreboard. If Pagan did not ask me his place in the lineup and I didn't have lunch with Jack Lightcap, the PA announcer, and provided him with the Pirate lineup, this would never have happened.

Fully realizing the unfortunate role I played in this folly I felt embarrassed and guilty. My eagerness to get lineups verbally diminished following that game, when Bob Prince personally took time to relieve my embarrassment. Thank God it didn't happen in a League Championship or World Series game. Hollywood or TV wouldn't use a script like that. However, I now believe it could have fit nicely into an "Odd Couple" script.

The broadcast schedule in 1967 was for Prince to do the first three innings, Woods the middle three. I would do play-by-play for the seventh inning, and Bob would finish the final two innings. If the game went extra innings Woods and Price would share innings. Listening to tapes of old broadcasts, I was amazed to how little conversation there was between announcers. The conversation was mainly between the announcer and the listener. Only occasionally would the other announcers be brought into the conversation. I think that made the games more listenable. Today there are so many promotional drop-ins, analyses, and statistical information that the flow of the broadcast is lost. It is especially annoying on television where you can actually see what is going on and one doesn't need verbal elaboration.

Vince Scully, who began doing Dodger games with Red Barber in 1950 at Ebbets Field in Brooklyn, has been doing them in Los Angeles since the team moved there in 1958. Doing broadcasts for over 50 years with one team is truly amazing. I had Scully as a pre-game radio guest at Three Rivers Stadium in the early 1970's and the conversation related to his longevity and the development of his style of broadcasting. He drew a word picture that illustrated it well. He related that when broadcasting a game he has the mental image of standing in his back yard leaning over the fence, sharing a beer and holding a conversation with his neighbor. He can see the baseball game being played, but the neighbor can't and he is simply describing what is happening down on the field. Rege Cordic, known as the best radio broadcaster in Pittsburgh history described it well stating, "The secret of radio is to get past the speaker, so you are having a conversation with only one listener, not a crowd."

Scully related to me the best advice he received came from "Red" Barber, during his first season in 1950 doing Brooklyn Dodger broadcasts. It concerned overcoming the fear of "dead air." The fear of having nothing to say spurs a need to fill time with meaningless statistics or press guide information. Barber told Scully, "Vin, if you don't know what to say, don't say anything. If nothing happens in the next ten or fifteen seconds, then you'll have something to tell listeners,

'There's nothing going on here.' " Vin said it enabled him to relax and let the game flow easily from him to the listener. In over 50 seasons of doing Dodgers games, his style never changed. He is among the few, or possibly the only, announcer who does not use an analyst or assistant. It's why Scully, working in the most competitive market in sports broadcasting, remained so consistently good over half a century doing baseball play-by-play for the Dodgers.

Bob Prince had a great comment that indicated how large Vince Scully's identity is in Los Angeles. Buzzy Bavasi left the Dodgers for the 1968 season to take over as General Manager of the expansion team in San Diego, it was rumored that Scully might leave the Dodgers to broadcast for Bavasi. When asked if he would like to replace Scully, Prince replied, "No, but I sure as hell would like to replace the guy who replaces him."

As an announcer you can't make a game sound exciting. It is or it isn't, but as an announcer you have the responsibility to make every game interesting. There is a big difference. In 1970, Gene Osborne joined me and Bob Prince in the booth and lasted only one season. In his lone season he had a style that endeavored to make each pitch and play exciting. Impossible to accomplish, it drew criticism from listeners. A fan letter best described Osborne's style, stating, "Gene Osborne is the only announcer who can make a ground ball to second base in the first inning sound like the second coming of Christ and the Normandy Invasion."

One of my most embarrassing moments came in 1969 at Bradenton when I tried to make a meaningless, spring exhibition game exciting. The game was in the last of the ninth inning, the bases were loaded with two out and the Pirates down by three runs. With power hitting Bob Robertson at bat, I attempted to make the situation exciting by embellished the importance of the confrontation. The count went to 3 balls, 2 strikes when Robertson hit a fly ball to left field that I lost, as did the left fielder, who I saw retreat quickly toward the fence. I described it thusly, "The runners are off and here's the pitch…Robertson hits a long fly ball to left field, the left fielder is back at the wall…" when I then noticed the shortstop waving away infielders and he caught the ball for the game ending out. Embarrassed I had to call the play at it developed, not as I had described it.

Jim Bunning, whom I had known when we played in the Southern Association in 1954, had joined the Pirates that spring. He approached me the following day and mentioned he was listening to the broadcast on his car radio on his way back to Anna Maria Island. Hearing my description of the final out he said, "That must have been a helluva wind blowing in from left field yesterday!" We both enjoyed a laugh and it eased my embarrassment. I never again embellished any situation. As I said and believed, it is either exciting or it isn't. The fans know when it is exciting and there is no need for the announcer to exaggerate.

My broadcasting the first two years was strained because of my anxiety and my relationship with Bob. In an attempt to gain his acceptance I played an overly obsequious role. The more obsequious I was the more domineering Prince became, however. I played that role until mid-season of 1969. The change came during a broadcast at Dodger Stadium and had an important and positive impact on our relationship.

The game was in the eighth inning when Bill Sudakis hit a ball into the gap in right center field for a sure double and possibly a triple. Sudakis was among the first players to take up the long hair trend then visible with the Viet Nam War protesters. It didn't sit too well with Bob, whose father was a lifetime Army officer, rising to the rank of Colonel. As Sudakis neared second base his hat fell off and as Bob described it,

"Sudakis' hat fell off and that long hair is blowing all over the place as he rounds second base and is now going to try for a triple."

Sudakis did get the triple and just beat the play at third thanks to a headfirst slide, but then called for aid from the Dodger bench. Prince then continued, "Sudakis is safe at third, but they have to bring him smelling salts. How do you like that? A young kid with long hair, and he needs smelling salts after hitting a triple!" I leaned over to tell Woods why Sudakis needed smelling salts. I explained that the head first slide caused Sudakis' testicles to be pinched by his protective cup and that can really take the air out of you.

When Prince saw me talking off mike with Woods, he showed me up on the air, shouting, "I asked you a question aren't you going to answer it!" As the inning ended, Prince was still fuming, throwing papers up in the air when I thought, "I'm either getting into this business or I'm getting out now."

During the commercial break I approached Prince and said, "Don't you ever show me up on the air like that again. If you do, I don't care if the game is in progress or not, I'm going to walk over and hit you right in the Goddamn mouth." I quit playing the obsequious role and we acquired a greater respect for each other as announcers and persons. We developed a very sincere relationship on and off air for the remaining seven seasons of outstanding Pirates' baseball.

Bob Prince had a rule that the only time the names of the announcers were mentioned was at the start and end of the game. I would open with, "Along with Bob Prince, this is Nellie King bringing you today's game from Three Rivers Stadium." On closing it was the same, "With Bob Prince, this is Nellie King saying goodbye from Three Rivers Stadium"

During our first NCLS in 1970 with the Cincinnati Reds, our broadcasts were picked up by a number of radio stations in National

League cities. We shared duties on both radio and TV. I did the first three innings on radio and Prince opened the broadcast on TV. Prince took over in the fourth inning and was informed that we were receiving phone calls and Western Union Wire messages inquiring who the announcers were. Bob informed listeners of the rule he had regarding the names of the announcers in pure Bob Prince style, "A lot of listeners are calling to find out the names of the broadcasters. We only mention our names at the start and end of a broadcast." He then stated, "We figure if we're good you'll know who we are, and if we're bad, we don't want you to know."

My first season of Pirates' broadcasting, I shared a post-game show with Jim Woods. It was my job to get the top player from the game for a post-game interview. I had no difficulty choosing the correct guest at Crosley Field in Cincinnati when the Pirates led 7-5, with two out and two on in the bottom of the ninth. The guest was to be Roberto Clemente who had one of his most dominating performances, driving in all seven Pirate runs. Woody Fryman, pitching for the Pirates, was facing Tony Perez, then in his rookie season.

Tony hit a walk off home run to win the game 8-7 and I had to find a replacement for Roberto, who, despite his 7 RBIs, was not eager to talk after the loss. I was fortunate to get Tony Perez. Unaware that Tony, in his rookie season, spoke only in broken English and had done few if any radio interviews, my first question to was, "What a dramatic way to win a game with a walk-off, three run homer in the bottom of the ninth. Where was the pitch Tony?" Using the clubhouse vernacular to describe location he replied, "Nellie, it was right down the COCK!" Flustered, all I could think of was to ask Jim Woods if he had a question for Tony. Tony Perez is now in the Hall of Fame and when we meet he always asks, "Where was the pitch Nellie?"

After a year or so of doing pre- and post-game interviews, I found out making up a list of questions to use as a road map was advantageous and diminished the anxiety of not knowing what to discuss. Thanks to my wife Bernadette's work as a psychologist, I learned the value of being not only an inquirer, but most important, a "listener." It came to fruition when we participated in a Parent Effectiveness Training Program. We learned how to open communication with our children as "active listeners" who listen not only to their words, but also to their feelings.

I remember the frustration I had first time I tried "active listening." It occurred when the school principal informed me that one of our daughters was cutting gym classes. It annoyed me, but I decided to try "active listening" in the attempt to understand my daughter's actions. One of the basic features of active listening is not to reprimand, but to search for the reasons for such action. I began with, "*It sounds to me* you don't like gym class." She said it was not the reason. I continued, "*It sounds like* you don't like the teacher" which she denied.

I was getting nowhere but decided to continue. After about five minutes she informed me the reason was because a group of girls were continually humiliating and berating her in gym class. She became aware that the approval of those girls was not important to her. She ignored them and never missed classes again.

When doing radio interviews I tried to determine the feelings of players–were they satisfied, proud, angry, confident, happy, etc. Once I hit on their feelings it opened communications and players honestly expressed themselves. When this openness occurs an interview can go into areas you never expected. An interview with Cubs catcher Randy Hundley in 1972 illustrated the importance of active listening. Randy had been a solid, everyday player for the Cubs from 1966 thru 1969, but suffered a severe knee injury halfway through the 1970 season. He played in just nine games in 1971. While doing a Pirates-Cubs game in Wrigley Field I was surprised when Randy beat out an infield hit. I thought how gratifying that must have been for him to be able to run without pain. I decided to do an interview with him the next time we played the Cubs.

The interview was at Three Rivers Stadium. I began the interview, "It must be satisfying for you to be able to run well again and return to the starting lineup." Randy then went off in a direction I was not prepared for. He told me of how he had lost his confidence in his ability and his faith in God. The interview then became focused on his search for the return of his faith in God. He also informed me of the guilt he carried for hurting the team for not playing at the level of his previous successful seasons. When I closed the interview Randy wanted to continue talking. It became a like a therapy session for him as I continued being an active listener. The post-interview conversation lasted almost 15 minutes or more before I had to end it in time to get the tape to the broadcast booth. It was an awakening for me about how being aware of feelings can have a positive effect on an interview, even though I never expected it to go down the path it did.

The most treasured interview I did was June 28, 1970 with Roberto Clemente between games of the doubleheader on the final day at historic Forbes Field. Roberto had a deep feeling for Forbes Field as he told me during that final day. He said, "This is great. Nellie, this is a big emotion for me. This ballpark means a great deal to me because I've been here sixteen years–almost half of my life I've been here." I then inquired how long he would like to continue playing. He said, "I would like to continue playing as long as I can help the ball club. Last year I played with a very bad left shoulder and it was very tough for me, I don't want to play like that because I hurt myself, I hurt the fans, and I hurt the Pittsburgh organization."

After a brief pause, in what was to be a sadly prophetic comment, Roberto said, "Nellie, I think I would like to play until I get to 3000 hits." He achieved his 3000th hit a year and a half later at Three Rivers Stadium on September 28, 1972. It was a double to left center field in the fourth inning against Jon Matlack of the New York Mets. It also turned out to be the last hit of his major league career. Roberto died on New Years Eve 1972 in a plane crash off the coast of Puerto Rico while on a humanitarian mission to earthquake victims in Nicaragua.

Danny Murtaugh handled the Pirates' managerial job until 1964 when he retired for health reasons. It would be difficult for Joe Brown to find someone with whom he could enjoy the close, personal relationship he had with Murtaugh beginning in 1953 at New Orleans. Joe Brown decided to go outside the organization and selected Harry "The Hat" Walker as manager. Walker, like Ted Williams, was addicted to discussing hitting at length with anyone. His fascination with this aspect of the game was evident in his three seasons with the Pirates, who led the league in hitting two seasons and finished second in the third.

The 1966 team and season was the most exciting and also the most disappointing. The team hit .279 to lead the league, with six players hitting .299 or better, including Matty Alou who led the National League with a 342 average. Willie Stargell had 33 homers and 102 RBI; Clemente had 29 homers and 119 RBI; and Don Clendenon hit 28 homers and 98 RBI. This trio had a combined total of 90 home runs and 319 RBI. The team also set an all-time season home run record with 158 and most total bases with 2,430.

Defensively, the Pirates' double play combination of Gene Alley and Mazeroski set the all-time team and major league record with 215 double plays. Despite those team and individual records, the Bucs finished third in a tight race, three games behind the Champion Los

Angeles Dodgers and one and a half games behind the Giants. It was a team that should have won the NL pennant, but didn't.

The disappointment of the 1966 season lingered into 1967. The Pirates never contended and finished a distant sixth, 20 and one half games out of first. Pitching again was a problem. It was humorously said that Harry Walker thought pitching was something you did until you got a chance to hit again. His handling of the pitching staff was always under question and evidently Joe Brown agreed, because he made another managerial change after the 1967 season.

If Harry Walker has no other claim to his three years in Pittsburgh, it is that Roberto Clemente blossomed under his tenure to become a truly dominating player. Players from those teams will tell you Harry Walker played a major role in Clemente's rise to a higher level of power-hitting. With most of the players from the 1960 Championship team gone, Clemente accepted the role as team leader, which he held until his untimely and tragic death. In 1966 Roberto won the National League MVP Award. In 1967 he captured his fourth batting title with a .357 average, the best of his 18-year career. He also hit 23 home runs, and drove in 110 runs to join Honus Wagner on the greatest all-time Pirates' list.

After the disappointing 1967 season Joe Brown chose Larry Shepard, a little known manager who had toiled long and loyally in the Pirates' farm system. Larry had acquired credentials for developing young pitchers. To add strength and experience to the pitching staff, Brown picked up veteran right-hander Jim Bunning in a trade with the Philadelphia Phillies. Bunning was a hard-nosed professional, who despite being hobbled by an early season groin injury in 1968, continued to take the ball every four days. He never fully recovered and finished with a with a very sub-par 4-14 record.

The addition of Jim Bunning to the roster in 1968 paid big dividends for the Pirates. Bunning took a personal interest in Steve Blass by sharing his professional attitude, work ethic, and pitching knowledge. His interest enabled Blass to have a break through 18-win season. From that 1968 season through 1972, Steve Blass compiled an impressive record of 78 wins, 44 losses (.639). In the Pirates 1971 World Series Championship, Blass had two complete game wins, including the clutch seventh game. He still credits Jim Bunning's interest and advice for much of this success.

Jim Bunning was a strong voice in the Major League Players Association in dealing with club owners. That was the only relationship he had with the Pirates' owner John Galbreath. Some owners of major league baseball teams portrayed a strong personal interest in their players, for others it was an investment with limited interest in their relationship with the players. John Galbreath, the very wealthy owner of the Pittsburgh Pirates, fell into that second category. His son and daughter were outgoing, friendly and very close to the team and the players. Mr. Galbreath's true love, besides Ohio State University, was horse racing, embodied in his large Darby Dan Farms, just outside of Columbus, and the home of many Championship horses, including Proud Clarion, the 1967 Kentucky Derby winner.

In 1969 the Pirates played an exhibition game against their top farm team in Columbus and the entire traveling party was invited to spend the afternoon at Darby Dan Farms. We dined in a large hall festooned with the heads of many exotic animals that Mr. Galbreath had shot during his African safari hunting trips.

We were to take an outdoor tour of Darby Dan Farms after lunch, but the weather was too cold and damp, so they decided to show the horses in a nearby walk-around-barn. Mr. Galbreath personally presented eight or nine horses, one at a time, identifying each horse, including the bloodlines of the sire and the dam. It took over an hour for the presentation and everyone agreed it was an impressive display of his knowledge and his personal interest in each horse.

As we returned to the dining hall, Steve Blass expressed to Jim Bunning his respect of Mr. Galbreath's personal knowledge of each horse. Steve was astounded when Bunning remarked, "I'll bet you the best steak dinner in Pittsburgh that he doesn't know *your* name." Steve jumped at the offer and said, "I won 18 games last year and I'm positive he'll know my name." Bunning then described how this would take place, "Tonight when Mr. Galbreath comes onto the field, you must walk up to him and say, 'Hi Mr. Galbreath', and if he says your name you win. If he doesn't, you pick up the check for the dinner."

Mr. Galbreath came onto the field that evening and was near the Pirates' dugout when Blass approached him, shook his hand, and said, "Hi Mr. Galbreath," to which he responded, "How are you doing fella?" Charming is not a word you would use to describe Jim Bunning, who said to Blass, "If he had asked you how many wins you had last year and you pawed the dirt 18 times like a horse, I'll bet he'd have known who you were."

The 1968 Bucs came in sixth. Roberto Clemente suffered a back injury in spring training and only hit .290. It was the first time in nine seasons he failed to hit .300. With these injuries to Bunning and Clemente, the Pirates finished 17 games behind the NL Champion St. Louis Cardinals.

CHAPTER EIGHTEEN

The Farm System Pays Off, Murtaugh Returns

The depth of the talent in the Pirates' farm system was obvious by 1969, and Joe Brown decided to go with youth. He did it at an opportune time as the expansion of teams to Montreal and San Diego diluted the talent pool at the major league level. In the next three years, Al Oliver, Bob Robertson, Richie Hebner, Freddie Patek, Dave Cash, Manny Sanguillen, Milt May, Rennie Stennett, Bob Moose, Luke Walker and Dock Ellis, all quality players from their farm system, came to the Pirates. Joining established stars like Clemente, Mazeroski, and Stargell, these young players came of age quickly to usher in the winningest years in Pirates' history.

The "Miracle Mets" won the 1969 pennant with a sizzling September performance. In all the excitement created by the Mets, few realized the Pirates were improving quickly. During the Mets' unbelievable run to the pennant in the final month, the Pirates were the only team to have an advantage over them. One of those September wins was Bob Moose's no-hit gem at Shea Stadium. The Pirates' farm system then was so deep in talent that, when All Star second baseman Bill Mazeroski retired in

1972, Cash replaced him as Willie Randolph and Rennie Stennett were still waiting in the wings. Also still in the minors were power hitters Dave Parker and Richie Zisk. Despite the death of Clemente in a plane crash and the retirement of Mazeroski in 1972, the Pirates captured two more division titles in 1974 and 1975.

With the Pirates' strong 1969 finish and optimism for the coming year, Joe Brown would make another managing change. At the completion of the 1969 season Brown asked former manager Danny Murtaugh for a list of names to interview to replace Larry Shepard. Murtaugh surprised Brown by putting his own name on the list. Don Hoak, a colorful star of the 1960 world championship team yearned and campaigned for the job, and was the leading candidate among the media. Murtaugh was given little or no media consideration because of his health problems.

In one of the greatest sports shockers in Pittsburgh history, Brown held a press conference on October 9, 1969 aboard the Gateway Clipper on the Monongahela River to announce the next manager of the Pirates. When Brown announced that the next manager of the Pirates would enter the room, Murtaugh entered. The media assumed he was not the choice, but was going to introduce Hoak. Brown astonished the media and everyone else by announcing that Murtaugh would return as manager in 1970. In an eerie and tragic sidelight, later that same afternoon, Don Hoak, at age 41, died of a heart attack in the Shadyside area of Pittsburgh while chasing a thief who had stolen a family member's car.

Murtaugh, in his return as a manager in 1970, left spring training with what he wanted: "A team that would be competitive the entire season." Overall, it was a young team, but had experienced players with Alley and Mazeroski at short and second, Clemente and Stargell in right and left field. The young players, Robertson, Hebner, Oliver, Sanguillen,

Patek, and Cash, all came of age as major league players to give the Bucs their first division title.

Murtaugh's handling of the pitching staff was superb, with five starters posting 10 wins or more. Dave Giusti, acquired from St. Louis in an off-season trade, failed as a starter in the early season, but then filled the biggest pitching need by becoming an ace reliever. With that piece of the puzzle filled in, the Bucs won the Eastern Division title by five games over Chicago. In the National League Championship Series, the Pirates played the Cincinnati Reds, a team that would prevent them from being the most dominant team in the 1970s. The Reds swept the series in three games.

Murtaugh guided the Pirates to the Eastern Division championship again in 1971, and then managed his second World Series Championship team. He retired after the 1971 season for health reasons. However, he would return late in September 1973 and manage through the 1976 season. The Pirates would dominate the National League's Eastern Division from 1970 through 1975, winning five division championships (1970-71-72-74-75) and another World Series in 1979. This was truly the most successful and exciting era of Pirates baseball. Bob Prince called those years the "Halcyon Days of Pirates' Baseball."

In an historic moment on June 28, 1970, the Bucs hosted the Cubs in a doubleheader for the final games at Forbes Field, which had been home for the Pirates since 1909. The Pirates opened the new multipurpose Three Rivers Stadium on July 16, 1970, losing to the Cincinnati Reds 3-2. Despite the move to a new downtown stadium and the Pirates' success, fans still longed for the charm and memories of baseball at Forbes Field in Pittsburgh's Oakland section.

Pittsburgh enjoyed another championship season in 1971, amassing 97 wins, more than any Pirates' team since the 110 wins by the 1909 club. Stargell, away from spacious Forbes Field for an entire season, had an amazing year. Despite being slowed down by a knee injury in early August, he belted 48 home runs and drove in 125 runs. In the National League Championship Series, the Bucs met the San Francisco Giants, who had to go to the final day of the season to win the Western Division. Gaylord Perry beat Steve Blass 5-4 at Candlestick Park in the opener, but the Bucs came back to sweep the next three games. Bob Robertson hit three home runs in a 9-4 rout in game number two.

Juan Marichal, who had to pitch the last game of the regular season for the Giants, made his first start as the series moved to Forbes Field for game three. Nellie Briles, who was to start, pulled a hamstring while warming up and wisely informed Murtaugh he could not pitch. Danny found a four-leaf clover when he chose Bob Johnson to pitch this important game. Johnson, acquired from Kansas City in the off season, struggled during the season but pitched the finest game of his career, beating Marichal 2-1. The Bucs went on to win the fourth game 9-5 on key home runs by Hebner and Oliver. The Pirates were on their way to the World Series in Baltimore!

In the opener, the Pirates opened with a 3-0 lead after two innings thanks to only one hit, a walk, and two Baltimore errors but that was all they would score against Dave McNally, losing 5-3. Riding back to the hotel the silence on the team bus bespoke the team's frustration. The disappointment of the first game was replaced by total embarrassment in an 11-3 loss to Jim Palmer in the second game. Pirates' pitchers were roughed up for 24 hits and 15 runs in the first two games.

The Baltimore media ridiculed the Bucs, declaring "this series could be over in three games!" Murtaugh's confidence never wavered and he replied, "Anyone who thinks the Pirates are dead is sadly mistaken!" He was right. That statement was immortalized and engraved on the cover of each box holding the 1971 World Series Championship rings presented to Pirates' players.

Down 0 and 2, the Pirates returned to Three Rivers Stadium where the questionable Pirate pitching became dominant. Allowing only 9 hits and 4 runs in 27 innings, the Pirates swept three games to take a 3-2 lead in the Series. Steve Blass started it with a 5-1 win, highlighted by a peculiar event in the seventh inning. The Pirates led 2-1 with nobody out, Clemente was on second and Stargell on first. Bob Robertson, the next hitter, faced Mike Cuellar and was given the sacrifice bunt signal. As he stepped into the batter's box, Clemente at second base was certain Robertson missed the sign and in an attempt to get Robertson's attention he began frantically waiving his arms to call time, but failed. It was a missed sign that turned out to be a blessing, as Robertson swung and hit a home run to right center that clinched the 5-1 win. Allowing only three hits, Blass picked up his first World Series win and the Pirates regained their confidence as a team.

Game four was the first World Series game played under lights. It didn't begin confidently for Pirate's starter Luke Walker. He gave up three hits, a wild pitch, one walk, and three runs while retiring two when Bruce Kison replaced him. Kison, who got the World Series butterflies out of his stomach in the second game, pitched confidently and aggressively. With his hard sinking and moving fastball, Kison kept the Orioles off the plate, hitting three batters. He gave up only one hit and no walks in six and one-third innings of shutout pitching as the Pirates battled back to tie the game at three.

In the Pirates' seventh, Milt May, another rookie, pinch-hit for Kison and delivered the game winning hit for a 4-3 lead. Dave Giusti continued his post-season excellence with a save that gave Kison a much deserved win to even the series at two games a piece.

The next afternoon, Nellie Briles allowed two hits while facing 29 batters in a 4-0 complete game shutout, giving the Pirates a sweep of the three games at home. The Pirates' pitching staff that looked so questionable in the first two games in Baltimore took control of the series. The Pirates were leading three games to two as the series moved to Baltimore for the final game or games.

The Orioles would not die, winning game six 3-2 in 10 innings, to put the Pirates into another exciting seventh World Series game. On TV following the Baltimore win of the sixth game, Joe Garagiola interviewed Steve Blass, the Pirates' starter for the seventh game, asking him how he was going to handle the pressure of this assignment. I remember Steve's reply; "Not many pitchers get this chance. I'm going to find out tomorrow how I can handle it." He handled it well, going the distance for the second time in an exciting 2-1 win and the 1971 World Series Championship.

Before the series, Orioles' manager Earl Weaver ridiculed Pittsburgh shortstop Jackie Hernandez, (who along with Bob Johnson, was part of the off-season trade with Kansas City) saying, "The Pirates can't win with Jackie Hernandez playing shortstop." In a fitting end to the series, Hernandez made an outstanding play, going well to his left on the first base side of second to throw out Merv Rettenmund for the final out of the Series. Roberto Clemente, playing on the big stage, proved how dominating a player he was at the bat, as a runner, and in the field. He was named the Series MVP and gained the national stature he long deserved.

The celebration for the 1971 Series wasn't as spontaneous as it was in 1960 because the Pirates won in Baltimore. But when they returned to Pittsburgh by plane that evening, families lined the Penn Lincoln Parkway from the airport to downtown to greet the team. I was privileged to be in that parade riding in an open convertible with coach Bill Virdon. The sincerity of the fans that evening is still vivid in my memory. There were no incidents of wild revelry, just families wanting to shake your hand to say, "Thanks." It got a bit hairy when we ran into a traffic jam after leaving the Fort Pitt Tunnel. Someone grabbed for Bill Virdon's tie and he strongly suggested they not do that. He and I gently removed our ties and gave them to the fans

After the 1971 championship season, Bill Virdon was chosen to replace Murtaugh. A quiet, strong, no-nonsense man, Virdon inherited a 1972 team that was expected to win another championship. It was a tough act to follow and Virdon was just a wild pitch away from pulling it off in the final game of the NLCS. In the minds of many people, even to this day, this team was better than the 1971 World Series Championship team.

The 1972 team waltzed to an Eastern Division title, finishing 11 games in front of the Chicago Cubs. Stargell again led the way with 33 home runs and 112 RBI, but for the first time played most of his games at first base. It was a sign that the knee injury and the battle with his weight were too much for outfield play. Clemente, with age beginning to be a factor, played only 94 games in the outfield, but was wisely used by Virdon, hitting .312 and gaining his 3,000th career hit. The pitching was stronger, with Blass going 19-8 and posting a solid 2.49 ERA. He was so consistent he took every start past the sixth inning that season. Established now as one of the top major league pitchers, the future looked long and bright for him.

The Pirates, in the NLCS again, had to meet their nemesis, the Cincinnati Reds. It would be one of the most memorable and disappointing playoff series in the team's history. After splitting the first two games in Pittsburgh, the Pirates won a thrilling third game 3-2 to tilt the series their way. However, Ross Grimsley allowed the Bucs only one run in a 7-1 loss.

The only run came on a Clemente homer. It would turn out to be the final home run of his career. It all came down to the fifth and final game. Steve Blass, who won the first game of the NLCS, started the game and continued his excellent post-season pitching with seven strong innings, leading 3-2 before giving way to Ramon Hernandez. Hernandez closed the door in the eighth and the Bucs led 3-2 going into the bottom of the ninth. With Bench, Perez and Menke, all right-handed hitters slated to bat for the Reds, Bill Virdon went with Dave Giusti, who in the third game had faced these three and saved the important 3-2 third game win.

Three outs away from a second straight NL Championship, Giusti faced Johnny Bench. On Giusti's first pitch, Bench pulled it foul and deep into the upper deck in left field. The next pitch was a palm ball up in the strike zone which Bench hit a line drive line that just cleared the right center field fence for a home run to tie the game. The Riverfront Stadium erupted with cheers. Giusti, so affected by the sudden impact of the home run and losing the lead, gave up a single to Perez who was replaced by a pinch runner, George Foster. Menke failed in his attempt to sacrifice Foster to second, pushed a single through the infield to right field. Giusti fell behind 2-0 on Cesar Geronimo and Virdon brought in Bob Moose.

Geronimo flied to Clemente deep right center and Foster tagged and moved to third on the play. Moose then retired Darrel Chaney on a pop out to shortstop for the second out to quiet the crowd and give hope to the Pirates. Hal McRae pinch-hit for relief pitcher Clay Carroll. Moose had a count of 1-1, when in the most heart wrenching way to lose a game, Moose uncorked a curve ball wild pitch that bounced away from catcher Manny Sanguillen, allowing Foster to score the winning run.

I always kept the scorecards I used for important games. So disappointed with the outcome, I can still see myself angrily tossing the scorecard into the now empty seats below our broadcast booth. I wish I hadn't because it had great significance, not just because of the outcome, but because it was to be the last game Roberto Clemente would play.

After the 1972 season Roberto held a "Bob Prince Day" in San Juan to show his appreciation for Bob's efforts to welcome him into the Pittsburgh community. I was invited to join the group along with Bill Guilfoyle (Pirates' PR Director) and our wives. Clemente expressed his admiration for Bob Prince by presenting him with his first Silver Bat, emblematic of leading the National League in batting average in 1961. Prince graciously accepted the award and guaranteed it would be returned to the Clemente family following his death.

We enjoyed three lovely days of San Juan weather and the opportunity to visit with Roberto and his family. Most appreciated was a personal auto tour of Puerto Rico from San Juan to a resort area near the coast where Roberto hosted an intimate party. Roberto spoke with pride of the charity and friendship of the Puerto Rican people. It was also a cultural learning experience that confirmed his strong personal beliefs and love for his native country.

We were amazed at the very visible admiration people had for Roberto when we stopped at the resort's parking area. The valet expressed his affection for Clemente and proudly displayed some of the artistic, handmade wire figurines he designed. When we left four hours later, the valet presented Roberto with a life-like wire figurine of him, he had made during our short visit. I was impressed with the humble and proud response Roberto displayed in accepting the gift. He was truly a man of the people who never forgot his roots. We returned to Pittsburgh the next day, unaware that it would be our last visit with Roberto.

On New Year's Eve in 1972 my wife and I were guests at a large party hosted by *Channel Four* newscaster Adam Lynch at his home in Monroeville. It was still in the early hours of the morning when we departed for our home in Mt. Lebanon. As we entered the Fort Pitt Tunnel, I recalled hearing Bob Kosic doing the 4:00 AM newscast on KDKA radio. When we arrived home our oldest daughter, Laurie, was waiting at the top step to the bedrooms to inform us that Roberto Clemente was killed in a plane crash off the coast of San Juan, Puerto Rico. I asked her where she heard the news and she informed us she was listening to a local FM station newscast.

Not hearing anything on the 4:00 AM KDKA radio newscast I doubted the report of the FM newscast. I decided to call Dave Kosic personally at KDKA for a confirmation on this tragic story. Kosic answered the phone and I told him of the reported death of Clemente in a plane crash in Puerto Rico. He was not aware of it so I asked him to please check the Associate Press newswire to confirm if there was any truth to what my daughter had heard. After a brief pause he returned with the sad news that Clemente had died that evening in a plane crash into the sea near San Juan.

My wife and I were crushed. I can't recall a family death other than my father's that affected me as much as Roberto's did. My grief was so deep I cried for weeks. Asked to represent the Pirates' organization at the Allegheny County Commissioner's meeting honoring Roberto, I had difficulty completing my comments.

The opening game for the 1973 season at Three Rivers Stadium began with the solemn ceremony of retiring Roberto's Pirates' jersey, number 21, with his wife Vera and three sons, Roberto, Luis and Enrique, in attendance. Clemente's loss and the empathy the fans had for him and his family was profound. There were not many dry eyes in the crowd.

The 1973 Pirates' season turned out to be heartbreaking for Steve Blass. Regarded among the best pitchers in baseball, he suddenly could not throw strikes. He finished with a 3-9 record, walking 84 batters in 89 innings; with a 9.85 ERA, and announced his retirement the following spring. The loss of Clemente and Blass was too much to overcome. Manager Bill Virdon kept the Bucs in the race just two games off the pace with three weeks to go, but Joe Brown, in a surprise move, fired Virdon and brought back Murtaugh. The magic didn't work this time. Murtaugh could do no better than split the final 26 games as the Bucs finished third, only two and a half games in back of the late surging New York Mets. With the loss of Clemente, Willie Stargell took over the leadership of the team. He had another outstanding season leading the league with 44 home runs and 119 RBI, but again missed the MVP honor. It would come to him finally in 1979, when the Pirates again won a World Series.

The Pirates won the Eastern Division Championships in 1974 and again in 1975, but never really challenged for a World Series until the end of the decade. They lost in four games to the Dodgers in 1974, losing 12-1 in the final game. In 1975 they were swept by their nemesis, the Cincinnati Reds, in three games. Murtaugh and Joe Brown continued their relationship for one more year and both retired in 1976. Harding Peterson and Chuck Tanner took over the Pirates' reins and in 1979 captured another seven game World Series Championship from the Baltimore Orioles.

CHAPTER NINETEEN

"The Great One" – Roberto Clemente

Three players dominated the halcyon days of Pirates' baseball: Roberto Clemente, Bill Mazeroski, and Willie Stargell. They were outstanding, dedicated players, who, despite all their celebrity, remained humble individuals who never forgot where they came from. Like all of those fortunate to have enjoyed a personal relationship with them, they left an indelible mark on my life.

I had the privilege of playing briefly with Roberto from 1955 to 1957, but did not get to know him personally until I joined the Pirates' broadcasting crew in 1967. It was then that I grew to appreciate his intense pride and dedication as a player, and equally important, the warmth and affection he had for people.

My first meeting with Roberto was during the Pirates 1955 spring training at Fort Myers, Florida. It was Roberto's first major league spring training camp and only his second season in professional baseball. Except for the pitchers, I was unfamiliar with the other players on the roster. After eight years in the minor leagues and only my second major league spring training camp, I was trying to survive and stay afloat in the competition for spots on the roster.

Like all rookies, Roberto suffered with anxiety his first year in the majors. He portrayed it well saying, "I was so afraid of making a mistake I developed tunnel vision when playing right field, I concentrated so much on the hitter I never saw the pitcher, first or second baseman standing between the hitter and me. After a couple of weeks, I began to relax and the first baseman, second baseman and then the pitcher came into my view. As I became more comfortable I started to see the shortstop, third baseman, then the left fielder and center fielder." He described it so beautifully: "Instead of being outside the picture, I was now in the picture, and could see it all."

He laughed as he told about the running bases errors he made. He would take off from first base on a fly ball to the outfield and round second base only to discover the ball had been caught. He knew he had to get back to first quickly and said, "I used to run right across the infield to first base, not re-tagging second base," and added "Sometimes I made it without the umpires noticing."

Only 20 years old when he came to the Pirates, Roberto had to overcome obstacles Jackie Robinson did not have to face when he broke the color barrier in 1947 with the Dodgers. Among them were race, language, and cultural differences. He had to deal with all of these obstacles while playing in the highest level of baseball.

Race was something he did not have to contend with in Puerto Rico. This, coupled with his innate personal pride, created emotional challenges. Language naturally was a problem. With a very limited English vocabulary, misconceptions between him and the media were embarrassing and almost constant. Cultural differences, largely overlooked by many, created most of the misunderstanding that to this day continue to cloud portrayals of him.

Following the event honoring Bob Prince, my wife and I joined Roberto and Vera as we journeyed to another location for a more private celebration. During the trip he proudly pointed out landmarks along the way and in a lengthy conversation described the warm openness Puerto Ricans have in their relationships with people. "In Puerto Rico, people wear their feelings on their sleeve. They don't hide emotions." He described it by saying, "Nellie, if people here tell you they love you, they will give you the shirt off their back. They also are very serious when they express their anger or dissatisfaction. When they tell you, 'I do not like you and if you come here again, I will kill you.' They are not kidding!" He went on to compare it to America, where people will say such things, but are playing "wolf," just trying to scare you. He said, "In Puerto Rico, they really mean it!"

Roberto had a dislike for anyone talking to him privately about someone instead of personally confronting the person. We call it "talking behind someone's back." Manny Sanguillen, whom Clemente mentored, translated this amusingly: "You are talking on the back of my neck!" Roberto told me how he handled such a situation in the early 1960s. A sportswriter came to his locker and confided to him, "Bob Friend can only beat teams like the Mets and Cubs, but can't handle the top teams like Los Angeles and San Francisco." To which Roberto replied, "Bob Friend's locker is right over there. Why are you telling me this? I will tell Bob what you told me." He then hollered across the locker room to Friend and told him what the sportswriter said. The writer angrily asked him why he did that. Clemente told him, "Don't tell me about Bob Friend, you go tell him yourself."

Cultural differences created misunderstandings for Roberto earlier in his career. One simple cultural difference, accepting compliments, confused him. He described it well that day on the motor trip through Puerto Rico. "If a fellow tells you, 'Roberto, I think you are the best plumber in Puerto Rico,' you are supposed to respond to him, 'Thank you. I feel I have learned my trade and I am proud of the work I do and am the best in my trade.' In Puerto Rico you are expected to accept a compliment. In the United States" he said, "if someone pays you a compliment, you shuffle your feet, say, 'Aw shucks, I'm not that good'…. and the person will tell you two or three times how good you are. In America you are expected to be humble."

This cultural difference plagued Roberto early in his career as his exceptional fielding, running, and throwing talents became obvious. A writer complimented him on his strong and accurate throwing arm and his overall ability to play right field. He responded saying, "Yes I feel I am very good and have dedicated myself to being the best right fielder in baseball." His response brought comments from teammates, other players, media types and fans: "Who does this guy think he is? He's been in the league only two years and he thinks he's the best right fielder in the game!" It came off as conceited and arrogant. It was misunderstood, as he was accepting the compliment as was expected in his culture.

A major problem for America in the world today is that we don't take the time to understand other people's culture, but arrogantly expect them to understand ours.

Pride and artistry were the true essence of Roberto Clemente as a player and person. As I got to know Roberto I felt the deep pride he had in his artistry and creativity on the baseball field. People who are artistic and creative see, hear, feel, and do things differently than most. We think of them sometimes as "strange" or "different." Roberto's artistry was displayed through his body, and his canvas was the playing field. Like a good artist, he was not going to paint a bad picture and put his signature on it.

This artistry and deep personal pride created other problems for him. He became known as a "malingerer" or a "hypochondriac" very early in his career because of the extreme attention he gave to his body. Like a good mechanic who can hear something wrong with a high performance engine, he could feel the slightest twinges in his body. He expressed those pains to trainers, players and managers. They thought Clemente didn't want to play for reasons other than physical. They questioned his courage and dedication to the team. It was whispered among players, writers, and broadcasters that he didn't want to face a certain pitcher or for other reason, which denoted a lack of "guts." It created a rift between him and teammates and managers, particularly Danny Murtaugh, with whom he did not have a good relationship.

Roberto's reasons for not playing were misunderstood. He said, "If I could not play my best because of the physical problems I felt, I should not play." Stating emphatically, "I would embarrass my family, my team, myself, and the fans." Americans' reaction to this attitude was completely different. You are supposed to "hang in there, spit tobacco juice on it and play." This was a sore point with teammates and still is today with his contemporaries. Bill Mazeroski had difficulty understanding why Clemente did not play certain games. Maz rarely took a day off and explained his reasoning by stating the obvious, "Clemente playing at 60-70% was better than anyone else they could put out in right field."

Ironically, when you look at the records, Clemente played more games than any Pirate in history. At age 38 he was still the best runner, fielder, thrower and hitter on the team. To play at that level at age 38 took great commitment and discipline, and Clemente applied both. Bill Virdon, a teammate and later Roberto's manager, appreciated the dedication it took to continue playing at the level he did in his final season.

Roberto had great respect for Bill Mazeroski and told me of a proposal he made to him at the end of the 1972 season. Maz decided to retire at the end of the 1972 season and Roberto tried to convince him to play another year. As Roberto explained to me, "I play right field and watch the play of second basemen. I told Maz he can still play better than the younger players, Cash and Stennett, who were expected to take over the job at second base. I invited him to come down to Puerto Rico for four weeks to work out with me to get in shape." Unfortunately Maz had a terrible genetic problem with his metabolism and confessed to Roberto that he could no longer fight the battle with his weight.

Roberto's obsession with his body did not escape teammates or writers. He knew it caused comment. But he had a mental side of his preparation for a game that was unique. Visualization is a new thing in sports now, but Clemente was doing that way back in his career, and to be honest with you, a lot of pitchers and hitters did, too, but not with the attention and dedication of Clemente. He used the power of visualization to prepare him for the pitcher he would face that night. He explained it this way, "I would go into the trainer's room, turn off the light and lie down on the rubbing table, close my eyes and visualize facing the scheduled opposing pitcher. I would visually bat four times against him; see every pitch he threw, and how he liked to pitch to me. I would see a fastball inside, a curve outside, and would hit it for a single to left. Next time I would see the curve ball, see a slider outside and hit it to right field. Next time I would see a fast ball outside, then one in on the hands and hit it to right center. I would see every pitch he had and would always get four hits. When I saw those pitches during the game, I would get hits off them, because I already had seen them and hit them. Some nights I would get one hit that way and on good nights, two, three or four hits." Roberto said,

"I know the players thought, 'Roberto is back on the rubbing table', but they didn't know what I was doing there."

Clemente told me of his dedication and the sensitivity to his body in our last visit. He said, "Every year since I have been playing baseball (he played 18 years in the major leagues), I have kept a diary and log of injuries I suffered during the season. In the winter, I get out the book and see what parts of my body have been injured. I know they must be strengthened. I have done this every year I have played." He said proudly, "In the winter, I work baseball. In the summer, I play baseball!"

His compassion and humanitarian feelings were not always visible to fans or even to players on his own team, but they were the core of his character. I recall Jim "Mudcat" Grant telling me of how Clemente took time to console him when he feared he was near the end of his major league career. The Pirates had picked up Grant from Oakland on September 14, 1970 to provide bullpen help down the stretch. His experience in Minnesota in 1965 when he won 21 and lost 7 with a Championship team proved invaluable to him. Working in relief he won 2 lost 1 in eight September games in 1970 as the Pirates captured what was to be the first of five Division titles in the next six years.

In the 1971 season, which was to be a World Championship year, Mudcat, now 35 and working out of the bullpen, had won 5 and lost 3. In late July the Bucs had an eleven game lead as they went on a West Coast road trip. They won the first two in San Diego but dropped the last two and opened a series in Los Angeles. "Mudcat" came on in relief in the 8th inning and gave up a three run home run to Bill Buckner in an 8-5 loss. He told me he sat dejectedly in front of his locker after the game, remaining in uniform as the other players showered and dressed.

Wondering if he could still pitch on a championship team, he thought the locker room was empty. It was then when Clemente pulled up a stool and sat next to him. Grant recalling that moment said, "For over twenty-five minutes he figuratively held my hand, telling me not to let this bother me, that I can still be a big part of this team. Here was a star player, who probably had two or three hits that night, but seeing the emotional pain I was in, took time to console me. In all the years I have played baseball never did I have anyone do that." The Pirates traded him to Oakland on August 10. Working out of the bullpen, Mudcat, with one win and three saves, played a big role as Oakland won the second of three consecutive Western Division Championships. "Mudcat" Grant still treasures that moment with Roberto Clemente.

A most poignant memory I have of Clemente and the impact he had on the leadership of the Pirates, then and even after he died, was the night before the 1971 World Series in Baltimore. Staying at the Lord Baltimore Hotel, my wife and I got on the elevator as Roberto and Willie Stargell entered. As we started up, Roberto said to Willie, "Do not press or try too hard in the Series, Willie. I will carry the team." He then said, "When we get off the elevator, come over to my room. I want to talk with you." I told my wife, "Roberto is a clever man. He knows if Willie can play as he did prior to a knee injury in August, Willie will carry the team. But if he can't, Roberto will handle the job."

It turned out that Roberto did carry the team, batting .414, fielding and throwing superbly and hitting a big home run in the fourth inning of the final game. Stargell, who struggled throughout the series, however scored the winning run in the eighth inning of the seventh game for a 2-1 win.

Years later I asked Stargell about that 1971 conversation in the elevator and what they talked about in Roberto's room that evening. He related that Roberto told him of the unusual excitement and media attention of his first World Series in 1960 and how difficult it was for him to concentrate and play at his best. Willie said, "He told me not to try too hard and that he was now ready now to handle this leadership role because his experience in 1960." Stargell then told me, "I did the same thing prior to the 1979 Series, gathering the younger players together to inform them of this, as Clemente did with me in 1971." Unsurprisingly, Stargell carried the Pirates in the 1979 Series and, like Clemente, was named the World Series MVP.

Roberto had strong feelings about who owned the financial value of players in a way that was not recognized or considered in the days before free agency. Owners could sell or trade players without players having any say in the matter. The trade of a player of the magnitude and financial value of Willie Mays from San Francisco to the New York Mets in 1972 truly annoyed him. The Pirates were playing the Mets in New York at that time and it made headlines in all the New York media.

During the bus ride to Shea Stadium that night I sat with Roberto and he expressed his dismay and anger that Willie Mays received no financial remuneration in the transaction. He said, "I told Joe Brown (GM for the Pirates) 'don't you ever try to do to me what the Giants did to Willie Mays.' Trade me to another team and not give me any part of the financial gain the Pirates would receive." He continued, "I told him I wanted to play the remainder of my years with the Pirates. He could trade me, but I would not report unless I got 80% of the sale price." As he put it, "The Pirates gave me the opportunity to play and develop my skills and they should receive 20% of the sale price." Of course the Pirates were not going to trade a player of his value, but

Roberto wanted it understood that he was not a piece of property. He had created his value and he must be rewarded.

Clemente, who had an illustrious career at Forbes Field, would play only three seasons in Three Rivers Stadium. But those three seasons gave him the national fame and acclaim that had escaped him for so many years. His brilliant performance in front of a worldwide audience during the 1971 World Series could not be denied or forgotten. He was named the MVP of the series, which he accepted with humility. Speaking briefly in his native tongue he took this moment to give praise and thanks to his parents. The following year, in what was to be his final season, Roberto compiled the 3000th hit of his career. By doing so, he accomplished a goal he told me about in an interview between games of a doubleheader on the final day at Forbes Field, June 28, 1970.

It really was not an interview; it was more of a conversation between friends. We talked about his wonderful journey from his childhood in Puerto Rico to the storied career he was enjoying in the major leagues. He had affection for Forbes Field and remarked, "I have played sixteen years here. Almost half of my life has been spent at Forbes Field." I then asked him how long he would like to continue playing. In what was a tragically prophetic reply, he said, "Nellie, I think I would like to play until I get three thousand hits." The record books show that on Saturday, September 30, 1972 at Three Rivers Stadium, the second to the last game of the season, he got his 3,000th hit, a double to left center field off New York Mets' pitcher Jon Matlack. He ended his career with exactly 3,000 hits.

The grief over Roberto's death was overwhelming in Pittsburgh and enlarged his identity, even with young fans today who never saw him play. A monument in his honor, dedicated before the 1994 All-Star Game ,was placed outside the main gate at Three Rivers Stadium.

A park on the riverfront adjacent to the stadium is also named in his honor. When the new PNC Park opened in 2001, the statue was moved to the new park. The Sixth Street Bridge became a pedestrian walkway to the new ballpark and was renamed the Roberto Clemente Bridge.

CHAPTER TWENTY

Willie Stargell – "Pops"

Not having been a teammate of Willie Stargell, my relationship with him was limited to the nine years I did Pirate broadcasts. A huge, powerful man, he had a gentle demeanor and respect for others that captivated everyone. Like Clemente and Mazeroski, Willie combined a deep sense of pride with sincere humility. They never put themselves "above" others. They had the strength of character Mr. Rickey said he always searched for when making judgments on players. Willie had developed the rare ability to compartmentalize his life.

In a conversation with him he related how he never allowed his baseball problems to interfere with his family life or *vice versa*. As he described it, "When I left home for the baseball park, I mentally closed the door on my family room. When I arrived at the park, I opened the door to my baseball room. When I left the clubhouse after a game I closed the door on the baseball room and opened the door to my social room." It is why he enjoyed a richly satisfying and successful life as a player and person. I don't know of anyone who had the pleasure of knowing Willie Stargell personally who didn't feel the warmth of his company and personality.

An intangible aspect of those successful Pirates' teams was the relationship the players enjoyed with each other. The continuity of the Pirates' roster during those years was an important factor, evidenced by the 1971 Championship team. Nineteen of the twenty-five players came through the Pirates' farm system, or played their entire major league career with the team. This created a strong bond between players that held together during the very difficult time when the assassination of Martin Luther King, Jr. and the Vietnam War were tearing at the fabric of the nation. Willie Stargell was an active facilitator in this process

Race was never allowed to be a hidden or whispered topic on the Pirates. It was always put out front where it was handled, not with acrimony, but with humor. I witnessed this in my first season broadcasting in 1967. The Pirates were playing at Connie Mack Stadium in Philadelphia and the Pirates' starting lineup had eight black or Latin players. The only white player was starting pitcher Dennis Ribant. It was an obvious topic for whispered conversation in the press room, but not in the Pirates' clubhouse. I remember Willie getting everyone's attention when he saw the lineup and announced, "Fellows, they will not be playing the National Anthem today." The statement caught everyone's attention and after a pause, Willie continued, "They're gonna play 'Sweet Georgia Brown'." Dock Ellis, who always got into any discussion, followed with, "We've got to get Ribant out of the game early and bring in Alvin O'Neil McBean, so we have nine brothers in the lineup."

Off the field, Pirates' players could use humor to disarm racial tensions. Following Dr. Martin Luther King, Jr.'s assassination in 1968, we opened the season in St. Louis. The newspapers featured photos of the riots in Newark, Detroit, and elsewhere. Traveling with the Pirates, who had eleven black players on their roster, you could feel the tension as we walked through the airport and entered the plane. We stayed at the Chase Hotel in St. Louis (where, in 1954, my first year with the Pirates, black players were not allowed to stay). As I entered an elevator to go to my room I nodded a hello to a perfect Norman Rockwell, middle American, conservatively dressed, elderly white couple. They nodded and smiled back.

Mazeroski entered, they nodded to him. Then Bob Veale and Don Clendenon, six foot, eight inch, black men, stepped on, followed by Maury Wills, Willie Stargell, Al McBean, Jesse Gonder, and Manny Mota. As the black players entered the elevator I could feel the apprehension of the elderly couple as they edged into the corner of the elevator. They had no idea we were all part of the same group.

As the doors closed and as is common in elevators, there were no conversations, until the doors opened when we reached the fifth floor. Mazeroski stepped off, and then held open the door with one hand and looking into the elevator loudly remarked, "Hey, how come all you guys have flat noses?" Well, the elderly couple straightened upright, expecting a fight to begin. Willie stepped out, held the door open, looked into the elevator, put his arm around Mazeroski, then turned to him and said, "By God, you know you're right, Maz. They do have flat noses!" Everyone, including the elderly couple, laughed. It perfectly illustrated the deft humor with which Mazeroski (a great practical joker), Stargell and the players defused the then very sensitive topic of race.

Another example of the ease and openness with which the team dealt with racial tensions happened during a series with the Cubs in Chicago. It was also the start of the NBA Playoffs. The Chicago sports pages were loaded with information about the Bulls' opening game at Milwaukee where Lew Alcindor (Kareem Abdul Jabbar) was then playing center for Milwaukee. I mentioned that I thought the Bulls, despite being a six-point underdog, could win the game. Willie heard my comment and quickly said, "I'll take Milwaukee and bet you for a fine bottle of wine." I wanted the 6 points, but Willie wouldn't go for that and I wound up losing the bet.

The next morning before going to Wrigley Field, I walked to a liquor store, or as Willie called them, "Sweet Shops," to buy that fine bottle of wine. Not being a wine connoisseur, I recalled Joe L. Brown ordering a high priced fine tasting wine named Fouille Pousse during a dinner he hosted at an upscale New York restaurant. Still annoyed I didn't get the point spread from Willie, I asked the salesman, "What's the worst bottle of wine you sell? He quickly identified it saying, "Well we have Thunderbird, which costs only .50 cents." I said, "Give me a bottle of that." Before I could give him the money I noticed a bottle of "Watermelon Wine" on the shelf and shouted, "That's it, give me the Watermelon Wine instead."

I took a cab to Wrigley Field, arriving ahead of the team bus and placed the watermelon wine in Willie's locker. As the players arrived in the locker room Willie noticed me and said, "Milwaukee won, where's the bottle of wine?" I replied, "I put the wine in your locker, but I should have gotten the points." He opened the bag, laughed and exclaimed, "Damn, Nellie where did you get this?" The brothers' back in Pittsburgh won't believe it—Watermelon Wine!" We had a good laugh and then I gave him the bottle of Fouille Pousse.

Willie was the type of power hitter who could carry a team, and proved it emphatically in 1971. It was the most consistent and awesome display of power hitting I had witnessed. Willie began the season by setting a major league mark hitting eleven home runs in the month of April. By the end of June he had set a league record of 30 home runs, and by the All-Star break had driven in 87 runs. Thanks to Stargell's hitting, the Pirates led the league by ten games at mid-way point.

His power hitting continued following the All-Star game finishing July with 36 home runs as the Pirates maintained their big margin in the National League. However, a knee injury in August slowed Willie down and the team's lead dropped to only four and a half games the third week of that month. Willie finished the season with 48 home runs 125 RBI's, a .628 slugging percentage and .398 on base average as the Bucs won the pennant by 7 games. Willie had an MVP season but did not get the award. Joe Torre of the Cardinals did with a .363 average, 28 home runs and 137 RBI's.

In the World Series, Baltimore manager, Earl Weaver made sure Willie Stargell didn't beat them. He drew 7 walks, only 5 hits a .208 average, with no home runs and only 1 RBI. Weaver took his chances with Clemente and paid for it as Roberto had his finest moment in the World Series spotlight. Ironically, Willie's fifth hit, a single to left field in the 8th inning of the final game, turned out to be the winning run of the game. He then scored all the way from first on a double by Jose Pagan in a 2-1 win and the World Series Championship. The 1972 season ended in a huge disappointment, when the Pirates missed another World Series appearance on a wild pitch of the final game at Cincinnati in the NLCS. The retirement of Bill Mazeroski and the tragic death of Roberto Clemente, following the end of the season left a huge gap in the leadership of the team. Willie Stargell quietly but with authority on and off the field took over the leadership role. He had another stellar season in 1973, hitting 44 home runs, 119 RBI's, batting .299, and a career-high .646 slugging percentage. Despite the amazing power hitting statistics, Willie failed to win the National League MVP Award. Pete Rose of the Cincinnati Reds who led the NL in batting with a .338 average and 238 hits captured the MVP Award.

Richie Zisk, then a young and promising outfielder, was in his first full season with the Pirates in 1973. Richie told early in the season how impressed he was with Stargell's wisdom and confidence as a hitter. "I was waiting in the on deck circle", he began, "Stargell was the hitter and he had just struck out his first time at bat. As he walked by me on the way back to the dugout he said, 'I'll see that same pitch in the 7th or 8th inning and I'll hit it out.'" Zisk in amazement said, "He was setting up a pitcher for later in the game when it would mean more. As a rookie, I could never begin to think like that. That's called confidence."

When the Pirates decided to make a change in the broadcasting team following the 1975 season it came as a shock to me. I had so thoroughly enjoyed the association I had with the players and the organization. Being fired from any job is humiliating and was especially so for me as a broadcaster of Pirates' baseball. When the news hit the papers, Jack Wheeler a radio personality decided to hold a noontime parade downtown to feed off the fan anger and hopefully change the Pirates decision. I agreed to participate along with Bob Prince. Willie Stargell called to inform me he and all of the Pirates' players then residing in Pittsburgh would be showing their support with their participation in the parade. I had a call from Bob Prince the night prior to the event stating that he was not sure he was going to join the parade. I believe he thought there might be a chance that Tom Johnson, one of the owners with whom Bob had a strong relationship over his 28 years, would be able to save him. Needless to say I was now feeling apprehension about my participation. Not much later I received a call from Willie Stargell and I informed him of Prince's decision. Willie comforted me saying, "I and the other guys are going to be there with you regardless." Unaware of the true feeling the decision had on the Pirates' fans, I had a restless night. I recall waking up often thinking, "what if only 50 people show up?" and how embarrassing it would be. Thankfully, Bob Prince showed up, as did the players. The parade and gathering at The Point gave us the opportunity we never got to say "good-bye" on the air and express our thanks for sharing so many wonderful seasons together.

Willie proved his leadership and confidence in the "We Are Family" 1979 team, sweeping the National League and World Series MVP Awards. He took over the Series in 1979, as Clemente did against Baltimore with the Series deciding home run in the final game. Willie ended his playing days after the 1982 season. He remained out of the game until 1985 when he reunited with Chuck Tanner as a coach with the Pirates. He accompanied Tanner to Atlanta in 1986 where he served as the batting and first base coach until May 1988. He then continued his association with the Braves as Special Assistant to the Director of Player Development.

During his years at Atlanta some acrimony developed between Willie and the consortium of owners of the Pirates. It centered on another "Willie Stargell Day" which he did not think necessary. He already was honored during his years with the Pirates and he felt he was being used to promote only a financial (attendance) purpose. Fortunately when Kevin McClatchy took over the Pirates ownership in 1996 he eagerly sought to have Willie join the organization. On February 11, 1997, in a welcome home signing at the Allegheny Club in Three Rivers Stadium, Willie was officially signed as Special Assistant to GM Cam Bonifay. Willie was happy to be return home with the Pirates, but was suffering with a lingering illness that physically slowed him down, but the smile and caring attitude was still there. He died the morning of the opening day of the season and the first game at PNC Park, April 9, 2001. A large statue in his honor was dedicated two days prior to his death and is on display outside PNC Park on Federal Street, not far from the Roberto Clemente statue and Clemente Bridge.

CHAPTER TWENTY-ONE

"Maz" – Bill Mazeroski

Bill Mazeroski is remembered for hitting the most dramatic home run in World Series history in the final inning of the seventh game to capture the 1960 World Championship for the Pirates. That legacy unfortunately hid the excellence and consistency of his overall playing for seventeen major league seasons. To me he was the best "money player" of the Pirates' halcyon days. His 1960 World Series home run was just the first and most treasured event in my opinion.

The first time I met Mazeroski was at the start of spring training at Fort Myers, FL in 1956. He was at the beginning of a long and glorious career. Having spent eight years in the Pirates' minor league system, I thought I was aware of every player in the major league camp that spring. I had never met Mazeroski, nor was I aware of him, as Maz, at age 18, had not had the time to build a reputation strong enough gain an identity.

The only thing I can remember about our first meeting was the wild, multicolored, ill-fitting pork-pie hat he was wearing. I can still see him standing in the doorway leading from the clubhouse to the field. It's an odd thing to remember about a player who would become one of the most memorable players in Pirates' and baseball history. The brashness of Maz's hat did not fit the personality of the man I have had the pleasure of knowing for more than 40 years now.

Mazeroski joined the Pirates from the Hollywood farm club in the Pacific Coast League. Nobody played second base again for the Bucs until 1971. It's a baseball trivia question: "Who played second base before Mazeroski?" (It was Forrest "Spook" Jacobs.) "Maz," as he was affectionately known, came to the major leagues with a wisdom and knowledge of the game far beyond his years. He credits his early sagacity to having played with older, better, and more experienced players in his early years. To this day, he recommends it to youngsters, saying, "You can gain wisdom fast by playing with players older than you."

Despite all of the acclaim he received during his time in the major leagues and since his retirement at the end of the 1972 season, Mazeroski remains a shy, humble, quiet person. Coming from Rayland, OH, on the banks of the Ohio River just outside of Wheeling, WV, he has never lost his small town innocence. He does not seek, nor does he desire, the limelight. To the contrary, it actually frightens and embarrasses him. Privately, however, he will proudly tell you of the many distinguished athletes who came from an area within ten miles of Wheeling, WV: Boston Celtics' great, John Havlicek; Cleveland Browns' Lou and Alex Groza; the Neikro brothers, Phil and Joe; and Gene and George Freese. Few areas of this size can claim a collection of such outstanding professional athletes.

Although Maz was only five feet, eleven inches tall, his sturdy 180 pounds combined physical strength with amazing athletic and mental gifts. Few people are aware that he was the second leading scorer in basketball in the state of Ohio during his senior year in high school.

The leading scorer was Jerry Lucas, who went on to greater success at Ohio State University and in the NBA.

Maz's shyness led some to believe he wasn't bright. How wrong they were! He was a quick study in anything that caught his attention. This became clear to me watching him take up the game of golf in the mid-1960s. I recall playing with him at the prestigious Laurel Valley Country Club in Ligonier, PA as guests of Joe Wentling, a prominent Greensburg businessman. Maz's swing, like most beginners, was outside in, causing him to slice everything. But his uncanny feel and touch, so noticeable in baseball, were visible around and on the greens. He knew how to score. Having played golf with him many times, I think he can get up and down in two from any place on a golf course.

Maz became so proficient at golf that he twice won the American Airlines Astro-Jet Tournament, which paired a major league and a NFL player. I have often told him that if he had taken up golf as a youngster, he would have done well on the pro tour. He quietly but confidently agreed with my assessment. However, his decision to play baseball was not a bad choice.

Best known for his defensive skills, Maz did not possess great speed, but made up for it with unbelievably quick feet and hands. He had a knack of making all plays seem routine – except for turning the double play. Again, even that was not considered exciting. It can best be compared to watching a skilled magician doing his trick and thinking, "How'd he do that?" Nobody in the history of the game turned the double play quicker or more consistently than Bill Mazeroski. The truly great players at the major league level do the routine things so consistently well they become unappreciated for their perfection. It is taken for granted.

So it was with Bill Mazeroski. Handling the pressure of these expectations by fans, writers, and contemporaries can create tension and invoke the most hated word in sports: "CHOKE." Maz told me that the most frightening choke he ever experienced was not during a game, but during infield practice in his first All-Star Game in 1958 at Baltimore.

He had been in the majors for three seasons and his reputation for turning the double play was well known by his peers in the National League. The American League players, with no inter-league play and limited TV exposure, had not witnessed his talent. As the National League players took the field for pre-game infield practice, the American Leaguers were warming up.

As Maz described it, "Suddenly, I noticed that every American League player stopped throwing. They wanted to watch me turn the double play." Performance anxiety hit him and he sheepishly admitted, "I took my biggest choke ever and it was only during infield practice. Nobody was coming at me trying to break up the double play, but I couldn't remember which foot to use when tagging the bag, how to catch and throw the ball with ease. I stumbled around, couldn't concentrate, and was really embarrassed."

Although long delayed, Maz's consistent excellence was finally rewarded when he was voted into the Hall of Fame in 2001. He will be remembered not only for his brief and warmly received acceptance speech, but also for opening the doors for other deserving defensive players who are certain to follow.

CHAPTER TWENTY-TWO

The End of My KDKA Radio Days

My relationship with KDKA during my early years was enjoyable. It changed after the 1969 season, however, when Bill Hartman became Vice President of KDKA radio. He was brought in to address the fragmenting of the broadcasting business that was cutting into KDKA-AM's dominant and steady ratings.

Following the 1969 season, Jim Woods left the Pirates' broadcast booth to join Jack Buck on KMOX doing St. Louis Cardinal games. Early in 1970, Ed Wallis, Bill Hartman, and Jim King, VP for KDKA-TV, invited me to a "power luncheon" at the prestigious Duquesne Club to discuss the broadcasts for the coming season. During lunch I was informed that Gene Osborne had been hired to fill the vacant broadcasting position and that my role on the broadcast team would not include doing any play-by-play. I questioned the move and was told that Osborne needed to gain more "audience identity." I told them I felt like they were preparing to go with only two broadcasters and the door was being opened for me to leave at the end of the 1970 season. They denied this, but it turned out to be true. KDKA did go with two broadcasters in 1971, but Gene Osborne was the one who left. His style and personality failed to gain the identity with Pirates' fans that KDKA hoped for. Also, his relationship with Bob Prince was never close.

Going into the 1971 season with only two announcers, Prince and I expected a salary increase. I discovered quickly that was not going to happen. During the previous years, Jim Woods and I did a post-game show as part of the agreement with Pirates' network affiliates. The total pay for both of us was $40 a show. Woods received $25 and I was paid $15. For the 1971 season I was asked to do the show by myself and wanted the $25 fee Woods had received. I held out for that fee when Bill Hartman informed me, "I can get a guy from Youngstown to come in and do the show for $12.50." I told him, "Go get him." He did, but the shows lost their immediacy and relevance.

In 1973, Joe L. Brown asked me to do the pre- and post-game shows, stating he personally was not pleased with Prince's interest in or preparation for the pre-game broadcast. Looking back, that was the first indication I had that Brown was dissatisfied with Bob's work. Earlier indications of KDKA's unhappiness with Prince came in 1971 over the control of seats in the large broadcast booth at Three Rivers Stadium. Bob loved being able to bring his many friends into the broadcast booth. They took up most of the seats, which annoyed KDKA management, who were also annoyed by Bob's habit of leaving the booth for long periods when not doing play-by-play.

The deteriorating relationship between Bob and KDKA was evident in these additions to our contract for 1971:

5. *It is understood and agreed that:*
   a. no unauthorized persons are allowed in broadcasting booth at any time.

b. *Unless physical arrangements make it unworkable, you will remain in the booth for the duration of each game, excepting for those times when moving to alternate locations for broadcast purpose.*

For the next five years, Prince and I did both radio and TV. Bob Prince rarely fought for a raise in 28 years and never received the type of money an announcer with his enormous appeal should have received. Thanks to his unique personality, he earned nearly as much income doing local commercials, endorsements, and speaking engagements as he did broadcasting Pirates' games. But Bob's salary affected the pay the announcers working under him received. I believe it was the main reason that Jim Woods left after the 1969 season.

In 1975 I was having trouble signing my contract for the coming season and needed to find out what Bob Prince was being paid. In 1971 I had to take over as the number one announcer without any increase in salary when Bob had an appendectomy and missed a number of games. Errol Miller, my lawyer, wrote to inform Ed Wallis of a change in my contract if I should again have to take over as a number one announcer for a longer period of time. He had to know what Bob was being paid and work out a percentage from that amount for the number of games I would do. He was informed Bob was making only $40,000.

As the number three announcer in 1967 I earned $13,000, and $15,500 in 1970. For the 1971 season, when we went with only two announcers, Bob and I were dismayed not to receive a sizeable raise. But we were really unhappy with the first contract from Ed Wallis. For the first time, Bob fought KDKA. It was not just for him, but also for me, which Bob expressed in a letter to Ed Wallis:

Nellie started out at a very low figure, and now as he enters his fifth year, he is being asked to assume a very important position *as well as a greater workload. In my case, I am bringing to the table a quarter of a century of major league broadcasting experience and my workload will be sharply increased; also, I should like to point out that in the past, I have gone several years in succession with little or no pay increase whatever. Additionally, with what we are asking for in basic salaries, neither of us will equal the salaries paid announcers in other comparable major league cities. Our basic disagreement is with the salaries offered. In the case of Nellie, he seeks an increase of $5000; I am seeking an increase of $7000.*

Our plea was not heard. I wound up signing for $19,500. Bob, I assumed, was making $40,000. Working with only two announcers created a problem for me in acquiring a guest for the post-game show. I now had to remain in the booth for the entire broadcast. I explained this situation to KDKA in the spring and was told verbally they would compensate me for the expense. I was able to solve the post-game guest problem at home using "Radio Rich;" on the road, I was able to get batboys to acquire the post-game guest. At the end of the season I sent a letter and an expense report to Bill Hartman listing the amount I had paid to Radio Rich ($146.00) and batboys ($100) — $246 for the entire season. Charles Peterson, KDKA's program manager, offered me 33 1/3 record albums, but no compensation for the expenses. I received this letter from Bill Hartman:

There was no agreement that KDKA radio would pay either Radio Rich or batboys for getting players for your post-game show. The only cost I agreed to was in the area of talent; you were going to pay the rest. In an inquiry with Mr. Peterson he verified this understanding. Mr. Peterson informed me that the record albums you referred to in your letter were not in lieu of compensation, but rather, a generous gesture on the part of the program manager.

I thought, "how damn cheap can you be to expect me to pay for the expenses doing a post-game show for acquiring guests on a show that was commercially sponsored?" As for Mr. Peterson agreeing with his boss, what a surprise! Those 33 1/3 albums given so graciously were now passé given new recording technology. So much for the generous gift!

I attended another "power luncheon" at the Duquesne Club in 1972. Bill Hartman informed me that KDKA was not certain they were going to continue doing Pirates' broadcasts because they were losing money on the games. I had a martini at lunch and it loosened my tongue. I said, "The Pirates just won the World Series last year. I sold radio time at small stations years ago and if you can't sell Pirates' games, you have either overpriced it or are lacking in salesmen." They sold advertising for the games in 1972 and continued to own the broadcasting rights for Pittsburgh Pirate games until 2007. So much for Bill Hartman's prognosis!

During the 1975 season, I took a day off for my oldest daughter's high school graduation from Mt. Lebanon High School. It turned out to be a very unpleasant day. In mid-afternoon, I received a call from Bill Hartman of KDKA. I said hello and his response to me was, "What's with this FUCKING lawyer letter you sent." I replied, "It is not a FUCKING lawyer letter, it's a letter from my lawyer."

My lawyer had sent a letter to Ira Apple, program director of KDKA. I never head from Ira, who evidently showed it to Hartman, who blew his top. The first paragraph described my lawyer's concern:

Dear Mr. Apple:

This letter is to confirm the understanding reached between you and Nellie King that effective at the conclusion of the 1975 baseball season, any attempt by KDKA to sell Mr. King's services when broadcasting sponsored announcements as part of a package deal to sponsors of the pre-and post-game shows involving Mr. King will not be permitted unless Mr. King is compensated for the use of his voice and personality in delivering such announcements.

My conversation with Bill Hartman never got to the point that we were able to discuss my appeal. It went on very long, though, until I informed him my wife and I had to get ready to enjoy graduation day with our daughter. He ended the conversation as I angrily slammed down the phone. I suddenly remembered the saying; "The boss is not always right, but he is always the BOSS." I don't know if this had anything to do with my firing after the 1975 season, but it didn't help.

CHAPTER TWENTY-THREE

My Final Broadcast: October 7, 1975

I n the deciding 1975 NLCS game against Cincinnati at Three Rivers Stadium, I witnessed one of the best performances of power pitching in the nine years I had been broadcasting Pirates' baseball. John Candelaria, then in his rookie season, struck out the first four Reds hitters and went on to compile 14 strikeouts in eight innings, but it wasn't enough, as Cincinnati again beat the Bucs 5-3 in ten innings to end the 1975 season. After the game, I did my usual post-game radio interview show. My guest was Tony Kubek of NBC-TV. I had no clue that this was to be the last appearance for me and Bob Prince as Pirates' broadcasters.

Late that October, following an afternoon of golf with Jack Berger and Manny Sanguillen, I returned home for dinner and my wife told me that Joe. L. Brown had called and wanted me to meet him at his Mt. Lebanon home at 7:00 PM. I had known Joe L. Brown for over 20 years and had never received such an invitation. I thought it so odd that my mind considered many reasons for the invitation. One of which was related to the renewal date of my contract with Westinghouse Broadcasting for Pirates baseball for the 1976 season.

Eager to confirm the renewal date I went downstairs to my files to confirm when it had to be renewed; the date was October 31, 1975.

As I was going down the steps to the garage to leave to see Joe Brown, my daughter Leslie asked, "Where are you going Dad?" I told her I was going to Joe Brown's house. She inquired why and I informed her that I had no idea and she humorously replied, "Oh Dad, he's probably going to fire you!"

Joe Brown's wife, Din, met me at the door and invited me to have a seat in the living room and offered me a beer, which I accepted. Joe Brown then made his entrance coming down the stairs from the bedrooms. After a brief greeting he abruptly informed me "You won't be returning to do Pirates' broadcasts next year, nor will Bob Prince." The thing I most feared had happened. It hit me like a sucker punch to the stomach.

Disappointed, I inquired why and he said, "Well, Prince has been having problems with Westinghouse Broadcasting management." I replied, "Hell, that's no secret, but what has that got to do with me?" His response—"Sometimes the water splashes over and hits other people" —left me speechless with anger.

I thought, "what a helluva way to lose a job!" To soften the blow, he offered me a part-time job with the Pirates doing PR work with the hope that I could also find additional work on radio in the Pittsburgh market. I felt like a beggar being given a crumb to ease his guilt. My response to his offer was, "I was not surprised by the Westinghouse management decision as I had little trust in them, but I am disappointed in you." I then went on to explain how I willingly did radio shows he requested due mainly to Westinghouse

Broadcasting and his growing lack of trust in Prince. With regard to his offer of a part-time job with the Pirates, I replied, "I'm so annoyed I don't know if I want to be associated with you or the Pirates at this moment. I'll have to think it over and let you know later."

He requested that I not mention this to the media as Westinghouse Broadcasting was preparing a press release for later in the week. He then casually mentioned he would be out of town for a week or more vacationing in Mexico.

Emotionally crushed and angry, I returned home to tell my family the bad news. They took it well and we had a laugh over what turned out to be Leslie's unfortunately prescient explanation of the reason for my meeting with Joe Brown. The way I displaced my anger then was to get a shovel and start digging in the yard or garden. I dug out a large space where I could have buried Ed Wallis, Bill Hartman, and Joe L. Brown. It became an outdoor cement patio located at the bottom of the steps leading from our kitchen.

Personally aware of what would be one of the biggest stories in sports broadcasting in Pittsburgh history, but asked not to divulge anything, was nearly unbearable. I informed my family and close friends, but did not contact any members of the media. Depressed and angry, I awaited the Westinghouse Broadcasting release, which did not happen for more than a week. Mt anger festered so much I finally had to tell someone in the media. By phone I informed Al Abrams, the Sports Editor of the *Pittsburgh Post-Gazette,* of the proposed change, but he never followed up on the story.

Barbara Holsopple of the *Pittsburgh Press* was the first writer to break the story, which created headlines and commentary for weeks. I was relieved the story was out in the open, as I could now voice my anguish about the unfairness of the situation.

Baseball radio broadcasters develop a unique personal relationship with listeners that is different than all other media or sports because of the length of the season. As a Pirates' announcer Bob Prince was a constant guest in the kitchens, living rooms, and cars of Pirates' fans for 28 years. During good and bad times, Prince had developed an unusual relationship with two or three generations of listeners. He was, indeed, "The Voice of the Pirates." To be dispatched so coldheartedly annoyed the fans. They held a noontime parade downtown to say good-bye and thanks to me and Prince. Although I spent only nine years doing Pirates' baseball, they were some of the most memorable and thrilling seasons in the team's history. To witness the fans' affection that day was heartening. It proved that Prince and I had enjoyed a special relationship with so many listeners. I still treasure it today when people share their memories of hearing those Pirates' broadcasts.

The door to Pirates baseball had closed. I have discovered, however, that when a door closes in your life, another one opens and in my case, it has always turned out to be better than the one that just shut behind me.

I had two months to make a decision on my career and inquired of possible broadcasting openings at Atlanta and with the Chicago White Sox. I was informed that they were looking for someone younger. I was 47. It was the first time I felt old.

I was fortunate to have had a two-year relationship in the winter of 1973 and 1974 doing the color commentary on Duquesne University basketball broadcasts with Ray Goss. In the fall of 1975, Clair Brown, the Sports Information Director at Duquesne, decided to leave to take another position. "Red" Manning, the Athletic Director, asked me if I could recommend anyone for the position.

I suggested a good friend, Howard "Huddie" Kaufman who was a sports writer for the Greensburg *Tribune Review.*

I thought nothing more of the position until I received a call from "Red" Manning and Jim McDonough, a Duquesne alumnus, inquiring if I might consider taking the position. The more I listened the more I felt that it was something I was capable of doing and would enjoy. The cut in salary was severe, but I was given the opportunity to do a daily radio sports talk show and color on Carnegie Mellon University football that eased the financial concerns. The Duquesne job also had the added benefit of free college tuition for my three daughters, Laurie, Leslie, and Amy. My oldest daughter, Laurie had just enrolled for her freshman year that September in Edinboro College. With two more daughters soon ready for college I eagerly accepted the position at Duquesne where I enjoyed an 18-year career as Sports Information Director.

All three daughters earned degrees at Duquesne. Laurie continued her education, earning a masters and Ph.D. in Social Anthropology at Indiana University in Bloomington, IN. Leslie earned a Nursing degree at Duquesne. Our youngest daughter Amy earned a degree in Communications and works as a graphic designer and director for *Mind Over Media,* a local video production company, handling a number of nationally known companies. My wife Bernadette decided to go to college earned an undergraduate degree at the University of Pittsburgh and a Masters degree at Duquesne in Psychology.

I retired from the Sports Information position on July 1, 1993 but remained active as the Duquesne golf coach until I retired completely on July 1, 2004.

Age is now taking its toll on me physically, but it has been a great journey. The memories and the many friends I've met are treasured. Most treasured by Bernadette, me, our daughters, Laurie, Leslie and

Amy were the pleasurable family times we shared on Anna Maria Island during the spring training years at Bradenton, FL. Listening to my heart has been the key to this journey and that "cur dog of happiness" Branch Rickey spoke of still remains close by my side.

EPILOGUE

The Biggest Save of my Career

I was enjoying 79 years of good health when I was diagnosed with cancer of the colon in June 2007 and very quickly had a partial colon resection. The operation at Mercy Hospital was a success and I was going through the recovery stage when another problem appeared.

In August 2007 my wife and I were residing in Schenley Gardens, an assisted living residence in the Oakland section of Pittsburgh. My recovery was going well, until I began having balance problems and suffered many falls. Further testing showed it may have been caused by a mild stroke and I was admitted to Mercy Hospital for physical therapy shortly after Thanksgiving in 2007.

The recovery again seemed to be going well when I was suddenly stricken with pneumonia. The cause was aspiration; I had serious difficulty swallowing and instead of food and liquids going into my stomach, they went in my lungs. Before I knew it I was intubated. The seriousness of the pneumonia was obvious to my wife and daughters, who became constant visitors at my bedside.

I was going in and out of consciousness and my oxygen saturation levels were not good. Daily x-rays indicated that the pneumonia was not clearing fast enough, and attending physicians suggested that my life support systems should be disconnected. My daughter, Amy, who has power of attorney, was against that decision and immediately contacted Dr. Landfair, my cardiologist, and Dr. Hospodar my neurologist, who after seeing my condition voted not to remove my life support.

During a period of unconsciousness I had an "out-of-body" experience that my flesh was leaving my skeleton. I recall thinking, "I don't want to go there!"

When I returned to consciousness I could hear Amy saying, "Dad, it's the last of the ninth, there are two outs, two on, and nobody is warming up in the bullpen." Hearing that I began to smile and uttered a small laugh. It was the turning point in my recovery. I decided to live!

It has not been an easy process, as I weighed only 140 pounds and was unable to swallow liquids and eat food at the beginning of 2008. I lived off a feeding tube for five months before I passed barium tests on my throat and succeeded in swallowing. I kept the tube until I decided to have it pulled in September 2008. I now am enjoying all foods and drinks and my weight is up to 174 pounds.

Thanks to the love of my family and the medical professionals in the Intensive Care Unit at Mercy Hospital, as well as the personal attention of Doctors Landfair and Hospodar, I made the journey from a "near-death" to new life. This event was truly the "biggest save of my life," and more precious and memorable than any I had pitching.

I currently reside in Friendship Village South Hills Health Center under the care of very caring nurses, doctors, and aides.

CPSIA information can be obtained at www.ICGtesting.com
Printed in the USA
267417BV00002B/76/P